THE STONE MASON OF TOR HOUSE

"*Jeffers takes the unhuman outer world for his real-ity, of which human spirit is a phantasmal and tran-sient by-product. The people in his verses have to act and suffer as intensely as possible in order to show at all against the magnificence he feels in the world outside them. He thinks the human spirit can find its peace by realizing its unimportance, and its value by realizing the beauty of the outer world.*"*

*FROM A COLLECTION OF
R.J.'S PERSONAL NOTES AT TOR HOUSE

THE STONE MASON OF TOR HOUSE

THE LIFE AND WORK OF
ROBINSON JEFFERS

BY MELBA BERRY BENNETT

FOREWORD BY LAWRENCE CLARK POWELL

THE WARD RITCHIE PRESS

ACKNOWLEDGMENT

THE ROBINSON JEFFERS POETRY IN THIS VOLUME AND THE SEVERAL
INTRODUCTORY PIECES FROM VOLUMES OF ROBINSON JEFFERS'
POETRY ARE COPYRIGHT AND ARE REPRINTED BY PERMISSION OF
RANDOM HOUSE, INC.

TO FRANK,

WHOSE INDULGENCE HAS BEEN

HEROIC

PREFACE

For DAYS AND WEEKS *and sometimes for months, I've sat here at the beautiful oak table in the dining room of Tor House, the work piled high before me—papers and manuscripts to be sorted or transcribed, letters to be answered, newspaper clippings to be dated and entered in the big scrap book. The large window frames the sea with its variable moods—an ever-present temptation to take my eyes from my work and to set my mind to wandering.*

Now Jeffers is dead. Now I have only my memories of those years—Jeffers stooping to come through the kitchen door with an afternoon snack of cookies for me; Jeffers sitting in the low chair by the little fire, idly rolling a cigarette, while the pale eyes steadily watch the curl of smoke and dancing flames; Jeffers on the bench opposite me, scowling over the autographing of a book or signing of a letter, as if the pen in his hand were an unfriendly alien that must be controlled by force. That dear, gentle, quiet man, whose deceptive serenity belied the inner intensity which burst forth in a hot flame of truth to sear humanity.

It was 1927 or 1928 that I first discovered the poetry of Robinson Jeffers. Although I'd had a thorough schooling in poetry, it hadn't prepared me for any scholarly appraisal of this strange and violent voice. As so many before and after me, I thought at first reading that it was a negative voice. Nor had Stanford University's courses in Psychology, Philosophy, or Comparative Religions prepared me for the encyclopedic knowledge of this man. He merited full understanding, so I began an intensive study *which, nine years later, resulted in the publication of my critique* of Jeffers' poetry.*

Its publication was due entirely to the encouragement of two friends, Theodore Lilienthal and Edwin Grabhorn, who shared my interest in the poetry of Jeffers. The Grabhorn Press and the Gelber & Lilienthal Book Shop were impressive sponsors. They had one qualification, however—that not only the poetry but the poet must be considered. I disagreed, feeling as Steinbeck had felt when he told Grabhorn, "I hardly dare to meet Jeffers because his poetry is perfect to me, and I don't think one should get the man mixed up with his work." Nor did I "dare" meet either Jeffers or his wife Una, being cognizant of their antipathy to strangers. Ted Lilienthal finally overcame my reluctance and took me to meet the Jefferses at Tor House in 1934.

The trees — cypress and eucalyptus — which Jeffers had planted when Tor House was built in 1919, had sixteen years of growth, so the little stone Tudor house was already hidden from the road although Hawk Tower still dominated the scene. We walked to the wooden gate, with its swinging wooden sign "NO VISITORS UNTIL AFTER 4:00," and as the latch clicked behind us the door of Tor House opened and a smiling Una greeted us.

She was small and plump, her brown hair wrapped around her head in braids. The most arresting thing about her were the large, blue, searching eyes. She gave Ted Lilienthal a warm greeting and then turned a critical look on me. I was to learn that Una didn't accept strangers lightly.

As we entered the low-ceilinged living room with its warm wood-panelled walls, Jeffers rose slowly from a settle by the small fireplace to greet us. It was his eyes, too, which held me, although they were hardly aware of me.

Ted explained the purpose of our visit—that I needed biographical material to complete my book. There was no reaction from Jeffers. Una looked me over again and then said briskly: "I'm sure you can find what you need by reading what has already been written about Robin."

I protested that I had already done so and that I'd found too many doubtful conclusions.

**Robinson Jeffers and the Sea.*

"Specifically what?" she asked.

"Critics," I answered, "have claimed that all of the poems in Jeffers' first book FLAGONS AND APPLES *were written to you." However it was obvious, I continued, that, although "Helen," his ideal woman, was Una, several of the poems had been written to other women.*

That was when I learned at first hand about Una's temper and her possessiveness. The little room shuddered with her indignation, and her eyes flashed with fury. She insisted that she was the only woman in her husband's life or poems, and I was given a very clear impression that I'd receive no cooperation whatever, ever! It could have been the end of the story, but my reaction, though mute, was furious, too. My fury included Ted who had led me to slaughter.

It was the goad I had needed, however, and within a month I had not only located the other "Helens" but had talked with them. Although I found no lurid past which might have triggered Una's fit of temper, I felt it urgent that I prove that I could get at the truth without her assistance, if need be.

I wrote the story as a "chapter" (although I had no intention of using it as such) and dispatched it to Tor House. Another stormy scene followed between Una and me, but it ended happily with our laughing at each other and our Irish tempers. From then on Una gave me her full cooperation, and I was able to deliver to Ed Grabhorn and Ted Lilienthal the material they had requested.

It was a result of my book ROBINSON JEFFERS AND THE SEA *that Jeffers and Una asked me to serve as his biographer—with one stipulation—that I publish nothing during his lifetime.*

Since Jeffers' recollections of his childhood were meager, my first port of call was Sewickley, Pennsylvania, where most of his mother's family still lived. Alexander Robinson, a cousin, introduced me to other members of the family and to the neighbors. It was he who arranged for me to visit Jeffers' birthplace and the other homes he had lived in. The story with which I returned to Carmel jogged Jeffers' memory so that he added other details. Later, another cousin and contemporary, George Evans, gave me further information to round out the story of those childhood years.

Una's friends during the time that she was married to Kuster,

Jeffers' college friends, the early Carmel friends—all have helped to bring alive those years before I knew the Jefferses or enjoyed their friendship.

From 1935 to 1950 I received one hundred and thirty-five letters from Una. After her death, Lee and Donnan Jeffers continued the correspondence, providing me with a year-to-year account of the activities of the Jeffers family.

As I gained Una's confidence she gradually allowed me to organize the mass of Jeffers' papers. After 1950 I had the full responsibility for them, as well as for answering the major part of his correspondence. It was about this time that I began the task of transcribing the notes (so many of which are quoted in this work) and manuscripts of which there were hundreds—on bits and pieces of envelopes, on discarded grocery lists, on the backs of advertisements, and even on the backs of other manuscripts or typescripts.

From these sources, as well as from the privileged relationship which I have had with all members of the Jeffers family, I have drawn the material for this biography. As the writing of it progressed and for as long as she lived, I had the benefit of Una's encouragement and sound criticism. She was tireless and generous in her efforts to help me, and for this reason it is as much Una's book as mine.

ACKNOWLEDGMENTS

THOSE TO WHOM I give my special thanks in helping me to assemble anecdotes and facts are members of the Jeffers family: Lee and Donnan Jeffers, Dr. Hamilton Jeffers, Alexander Robinson, Alice Robinson, George Evans, and Harriet Hampson. Also to their friends Hazel Pinkham, Nettie Carter, Daniel Hammack, Dr. Robert Cleland, James Hopper, Adele and Frederick Bechdolt, James Rorty, Maud and Frederick Clapp, Phoebe and Hans Barkan, Blanche Matthias, Dame Judith Anderson, Noel Sullivan, and Albert Bender. And, without whom I would never have had the temerity to begin this book: Frances and Theodore Lilienthal and Edwin Grabhorn.

MELBA BERRY BENNETT

CONTENTS

xi

ILLUSTRATIONS

JOHN ROBINSON JEFFERS, 12 YEARS OLD, JANUARY, 1899

UNA. A. B. DEGREE CAP AND GOWN. MARCH, 1908

TERMINAL ISLAND. UNA. 1908

ROBIN JEFFERS. HERMOSA BEACH, JANUARY, 1912

ROBIN, GREAT AUNT MARY, UNA, BILLIE, BELLE MÈRE. LOG CABIN, CARMEL, 1915

CHEROKEE AND BANKSIA ROSES ON SLEEPING PORCH AT ROBIN'S FATHER'S HOUSE, 822 GARFIELD AVENUE, PASADENA, APRIL, 1914

Following page 176

UNA AND BILLIE. CARMEL, 1915 OR 1916

ROBIN, UNA, BILLIE, AT TOR, WHERE TOR HOUSE WAS BUILT, 1918 OR EARLY 1919

ROBIN, UNA, THE TWINS AND GOATS AT THE POINT

ROBINSON JEFFERS. TOR HOUSE, CARMEL, 1928

TONY LUHAN, DONNAN JEFFERS, ROBINSON JEFFERS. TAOS, NEW MEXICO, 1930

ROBIN LAYING STONES

1939. HAWK TOWER, TOR HOUSE, CARMEL. ROBINSON JEFFERS

JEFFERS WITH HIS TWO SONS, DONNAN AND GARTH, IN 1944

TOR HOUSE AND THE TOWER

ROBIN WITH HIS GRANDDAUGHTER UNA. TAKEN BY HIS BROTHER HAMILTON

FOREWORD

BY LAWRENCE CLARK POWELL

I HAVE READ *this first biography of Robinson Jeffers with rising admiration for its author. Melba Bennett has rendered unique service to readers and students of the Carmel poet by her selfless and unswerving devotion to the poet while he was alive and to his reputation since his death.*

Although it is true that a definitive biography of an author cannot be written during his life or soon after his death, this does not mean that a beginning toward such cannot and should not be made. Without this invaluable beginning by Mrs. Bennett, biographers fifty years hence would be critically handicapped, for many of the materials now forming her book would have been irretrievably lost, or, more serious yet, have never been called into existence.

It was she who had the vision, the determination, and the energy thirty and more years ago to begin to assemble, evoke, preserve, and sort out the facts, the fictions, and the folklore that were fast cohering into the Jeffers myth. I cannot imagine anyone other than Melba Bennett having the combination of audacity, sophistication, and gaiety to establish contact and to stay with Una Jeffers through the years of their friendship.

For Una was a formidable woman. Possessive, jealous, violent, ambitious, snobbish, reactionary—true, all true—but add, and more important, as indispensable and inevitable a part of the poet's genius as sunshine to life. No Una, no Robin of the great poetry of his prime, their prime. Melba Bennett never questioned this primacy of Una's role, and she was able to obtain the wife's understanding and cooperation as no other writer ever did.

Una regarded herself as Robin's ultimate biographer, and she would have made an extraordinary one. She expected to outlive him, and he believed she would. Fate in the form of cancer ruled otherwise. Her death in 1950 left her book unwritten, and worse, left her husband to drag out the final sorrowful, sterile years of his long life.

To Melba Bennett we are grateful for preserving manuscripts and memorabilia Una made no provision for, and to which Robin was characteristically indifferent. The Robinson Jeffers collection at Occidental College has assumed responsibility for the custodianship of the Jeffers archives transferred to it by Mrs. Bennett and by Donnan and Garth Jeffers, the poet's sons and executors.

I have said that this book is a beginning, a statement which the author would second. Much remains to be recovered and studied and related. Hints and clues are found throughout its pages. Robin's relations with other women, particularly in the early years, his sources and influences—Lucretius, for example—and the questionable role played by Mable Dodge Luhan—there will be theses and studies and entire books written on these and other topics only broached by Mrs. Bennett.

And so it is on this note of gratitude that I close, to Melba Berry Bennett for bravely and boldly having done so usefully what no one else even attempted to do. Hopefully it will lead someone next to fill the great need for a critical edition of Jeffers' work. As she truly observes, he has been poorly served by his publishers. Thus Melba Bennett's book should prove both illuminating and stimulating. The prospect for Jeffers studies is furthered and brightened by it.

University of California
Los Angeles

THE STONE MASON OF TOR HOUSE

I

THE YOUNG ROBIN

H<small>E WAS SUCH A LITTLE FELLOW</small>, sitting on the top step of the broad veranda of the big brick house. His hands were tucked deep into the pockets of his short coat, and his stockinged knees, beneath the tight wool breeches, hugged each other tightly. As he stared solemnly at his high black shoes, he shivered. The serious little face looked older than his nine years because of his immediate worry. Having failed in both his Latin and algebra assignments the day before, he had been denied his play time, and he was doubtful that today's lessons would show any improvement. As punishment, his father permitted him to run around the big oak tree only once—for exercise, not for pleasure.

Shifting his position, the boy's attention was directed to the large maple tree, and his eyes followed the lonely flight of its bronze leaves, for it would soon be winter in Sewickley. His play hours would be limited by the weather as well as by his father's disciplinary measures. Each beautiful autumn hour lost would lengthen the winter days.

"Robin?"

Hearing his name, he jumped quickly to his feet and answered, "Yes, Father. Ready."

"Your school books, Robin?"

The boy stooped to lift them from the steps and then followed the dark figure of his father down Edgeworth Lane to the station. As they passed Harry Irwin's house, Harry called to his wife,

3

"There are the big Indian and the little Indian going by—set your watch, Lilly." For the two Jefferses, father and son, were irrefutably punctual.

Although many of his neighbors whispered that this tall, stooped man, with the high cheek bones and inscrutable expression, had Indian blood, others, fascinated by his shiny black clothes, his long frock coat, his coarse, bushy, untrained hair, referred to him secretly as "old Ichabod Crane." They shook their heads sadly over the young boy with the aging father.

The father, Dr. William Hamilton Jeffers, A.B., D.D., LL.D., held the chair of Old Testament Literature and Exegesis at the Western Theological Seminary (Presbyterian) in that part of Pittsburgh known then as Allegheny. And the previous year, in the fall of 1895, the seminary had further honored him by giving him the Chair of Biblical and Ecclesiastical History. A brilliant scholar of Latin, Greek, and Hebrew, he was intolerant of the lack of interest his young son had recently shown in his Latin lessons. The child had a tendency to be distracted by frivolous interests. Two years before, when the doctor himself had tutored him in his first Latin lessons, Robin had seemed quick and eager to learn, but when his interest had been rewarded with longer study assignments the boy began to complain of headaches and was sullen when forbidden to play with the neighborhood children. Nearly sixty years old and constantly concerned with his own health, the doctor lacked patience. He reluctantly turned over the responsibility for his son's education to the Park Institute in Allegheny. He kept close check on the assignments and the results and was too often disappointed in both the school and his son.

A taciturn man, the doctor confided none of these thoughts to his son Robin who sat beside him in the train, his young head lowered over his Latin book.

On their return home from Allegheny that same afternoon, Robin saw his mother waiting for them on the porch. Her smiling face held a promise as she waved a letter to them.

As gay as her husband was serious, Annie Robinson Tuttle Jeffers at thirty-six was healthy and vital. Her hair was as warmly brown as when she married eleven years ago, and her large brown eyes were as ready for laughter.

As Robin ran ahead of his father, his mother held out the letter to him and asked teasingly, "Guess who is coming for a visit?"

He answered quickly, "Harriet!"

Robin knew that his mother had invited her young cousin for a visit, and he had been anxiously awaiting her answer. Each day he had asked his mother if she had heard from Harriet.

A happy smile warmed the serious little face. Now there would be someone young in the house. Hamilton, Robin's three-year-old brother, didn't count—he was too young. And the other members of the household were all too old to play with him. His father, when he was home, closed himself off in his study back of the parlor. His mother was preoccupied with Hamilton and housekeeping and had even stopped giving him his music lessons. He had enjoyed those short periods, sitting there at the big piano with his mother, searching out the notes to the little pieces in *Nursery Singer Plays*. He could still play "The Little Men" and "The Lamb," though he was vaguely ashamed that he could. As he had shown no talent for music and had made no progress, his mother had stopped the lessons.

Another member of the household was Cousin Mary McCord who was really a half-aunt of his mother's. Sis, as they called her, had come from her home in North East, Pennsylvania, for a visit and had remained to live with them. She was good company for his mother and helped her to run the big house, but she was no fun for a boy of nine. She was even older than his mother and nearly as old as his father.

Then there were William Hicks and his wife Mary. William took care of the garden and drove the carriage, though William was, Robin had discovered, deathly afraid of horses. Mary cooked for them, and, though tolerant of Robin's visits to her kitchen, she was no companion for him. There was also Lizzie the nurse. Lizzie had taken care of the house before he was born and had helped his mother with his care when he was a baby, returning to them when Hamilton was born. But Robin had a young man's scorn of nurses.

His life was tediously dreary, spent as it was between home, train, school, train, and home work. A young girl in the house at "Twin Hollows" might liven things up a bit. Harriet would, he hoped, bring copies of *St. Nicholas* magazine and the *Youth's*

Companion. Robin hunched his shoulders with delight, certain that Harriet would share them with him. His father had forbidden the magazines in the house, considering them a waste of time, insisting that Robin devote his leisure to the reading of *Quo Vadis*. But Harriet was fourteen years old, a guest, and a girl, so perhaps she would be exempt from the doctor's discipline.

What sort of entertainment could Robin offer his cousin? He could, of course, show her the woods. "Twin Hollows" sat on a hill with a natural ravine driveway on either side. The extensive grounds around the house were mostly lawn, with lovely old maples, chestnuts, and tremendous oaks. In the summer the woods were full of song birds and the elusive fragrance of the trailing arbutus. Now, though, it would be different. The wind had flirted most of the leaves from the trees, and the birds had gone south for the winter. There were too many days like today —too cold for family picnics.

Mentally Robin scanned the neighborhood for ideas. Suddenly the serious little face lighted with pleasure—he had thought of Mr. Shannon's cows: Mr. Shannon kept blooded cows from the Isle of Jersey—kept them in the yard outside his wife's parlor window—right in the heart of the fashionable Edgeworth residential section. Harriet would surely be amused to see the old Jersey bull, hitched to the cream separator, being led around and around like a wheel, with old Shannon either wheedling or yelling at him.

But when, at last, Harriet arrived at Edgeworth, she showed no interest in Robin's small pleasures. The truth was, he was too much like his strange father—addicted to long words, faultless diction, and endless quotations from the classics. Harriet felt self-conscious with him, finding it difficult to be natural with a boy of nine who could converse in Latin. It was inevitable that she should find it far more pleasant to be with Robin's mother whom she thought both fascinating and glamorous.

The winter dragged on, Robin's dull routine unbroken. Not until late spring did the picnics, arranged by his mother and Sis, make life at "Twin Hollows" a little brighter for him. These picnics always included Philena Robinson, wife of his mother's cousin John, and any of the visiting nephews, nieces, or young cousins. They also included Aunt Kate and her son, Alex Robinson's wife, their three young boys, her sister Louise Way and her three children.

It was on one of these picnics that Aunt Kate asked Robin's mother whether or not they had decided to go abroad for the summer. Robin held his breath, dreading the answer, for he didn't want to go abroad again. Before Hamilton's birth, his parents had twice taken him to Europe for the summer. Living in *pensions*, going to museums and band concerts, or shopping with his mother wasn't Robin's idea of fun. After Hamilton was born, they'd spent the summer at a Methodist resort on Lake Chautauqua; it had been Robin's most exciting experience and he hoped to spend another summer there. So he sighed with relief when his mother told Aunt Kate that the doctor had decided not to go abroad that year.

It was after the family returned from Chautauqua and Dr. Jeffers had gone to visit one of the outlying parishes that Robin wrote his first letter to his father:

August 23, 1897

"Dear Papa,

The baby and I were out in the garden when I saw a snake which afterwards measured 22 inches. I called William and ran to get a club. But William called me back to help him hunt for it. I ran back and found it and he got it under his hoe and I ran away to get a stick. When I came back he was about two rods away and I thought he had killed it but when I asked him he said no it was in the row of beans just above the garden. I saw it in the beans and William poked it out with the hoe and then I killed it with my stick. I think, it was a garter snake. It was white undernearth, black with green speckles on top, a greenish yellow band ran along its back, and large brown stripes ran lengthwise along its sides. Mr. Shannon's road is being filled up fast. We go out for a ride every morning: before Grandma[1] went away we took her; since then we have been taking Mrs. Knox. Yesterday we went to the U.P. Church. Goodbye.

Your loving son
John Robinson"

[1] John and Philena Robinson were always called "grandpa" and "grandma" by Robin and Hamilton.

The following spring, Robin wrote his first poem. It, too, was about a snake. One of his cousins found the poem most amusing and kept a copy for many years before mislaying it.

Another cousin, George Evans of Ohio, who often visited the Robinsons, wrote his impression of Robin and his family at this time:

"I felt older enough than Robin to be quite superior to him in the Sewickley days. His family seemed always moving from one fine house into another. The last home I remember them in near Sewickley was a place of large acreage in what seemed a woodland of trees, with little rills and hills of its own where we played Indian. My twin brother and I usually made Robin the Indian to be shot. When he solemnly objected to this at last, the game would stop. His solemnity in games was something I still remember. He got his youthful solemnity from his father, by no means from his blithesome mother.

"Dr. Jeffers walked along always with a stoop, his hands often clasped behind him, his very light blue eyes seeming to gaze at an idea. He always seemed enormously tall.

"Robin got Latin and Greek from the very start. I can recall playing at tennis with Robin on the Robinsons' grass court, when he was about seven or eight years old, and having him suddenly stop the game, much to my boyish disgust, to tell me scenes from Xenophon's *Anabasis* that he had been reading in the original that morning with his father. I remember saying to him, 'You'll soon know enough words to understand what our fathers are talking about.'"[2]

²Letter from George Evans to M.B.B., August 8, 1943.

FAMILY BACKGROUND

ANNIE JEFFERS, Robin's mother, was one of three daughters born to Edwin and Mary Sherwood Tuttle, of North East, Pennsylvania. Edith, the oldest daughter, was born on November 17, 1858; Annie Robinson, on September 5, 1860; Mary Georgiana (called Minnie), on May 19, 1863. A few months after the birth of Minnie, Edwin Tuttle died. Mary Tuttle was in frail health, though only thirty-one years old, and she deeply mourned the death of her beloved husband. An old tintype shows her to be a very pretty young woman, with delicate features, large soft eyes, a sweet, full mouth, and neatly-dressed brown hair. She wore her clothes with fastidiousness and taste.

In a diary she began writing about five years after the death of her husband, she gives us an intimate picture of her struggles and her way of meeting her problems.

Mary Tuttle's "Record" [in part]

January 1, 1868   Rain, sleet, and snow.

I, Mary E. Tuttle, Resolve to keep a record of each day of the year which begins today. I have spent the day very pleasantly with Mrs. Rogers and Mrs. Pettys at Mrs. P.'s house. Went to prayer meeting this eve. Earnestly desire to live nearer to my Saviour to make my life more like his. Commenced to read Bible by course.

Thursday 2   Calm but not bright.

Made Minnie's bonnet today. Went down town towards night. Learned that Julia was sick so I went to see her. Oh, what shall I do?

9

I am *willing*, God knows, to do all for them that they need, *but* is it justice to my children? God help them, and me. . . .

Friday 3   Weather the same as yesterday.

Made bonnets for Edith and Annie today. Went at four o'clock and studied my German. Then in the evening went to singing school. The first of the course. Think I shall like the teacher. My life is all excitement and hurry. Yet at night when the excitement is over, oh, how lonely. I have Christ. God help me to be at peace.

Monday 13   Pleasant.

A nice quiet day at home. I am *glad* that I am, at last, learning to love home even without the dear Presence which *made* it home for me. It is more than four years since My Husband left me, and only now I begin to love home without him. Thank God for the softening hand of time. Spent the evening at Mrs. McNutts.

Tuesday 21   The most stormy day of the year.

Wind and snow. I am not at all well. Have kept to the sofa nearly all day except that I baked bread and made mutton pie for dinner, of which I was too ill to taste. My darling Minnie favored me with frequent visits and numberless kisses from the rosiest and sweetest of mouths. Truly I am blessed in my children. *All* of them.

Sunday 26   Steady snow.

But very few at Church, on account of the storm. Still less at Sunday school for the same reason, I suppose. Didn't go out this evening. Have been reading the "Guardian Angel." Wish I could have an hour each day just for myself, to do what I please. I want to write. Wonder if Mr. B will write me again.

Thursday 6   Snow and wind.

Mr. and Mrs. Forsythe were here for tea, and against my hopes spent the evening. Dr. Stillman called. How good he is. Was so sorry they were here. "God help me to do my duty and not faint." I will try with God's help to be a good woman.

Sunday 9   Very stormy, wind and snow.

. . . am not well and must take care. I wish I could leave wishing and planning for things which I am not sure that would be best for me to have. I desire to be pure and single in my heart and life.

Friday 14   Pleasant.

A somewhat eventful day. Went down and had a tooth pulled. The dentist, Dr. Stillman, gave me such a lovely bouquet from his plants, a rose surrounded with geranium leaves. Sat for my pictures.

These excerpts from the diary of Annie's mother end in July of 1868. She continued to comment with favor on Dr. Stillman, but since there is no record of a marriage, Mary Tuttle's prayers for a "single life" were evidently answered. Little is known of her life from 1868 until her death six years later.

Upon their mother's death, the three sisters lived for a short time with relatives in North East and were then invited to visit their father's first cousin, John Robinson, and his wife Philena, in Sewickley, Pennsylvania.

According to Alex Robinson, "Edith, the oldest of the three, had, as I remember, gone from North East to Massachusetts to work in some occupation. . . . They were not invited to come to stay permanently, but after their arrival Edith died suddenly, and my uncle and aunt, in the kindness of their hearts and having no children of their own, invited Annie and Minnie to remain with them, especially as they had hardly any means of their own."[1]

At this time, Annie was fourteen, her sister Edith was sixteen, and Minnie was eleven. Philena and John had recently moved to Sewickley, a suburb of Pittsburgh, on the banks of the Ohio River. Their house was spacious and handsome, set back from Beaver Road in a grove of beautiful trees. John Robinson, a member of the banking house of Robinson Brothers, was obviously a gentleman of means.

George Evans gives us a picture of his uncle:

"His treatment of us visiting—and we must have been bothersome nephews and noisy, too—was a combination of dignified austerity and twinkling amusement. He had one of the most beautiful, soft voices I ever heard, but he rarely talked to us, except to correct our manners. We were definitely afraid of him, without any real reason, except that his manner was entirely aloof. He never used liquor or smoked, always conducted family prayers in that beautiful voice, keyed specially for conversing with the Deity into almost a singing tone. He was the nearest thing to what seemed like royalty in our family connection. We never climbed into his lap. The nearest I ever got to him was to sit in the front seat of the carriage of an evening, alongside of him, and watch the way he managed his lively sorrel team. Always there was a ride of a summer evening, and we youngsters took turns to go.

[1]Letter from Alex Robinson to M.B.B. March 13, 1949.

11

"Aunt Philena, my mother's sister, was one of the most lovely characters I have ever known. She was gentle, handsome, good-natured. Having no children of her own, she enjoyed her nieces and nephews. Her husband always handled the purse strings. If she had to shop, or pay the hired girls or the coachman, she stated how much she needed at the time. And she seemed ideally content to have it that way.

"I never heard him discuss money with the family, except to groan at the taxes he had to pay year after year. When Uncle John died, the estate was not as great as we had all supposed it might be. When everything was settled, all debts paid, his widow, Aunt Philena, provided for, about twelve of us nieces and nephews who had no real claim, were surprised each of us to receive some $10,000.00."[2]

For seven years young Annie studied music and taught piano lessons to the neighborhood children at John Way's Edgeworth Seminary. On Sundays she played the organ in the Presbyterian Congregational Church of which John Robinson was an elder.

About this time, Dr. Bittinger, pastor of the church, complained of poor health and asked for a supply preacher. The elders of the church contacted the Western Theological Seminary and through them obtained the services of Dr. W. Hamilton Jeffers.

When he came to preach in the little Sewickley church, Dr. Jeffers was a shy, scholarly widower of forty-eight. He was over six feet tall but so stooped that he gave the impression of being a much shorter and older man. He was an odd mixture of Irish and Bavarian blood. His father was from County Monaghan, Ireland, and his mother, Barbara Moore, was a Rosenberg whose father came from the Palatinate, Bavaria. Dr. Jeffers was born of these parents in Cadiz, Ohio, on May 1, 1838.

Before coming to Allegheny, Dr. Jeffers had been pastor at the important Euclid Avenue Church in Cleveland, Ohio. When the Presbyterian seminary was established in Pittsburgh, Dr. Jeffers was called there and came willingly, since his first wife, Maria Robinson Jeffers,[3] and his two sons were no longer living.

Seminary professors were expected to preach wherever they were invited—anywhere in the district of their seminary. Dr. Jeffers was a popular preacher, and, although he was not an in-

[2]Letter from Evans to M.B.B. August 8, 1943.
[3]No relation to the Sewickley Robinsons.

spiring orator, he had no difficulty in holding the attention of his congregation.

Visiting preachers were invited for dinner and to spend the night in the homes of the elders of the church in which they were preaching, so Dr. Jeffers, when preaching in Sewickley, was often invited to John Robinson's home. This pleased the doctor as he found Mr. Robinson's niece Annie, the pretty young organist at the church, extremely attractive. Annie was full of fun and laughed easily, and her merry, brown eyes rested with admiration on the new pastor.

It was a distinct shock to both John and Philena Robinson when they realized that Dr. Jeffers was seriously interested in Annie. Although they respected him as a man and a theologian, they couldn't entertain the idea of his marrying their twenty-one-year-old niece. The doctor asked John, "What is your objection to me?"

John replied tersely, "My objection is, you!"

In a letter dated February 10, 1885, Annie wrote her own version of the courtship to her Aunt Hetty Bosworth:

"A gentleman called here one evening, requesting a confidential talk with me, and when he went, I found myself engaged to be married! Just think of it! It happened a week ago, and I have hardly been able to take it in yet. I know you are surprised even more than I am, and I am *awfully* surprised. He never paid me the least bit of attention publicly, and he lives in Allegheny, so it will be a perfect surprise for everybody here. What is his name and business, and what does he look like, you say? Prepare for another surprise, and perhaps a little disappointment. His name is Rev. Dr. W. H. Jeffers, and he is a deal older than I am, and not a bit handsome; very tall and, in fact, quite homely, but so good! And so good and kind and thoughtful for me. I am happy, and will be happy, though he is nearly twice as old as I am. We expect to be married in May...."

The perseverance of the doctor finally won out over the objections of the Robinsons, and, on April 30, 1885, he and Annie were married in the Robinsons' parlor. Philip and Alice Robinson, nephew and niece of John Robinson, carried the ribbons which were to mark the aisle and stood awaiting, tremulously, the entrance of the bride. Annie, young, beautiful, and proud, preceded

13

by her sister Minnie, walked through the parlor doors and down the aisle of ribbons to be joined in marriage to the scholarly Dr. Jeffers.

As the seminary school term was still in session, Annie was taken immediately from her wedding to the austere seminary house at 723 Ridge Avenue in Allegheny. It was no vine-covered cottage, but a three-story double dwelling, with a staid brick front flush with the sidewalk. Across the street was a block-square park, and on the opposite side of the park were some of the finest homes of the suburb.

In the other half of the house lived one of John Robinson's many brothers, Dr. Thomas Robinson, his wife Mary, and their rapidly increasing family. Dr. Robinson was also a professor at the seminary.

On the first floor of the Ridge Avenue house was a long hallway, off which were the parlor, living room, dining room, and kitchen, then a sizable back porch, and a very small and very dreary back yard. On the second floor was a large front room which the Jefferses were to use as their living room. Off this was a pleasant bedroom with a fireplace. Here, a year and a half later, Annie's first son, John Robinson Jeffers, was born.

To this house, then, came young Annie Jeffers to take her place in the society of professors and their wives, and the students of the seminary. Since the rules of the seminary called for the professors to hold open house for the students, Annie, as an inexperienced bride, had no time for romantic reveries.

When the seminary closed for the summer, the doctor took Annie to Europe for their delayed honeymoon, returning to Allegheny only in time for him to prepare his notes for the fall term. He now held the Chair of Biblical and Ecclesiastical History and the History of Doctrine and continued to teach Old Testament Literature.

That winter was a difficult one for Annie, removed from her family and friends in Sewickley, adjusting herself to the rigorous demands of seminary life. The doctor was content to dispense with any social activity as even the minimum upset him, and he used his poor health as an excuse to avoid accepting invitations or inviting friends in for an evening.

Hoping that a change of climate and scene would improve his

health, the doctor again took Annie abroad for the summer of 1886. By the time they returned to Allegheny in the fall, Annie was looking forward to the arrival of her first child. From her "Early Chronicle of the Life of John Robinson Jeffers" we learn that:

"At ten o'clock, Monday morning, January 10, 1887, my baby, a strong healthy boy, was born. Having been long expected and eagerly wished for, he received a very warm welcome, and both his parents were very thankful and grateful for such a blessing.

"At first, as all babies do, he slept a good deal; always being very good at night. His nurse stayed with us for six weeks; before that time, he began to laugh a little. He had presents in those early days, and many people were anxious to see this wonderful baby, with big blue eyes that weighed eleven pounds. . . ."

And on April 30, Annie wrote:

"Today being the anniversary of our wedding we thought it a very appropriate time to have the baby baptized. After considerable thought and discussion pro and con we decided to call our boy John Robinson. Cousin John seemed pleased, and shows his appreciation in various ways; one way was by sending him a beautiful new dress for his baptismal robe. We invited a family party. . . .

"Cousin Thomas administered the baptism. The baby was just as good and sweet as possible all through the service; but afterwards when everybody began to talk and to crowd around him he looked around with a frightened gaze, his lips trembling and then such a piteous cry burst forth. He was soon pacified however, and just as good as ever. . . ."

But Annie says nothing of her own torture in bearing this large baby. In using forceps to aid in the delivery, a doctor's carelessness injured the baby's right eye with one prong of the forceps. Jeffers, writing of this later says, "As to the eye: it remained invalid and now has a cataract. . . ."[4]

---

[4]Excerpt from unpublished poem, Tor House collection.

MATERIAL FOR BIOGRAPHY

To GET THE BABY out of the heat of the Pittsburgh summer, the doctor took him and Annie to North East where many of the Tuttle family still lived and where some of the Robinsons spent the summer months. Since the doctor could be with them for only short periods, Annie avoided boredom by taking music lessons and by writing daily reports to her husband on the baby's development. On the baby's eighth-month birthday, the doctor wrote Annie advising her to have him weighed, to "ascertain his avoir du pois as soon as convenient & enter it in your chronicle as material for biography."

By the time Robin's first birthday came around he had had his first fall, and his mother reminded herself of the superstition that a baby will not be bright unless he falls out of bed at least once. She reported in the "Chronicle" that:

"He weighs twenty-six pounds; creeps all over, can pull up easily to his knees by anything, and often to his feet; he says mama, sometimes he will try to say papa, & he begins to try to say a few other words, to call his nurse, 'Annie,' 'boys,' 'bears,' etc.; but says nothing distinctly. He wears little white dresses and gingham aprons. He has beautiful blue eyes, light brown hair with a little curl in it, & eight teeth. . . . His diet is chiefly milk from his bottle; he does not care to eat at all, does not seem to like things."

From now on his mother records only what she considers important events in the progress of her child — the fact that he would stop anything he was doing, even crying from a hard bump, to look at pictures which were his chief delight. His first step, taken on March 13, was of course a great achievement in the eyes of his mother.

It is surprising that Annie made no note of the purchase of two lots on Thorn Street in Sewickley in January, 1888, nor of the building of their new home there. Dr. Jeffers had inherited $60,000 from the estate of his first wife, enough to indulge in luxuries not permitted by a seminary professor's salary. He had found it increasingly difficult to live happily in the seminary house, and very trying to have his intellectual contemplations interrupted by the demands of the students. It was this problem which prompted him to buy the Sewickley lots which John Robinson had been urging him to purchase. He was gravely criticized by the trustees of the seminary when it was learned that he planned to establish a residence away from the seminary, as they felt that he was shirking his responsibilities by not being available to the students. Because of his ill health they finally, reluctantly, made an exception to their rules.

Thorn Street was a quiet residential street which ran into Academy Road. Around the corner from Academy, on Beaver Road, was the home of John and Philena, and about half a mile down Beaver was the Sewickley Presbyterian Church, conveniently situated for the doctor when he was a visiting preacher there. The Quaker Station, where he could catch the train into Allegheny for his daily classes at the seminary, was only a short walk from Thorn Street.

With the assistance of John Robinson, who supervised the building, Dr. Jeffers erected, on the Thorn Street property, a handsome, three-story brick house, set back from the street with a generous breadth of lawn. The inside of the house was not so pleasant, the dark woodwork preventing the rooms from reflecting any stray ray of light which might have crept past the brown shutters. Annie had no taste in furnishing, and there was no gay note to lighten the stuffy lines of the "Mission" ensembles. But at the back of the house was a spacious yard where a growing boy could run and roll in the grass and could look up into the trees. Here the sky was bluer and the air sweeter than in Allegheny.

The Jefferses moved into their new home in the fall of 1888, and to celebrate the event Aunt Kate had a family party on

Thanksgiving Day. It was a very special occasion for Annie, to be back in the bosom of the Robinson family and to be in the same neighborhood with her cousins and young friends, free of the obligations of the seminary.

The early months of winter passed happily in the new home. Annie saw her Family Robinson daily, and Robin grew rapidly, a handsome little boy with fair hair and bright blue eyes. Christmas was cold and white and would have been gay but for the fact that Minnie, Annie's sister who was living with them, became seriously ill with a lung affliction and showed no will to live. On the first day of the new year 1890, Minnie died. It was a great loss to Annie, and, with her sister's death, Annie's girlishness entirely disappeared. She seemed to change overnight into a young matron, seriously aware of her position as the wife of the eminent and scholarly Dr. Jeffers and the mother of a growing son.

During 1890, Annie made only five entries in Robin's "Chronicle," to report a strong and healthy baby who was "bright but not an especially remarkable boy for brightness" despite the fact that at three and a half years old he knew all of his letters, could repeat the days of the week, and had learned to read three pages in his book, *The Reformed Primer*. In September, Robin began accompanying his parents to Sunday services, and, according to Annie's diary, "he considers it a great privilege and is generally very quiet."

George Evans writes of Robin about this time and says:

"During times when they lived within easy walking distance from Aunt Philena's the Jeffers family usually came over in the evening. My first pictures in memory of Robin are of a child about four, being pushed in a child's carriage by his father, who seemed to arch forward over it almost dangerously and gaze straight ahead at nothing. Then there came a couple of years later another baby, Hamilton, who took his place in the carriage. Sometimes the mother would be pushing, and in that case, the Doctor would be ambling on ahead, followed by Robin who would be imitating his father's very walk and stoop and long steps."[1]

Little Robin was always happiest when his father was working in the garden, and he could help him push the lawn mower. He

[1]Letter from Evans to M.B.B. August 8, 1943.

was still too young to join the neighborhood children in games but was allowed to watch them from the front porch. Next door lived the four Charnley boys with their widowed mother. The youngest was six and the oldest fourteen when the Jefferses moved to Thorn Street, each with a high-wheeled bicycle. Then there were the two Scott boys who lived across the street and were about Robin's age, while down the street were the three Atwell girls. When Robin was about five, he eagerly joined the group of children, and his father, annoyed at having them playing on his front lawn, planted a hedge around the front of the lot, setting the house off from the others on the street and causing unfavorable comments about his unneighborliness.

The Charnley family kept chickens which the older boys tended and which Robin found a big attraction. Most of them were bantams, and there was a trick hen that would wait on the Charnley's back porch until someone opened the screen door, then she would walk into the pantry, hop onto a shelf and lay an egg in a basket. One day Robin tried to crawl into the chicken coop to join the chickens. As he bumped his head, he ran a nail into it, and cut a bloody gash. This incident caused Robin's parents to restrict him to the confines of his own yard. The doctor tried to use up the child's energy by allowing him to run down the street to a certain tree, then back to the house where the doctor stood, calling directions.

But Robin managed a few excursions on his own. The Semples, who lived down the street, had horses, and Robin liked to play around the stables. Back of the Semples' was a field where people tethered their cows, and here the neighborhood children played baseball. Though Robin was still too young to play the game, he was happy to run after the wild balls.

Despite Robin's having every reason to resent his father, Annie wrote in her diary that Robin and the doctor were great friends and companions. The unnatural vigilance may have been in part due to concern for the child's safety, but in all likelihood, considering the doctor's peculiarities, it was a desire to discourage associations which would eventually find their way into the house and disturb his prized seclusion. Certainly little Robin must have already been aware of being "different," as even his small manifestations of wilfulness were severely dealt with.

IV

SCHOOL ABROAD

THE SUMMERS OF 1891 AND 1892 Robin had spent in Europe with his mother and father. The clearest memories of these journeys were his seasickness on the crossings and his physical weariness, trailing his tireless mother. Wherever he went, his mother took "language lessons," and, from her and the kindergartens which he attended, he had his first lessons in German and French. Annie had abandoned the "Chronicle" of John Robinson, but she kept a daily diary of the European trips.

She notes: ". . . a dear, good little traveller is Robinson, no trouble at all." She tells of getting lost in Paris and walking for hours in the rain, "but we bore it with cheerfulness, and Robin was so good and patient. Not one murmer escaped him; he is just a darling; there couldn't be a better boy. We got home tired, muddy and wet, but cheerful. . . ."

Every day the four-year-old boy was taken on walks to the park, shopping, visits to his parents' friends, to the galleries, and to concerts. His mother wrote, "Robin seems to be interested in all these things." After a two-and-a-half-hour Händel oratorio she wrote, "[Robin] was a little restless at times but very quiet. After one grand chorus to which he listened attentively he said to me that he wished I would teach him to be a musician."

There seemed to be few things planned for a little boy's pleasure. Once, walking up the Champs Élysées, they passed a merry-go-round, and Robin exclaimed, "It will make me *so* happy if you will let me ride on that." His mother added, "So we could not resist." Another time he was allowed to ride an elephant in the Bois de Boulogne, but these are the only two instances noted in his mother's diary where Robin's amusement was catered to.

Robin's first introduction to kindergarten was in Zurich on June 22, 1891. He was allowed to dig in the sand to make a little garden, planting his own seeds, the bloomings to be eventually enjoyed by some other little boy since Robin was taken out of the school in three weeks. The following summer he was entered in a kindergarten at Lucerne where he stayed for a somewhat longer period.

Jeffers remembers that when he was in Paris this year his parents bought him a little military cape, blue on the outside and red inside. As they walked out of the store, he stumbled on the curb and fell into a gutter full of sewage. He was not only scolded for his awkwardness, but his handsome new cape had to be thrown away. This is probably the only piece of wearing apparel that he thought of twice in later years.

He couldn't remember the kindergarten in Lucerne but did remember liking to collect snails on the way to school—sometimes as many as twenty of them—which he turned loose on the garden wall. He also remembered paintings of Keats and Shelley, hanging side by side in a gallery in London, and Arthur's Seat, the hill above Edinburgh.

In the fall, the family returned to the Thorn Street house in Sewickley. But the many distractions of the neighborhood made it increasingly difficult for the doctor to concentrate on his studies or to obtain the necessary rest that his poor health demanded. Despite his father's protests and his mother's warning, Robin had opened the doors of his home to his playmates. According to Alex Robinson, this was too much for the doctor, and he knew of only one way to correct the situation—to move to another neighborhood. So, in October, 1893, he sold the Thorn Street house and bought Margaret Nevin's home, "Twin Hollows," at Edgeworth. It was situated out Beaver Road about a mile from John Robinson's house, past the pond where the children skated in the winter. It was far enough into the country to afford the doctor the privacy which he cherished and too far for a six-year-old boy to keep in touch with his friends. Robin had to depend on the companionship of adults and books. Phenomenally gifted, he absorbed book-learning readily, but it wasn't long before his speech became pedantic from his close association with his father. It was no wonder that, after three years of the restrictions of "Twin Hollows," the little boy looked forward hopefully to Harriet Hampson's visit. His ensuing disappointment was, however, somewhat assuaged by an unexpected diversion the following spring when his father built the chalet.

The chalet could easily be "Exhibit A" if anyone doubted the doctor's sanity. It was an impractical, spontaneous gesture which a man of unlimited means might make to indulge a flighty wife. But in no way was it congruous with Dr. Jeffers or Annie as we know them. When they took their evening walks in good weather, they would cross the eastern ravine and climb the rise on the other side to watch the sunset. One evening Annie said to her husband, "Isn't it a pity that the house wasn't built on this spot instead of in the hollow?" The doctor made no promise at the time, but a few weeks later a load of lumber arrived and was dumped on the rise. A few days later stilts were erected, and on these a Swiss chalet gradually took shape—a surprise from the doctor to Annie, a front row seat from which to observe the sunsets. How much of a surprise and shock, Annie never admitted to anyone. She had not been consulted about either the building or the furnishing, and there is no record that John Robinson was invited to have a say in it either, and he must have been terribly disturbed over such an impractical expenditure.

The chalet was an atrocity, from the description by family and friends. The lower floor, which was constructed out of unsightly building blocks trimmed with ornate woodwork, was supported on spindly stilts. Even the two huge oak trees nearby were unable to conceal its ugliness. Although the Jefferses actually tried living in it for awhile, it was not long before the household was forced, due to the chalet's functional deficiencies, to move back into the comforts of the big brick house. Probably the only good purpose it ever served was a diversion for the two little boys, Robin and Hamilton, during its construction.

The chalet was the fourth home which Robin had lived in during the ten years of his life. Besides these three moves, his summers had been spent in North East, at Lake Chautauqua, and in travel. He had attended two kindergartens in Europe, a private school in Sewickley, the Park Institute in Allegheny, and the Pittsburgh Academy. Robin was well advanced in his school work but was beginning to feel resentment towards his father because of the grind of studying which closed him off from normal contact with other boys and made him feel stiff and unnatural during the few opportunities he had to share in their sport. Robin's mental discipline for Sundays was, for example, to commit to memory the Presbyterian "Shorter Catechism" (really quite long).

If Annie was aware of her son's growing resentment, it is doubtful that she tried to interfere with the doctor's discipline or criticised it. But it is difficult to understand this young mother's enduring the austere solemnity of her child. Perhaps she underestimated the extent or importance of his present unhappiness and believed that some sacrifice must be made to insure a brilliant future for him. It is certainly obvious from her "Chronicle" that she had great hopes that her son would become a man of unusual abilities, so it was likely that she may have encouraged the doctor by her complaisance.

The doctor's impatience with the schooling his son was receiving brought him to the decision to put Robin in European schools, so Annie spent the next four years abroad with her two sons, until Robin was fifteen years old. Dr. Jeffers joined his family during the summer, returning to Allegheny in the winter. Although he did not sell "Twin Hollows" until 1901, he must have closed it because during these years he lived in a room which he rented from Dr. James Kelso at 725 Ridge Avenue.

Later Robin writes of this period:

"I had little or no companionship with other children, and spent much time in daydreams, but I don't remember imagining companions (meaning playmates). I was usually alone against the (imaginary) world, astonishing a curious or hostile people by my exploits—a flying man or an animal-companioned man, like Kipling's Monagh. Thus, up to fourteen or so, when I found satisfactory companionship of my own age. Occasionally after that, when circumstances isolated me again!"[1]

[1]In answer to a question from Grace Besthel, Shenandoah, Pennsylvania, 1940.

The first six months that he was in Europe, in 1898, Robin attended a Leipzig day school. The teachers in this school were very demanding, and Robin studied hard. He was up at six in the morning, drank a glass of hot milk, and was in school by seven. He was evidently a good student and obedient, because, though many of the boys were slapped, Robin was never punished. Being a sensitive boy, he was shocked to find that the boys were not above carrying tales or compromising with the truth. He was totally unprepared for the moral laxity of the average European youth. Nor did he like his German teachers very well.

He was not averse to changing schools when he returned to Europe the following year and was entered at the Villa La Tour, a small school at Vevey, surrounded by vineyards. However, the first few days he was there he hated it so that he didn't think he could endure it and told his father so, begging him to let him change schools. His father was unexpectedly sympathetic and placed no objection in his way. But Robin suddenly decided to remain, discovering that he liked the school and its environs. The lakes and mountains lured him on his holidays, and he soon earned the nickname "Little Spartan" from his teachers and classmates because he swam the lakes in any weather and climbed the mountains, usually alone.

He could now speak German and French fluently, had a thorough knowledge of Latin, and could read, though not converse, in Greek; and he was only twelve years old.

In a letter from Vevey, dated September 14, 1899, Annie wrote to her Aunt Hetty Bosworth, admitting her loneliness without her husband. She said that Hamilton was going to a French day school but that:

"Robin doesn't live with me; he is in boarding school and seems very happy and contented. It is such a joy to me that he is satisfied for if he wasn't, it would be perfect misery for everybody. I see him very often, and he always comes to me Saturday afternoon. . . ."

Sis McCord joined Annie in October and remained until the doctor returned in May. Early in the year 1900, however, Robin did change schools, going to the Château de Vidy at Lausanne, where he stayed for a year. This school was operated by the Christens, a Swiss couple who had been missionaries in Chile.

It was a small school, and there were many South American as well as German, French, and Italian boys. Robin found the mixed company particularly confusing, for he had not yet learned to make friends easily. His energies seemed constantly devoted to adjusting himself to the changes of schools and teachers and languages. Now the complete lack of reverence of these boys for all that Robin had been taught to respect was a burden for him to handle alone. He had no friend in whom he could confide and with whom he could share his disgust, or who might have helped him to understand the immorality which offended him and which he instinctively feared. So although here too, as at Vevey, he was taunted for going off alone, it was necessary for the child to do so if he were to maintain his spiritual balance.

Hamilton remembers an incident at Vevey that made a lasting impression on him. Sis, who had joined them at Vevey, was persuaded by Robin to make him a pair of wings (no doubt suggested to him by the story of Icarus and Daedalus). Sis fashioned them of cloth and ribbons which could be attached to Robin's arms. There was a farm adjoining their *pension* with a large manure pit. It was here that Robin, with his young brother a breathless spectator, made his take-offs from the top of the pit, always landing ignominiously in the heap of manure. Nevertheless, Hamilton was extremely proud of his brother's prowess. This is interesting in view of the fact that it was Hamilton who later flew his own plane and Robin who admired the flight of every bird but dreaded to be air-borne.

He sometimes attempted to realize his daydreams. For instance, one morning he read a story telling of people who lived in jungles and fed on berries. At noon dinner he looked about at his schoolmates and inwardly scoffed at the softness of their civilized living, wishing fiercely that he could forage for his food. Abruptly leaving the table, he decided that he would go out in search of berries. Since it was not the season for berries, he settled for a pear tree, climbed it, and prepared himself for a new and hardy life. He spent the afternoon in the tree, made his supper on pears, spent the night in the tree, and somehow, despite his cramps, managed to breakfast—lightly—on pears. After this, his interest in rugged living lagged, and he was happy to descend to solid earth and civilized food.

The Château de Vidy had charm, set as it was behind high, thick laurel hedges. In the yard was a linden tree under which Napoleon was supposed to have rested. The beauty of the wild briar roses in a corner of the garden lived long in Robin's memory, as did the enormous poplar tree which he loved to climb, although the smell of it always made him ill. He loved, too, the walled vineyards which stretched out lazily in the sun, down to the edges of the lake.

Appealing to his imagination was the mountain La Dent d'Oche, across the lake from Lausanne, and he made up his mind that he would climb it some day. Early one spring holiday, he ferried across the lake, expecting to reach the mountain by noon, climb it in the afternoon, and return to Lausanne by evening. But it proved to be farther than time or a boy's strength could stretch in a single day. Although he hurried, it was noon before he came to a little hamlet near Bernex, in Savoy. He stopped there and had a good lunch and a bottle of wine, swallowing it quickly in his eagerness to be on his way. Walking with great speed, he reached the foot of the mountain by late afternoon. He was tempted to spend the night there and climb the mountain the next morning, but he knew that his mother and Sis would worry about him. Despite his enormous disappointment, he hiked back to Evian-les-Bains, intending to take the evening ferry. He was too late, so he used what little money he had to wire his mother the reason for his delay, and to buy himself a roll and a bar of chocolate for his supper. Spending a cold night in the street without even a coat, he had to wait for the early morning ferry, suffering from apprehension that the date on his round-trip ticket would be questioned, but fortunately it passed unnoticed, and he took his place with hundreds of farmers with their baskets of fruit and vegetables which they were taking to Lausanne. The color and movement, the good-natured shouting and squabbling amongst the farmers were a tonic to Robin, and he felt recompensed for his disappointment.

The next year Robin was placed in a larger school—the *pension* at International Thudichum at Geneva. This was a well-organized school, and there were many South American boys here too, as well as Greek, Turkish, two or three British boys, and one other American. Robin was more distressed by the constant tale-bearing than he was by the lack of moral integrity of the boys, which he had, by now, learned to expect. Here his Greek professor pronounced Greek in the modern manner and changed Robin's classical accent. This resulted in many arguments between Robin and his father.

Whether the doctor had an irrational compulsion about leaving his son in any school longer than a year or whether he had some definite plan, we don't know, but every year that he joined his family in Switzerland he removed Robin from whichever school he was attending and placed him in another one. It is no wonder that Robin kept to himself. He probably felt that it was not worth the terrific effort it cost to make new friends, only to be snatched away from them. It possibly never occurred to the doctor that friendship might include human beings as well as books.

The latter part of 1901, Robin, true to form, was transferred from the *pension* at International Thudichum to Villa Erika at Zurich. Hamilton, who was now seven, also attended this school. Villa Erika did not match, scholastically, the school at Geneva, and the students had worse morals than in any other of the European schools which Robin attended; so nothing constructive was gained by the change.

While the boys were in school, Annie attended the Academy of Music at Zurich. In a letter home, dated January 29, 1901, she wrote:

"We expect to spend this coming winter here at Zurich. There is a fine orchestra connected with the Academy of Music and during the summer there are open air concerts every evening. We are now in Lucerne for a week. It is a lovely place. I would like to spend weeks here, there are so many things one can do. The drives and the walks are lovely—then there are the excursions by boat to so many points of interest. Both our boys are going into a boarding school where they will have to speak German and French. . . ."

Perhaps it was Annie's own restlessness which caused her to persuade the doctor to find a school in another part of Switzerland for the boys each time he joined them.

At fourteen, Robin was definitely showing an interest in poetry and tried his hand at writing some simple verse. His father had given him two small, paper-bound books, the poems of Thomas Campbell and of D. G. Rossetti. Robin was not familiar with either of the poets and, although he soon laid aside the book by Campbell, he was completely intoxicated by the poetry of Rossetti, and thrilled to every poem "from 'The Blessed Damozel' to the least last sonnet." His pleasure was free of all analysis. Those were the first verses that he loved, his first passionate springtime.

Evidently Robin's European education had been completed to the satisfaction of his father because the following year the Jeffers family returned to America, and Robin was entered at the University of Western Pennsylvania (now the University of Pittsburgh). The family had subleased the seminary house on Ridge Avenue, and Robin lived at home and attended the university as a day scholar from September, 1902 to April, 1903.

FIRST POEMS

Although the European schools had demanded a considerable reconciliation of his values and had contributed little to his happiness, they had undoubtedly given Robin a firmer foundation on which to stand for the next few years of his life, forcing on him the necessity of adapting himself to the customs of foreign countries. For although he was separated from his companions by a difference in moral values, two hazards had been removed. In Europe he was not looked upon as a prodigy, since mental precocity was usual, and he had the privilege of companionship if he wanted it. For the long winter months he had been relieved of his father's authority and morbid company. As his fear, self-consciousness, and shyness diminished, his spirit and personality expanded. Self-expression flowered into youthful verse-writing.

Young manhood now took the place of childhood. With it came a sense of independence and an increasing tendency to show a "will of his own," which his mother had noted in his early "Chronicle." He entered into a far more normal adolescence.

The doctor was now sixty-seven years old, and his trips to Europe had not, apparently, improved his health at all. So he decided to leave not only the seminary but the East, and to try a warmer climate. In 1903 he took his sons out of school and moved to California, renting a cottage at Long Beach. Neither Jeffers nor his brother Hamilton remember just how long they lived there, but it was probably for just a few months. In the meantime, the doctor had purchased land at Highland Park where he built a handsome, two-story frame house for $4,000, at 346 Avenue 57.

A college had to be selected for Robin, and the seminary had recommended Occidental College at Highland Park. It was a small Presbyterian school with an enrollment of about two hundred students. In answer to the doctor's request for information, the college sent as emissary Daniel Hammack, a young student who had just completed his sophomore year. Hammack evidently did a good job of representation since, as a result of his visit, Robin was entered for the fall term of 1903. Until completion of his family's house in Highland Park, Robin boarded with a local family.

Although only sixteen, Robin was so advanced in his studies that he was given junior standing at Occidental. But this apparently was not held against him by his classmates and it didn't take him long, in spite of his diffidence, to enter into the activities of his class. Neither aggressiveness nor an acute social sense was a necessary tool with which to make friendships in this small college. A similarity of tastes was all that was required to become one with this group whose members were as steeped in the classics as was Robin. They had as serious an approach to their week-end hikes and athletics as to their academic studies. These associations and circumstances were ideal for Robin's development. He felt no self-consciousness and, instead of solitary excursions, he joined the other students on week-end trips to the mountains and nearby canyons. He quickly gained in popularity and soon became known as "Jeff" to his intimates.

His inner freedom developed, and he wrote more poetry, contributing to the student magazines, *The Aurora* and *The Occidental*. Thirteen of Robin's poems were printed during the years 1903 and 1907 (twelve of which have been reprinted in Sydney S. Alberts' *A Bibliography of the Works of Robinson Jeffers*). The name of the student publication was changed from *The Aurora* to *The Occidental* in 1904 when Robin was editor of the magazine in his senior year.

In June, 1904, *The Youth's Companion* printed Robin's poem "The Condor," which has been reprinted many times. It was the first time that he received payment for a poem, and his brother

Hamilton remembers being deeply impressed on seeing the check for $12.00, a magnificent sum for those few lines of verse.

Robin's writing revealed his preoccupation with nature and his lack of interest in people, a trend which strengthened with maturity.

Rossetti gave place to Swinburne, who was shortly joined by Tennyson and Shelley. It was inevitable that Robin's early verse showed the influence of these poets whom he admired, though it was stamped with an identifiable style.

Robin was a good-looking boy with a quiet poise. He walked with a rhythmic gait, swinging his shoulders slightly as he moved. He had an amazing amount of energy, but it was used up in exercise and study. Probably from lack of interest, he never appeared well-groomed despite his handsome tweed coats. He was still, however, fairly young to give much attention to grooming.

The doctor was restless and again moved his family, this time to Manhattan Beach. Hamilton Jeffers recalls that their first house there

". . . was about a block from the ocean, near Third Street. That was where the seniors had their picnic. Later we moved to a house my father built, also near Third Street, but a mile or so back from the ocean in the 'Carnation Heights' . . . . The farm (my memory suggests twenty, not eighty acres) was also in Manhattan Beach on what is now the main street, perpendicular to the ocean, and about a mile back. My father subdivided these acres . . . there may still be streets in the 'farm' area named after the family, like 'Robinson', 'Hamilton', etc.

"There was only one house on the 'farm', a dilapidated shanty surrounded by eucalyptus trees, that we called the 'rotten house'. The chickens from Highland Park were installed there and, for a time, Nellie the horse. The horse was later moved to a barn at the 'Carnation Heights' house, but the chickens were killed and eaten by some wandering hobo."[1]

Hamilton was twelve and a problem to his parents, as he was less tractable than Robin had been and resentful of too much discipline. The doctor was hopeful that Hamilton would be happy

[1]Letter from Dr. Hamilton Jeffers to M.B.B. July, 1964.

31

on the farm and was pleased when Robin spent his first vacation there, taking long horseback rides into the hills and long walks along the beach.

For the first time since he had started school, Robin continued in the same school the following year, taking his senior year at Occidental. He found it a wonderful relief to be released from the strain of establishing himself with new teachers, students, and customs. Already accepted, he could devote his attention to his studies and have time for outside interests, principally making new friends—the first time in his life that he had enjoyed this experience. He excelled in all of his subjects: Biblical Literature, Economics, Geology, History, Greek, Rhetoric, and Astronomy.

The course in Astronomy took him, with other members of his class, on frequent trips to Mount Wilson and to Echo Mountain where there was an observatory maintained, after a fashion, by the Pacific Electric Company. Sometimes the boys worked all night on the mountain. Other students, not members of the class, would occasionally join these excursions. Much laughing and talking accompanied the work.

Because of his youth, Robin was too undeveloped physically to be outstanding in athletics. He became, however, a member of the track team and ran the two-mile, "displaying rare nerve." He also had great endurance which he proved on some of the trips which he took with classmates and professors.

Dan Hammack told of one such trip—a hike up San Gorgonio (Grayback) Mountain. The highest peak in the San Bernardino range and about seventy-five miles southeast of Highland Park, it stood 11,485 feet high—a challenge to all embryonic Alpinists. Late one fall, Robin, with Dan Hammack, Robert Cleland, and a man named Nevins, took the electric car from Highland Park to San Bernardino. Arriving there at eight o'clock in the evening, they started off, walking until midnight, when they stopped to make camp in the Santa Ana wash. The next day they continued their walk and about the third night reached Bear Valley and made a camp on the north side of the mountain. At dawn they got off to an early start with no breakfast. Fortunately they had not gone far when they found a small camp where they were able to get a little food. They stayed here two days and then moved on to

Seven Oaks, where they found a man by the name of Louie who took them in. Louie had a small cabin, a pet deer, chickens, and innumerable cats. He took a liking to Robin because the boys had told him he was a poet. Louie kept asking him to recite poems, so Robin accommodated him by reciting passages from Tennyson and Homer.

San Gorgonio is usually climbed from the south side, but the boys had decided to take it from the west side, so at two in the morning they began the ascent of the peak from Louie's place. At Horse Meadows the boys got off the trail and had to backtrack. When they finally found the trail again, they still had a 1500-foot scramble to the peak, which they scaled about noon in a screaming wind. But the magnificent view of the Coachella Valley, the San Bernardino range, and the surrounding country made them forget their weariness.

Descending, they reached Louie's place at five in the evening and found that the old gentleman had killed a chicken for their dinner, by way of celebration.

During the next day the boys came to Big Bear Lake; hot and dusty they decided on a swim. They undressed, climbed on a rock and, at the count of three, all dived into the icy water. Hammack, Cleland, and Nevins, gasping for breath, hurriedly swam for shore, shivering with the cold while they waited for Robin. But their Spartan companion evidently felt no discomfort and swam leisurely and with evident pleasure for a good half hour.

By now they were familiar with his stamina. At the end of a day's hike he was never tired and always ready to do more than his share of the camp chores. On the trails it was exhausting and almost impossible to keep up with him. With the cooking utensils packed on his back in a gunny sack, he would swing along the trail, with pans banging, while he poured forth long passages from the classics. He would pause occasionally to study a flower, tree, or bit of rock, or to help a small bird back into its nest. On the way down the trail his poet's eye made note of all the mountain's beauty, which he later used in a poem called "Stephen Brown."[2]

[2]*Californians.*

—In the San Bernardino Mountains,
Traveling from sky-peaked Grayback to Bear Lake,
In a deep-shaded dell I saw great fountains
Of shining water from the black earth break,
And pour through heavy-fronded ferns below,
And down the dark ravine a turbulence make
As of immortal footsteps, when they go
Assured and at their will the wide world to and fro. . . .

The fact that Robin wrote poetry for the college publications, and that he showed more interest in poets and poetry than his classmates, led them to assume that he would probably choose poetry for his profession. But they treated the idea soberly; they found nothing remarkable in his choice. His gift was accepted without challenge or ridicule.

Robin became a member of the Stevenson Literary Society of the college, and was one of the two associate literary editors of the yearbook, *The Occidental*. Of the senior class this magazine wrote prophetically:

"Reverend and grave, with cap and long funereal gown,
The Austere grand Senior paces slowly up and down,
What be his thoughts, you ask, his meditations deep?
What fires those eyes wherein great projects seem to sleep?
Plans he to save mankind? To ease the people's woes?
What is he thinking of? I answer, *NO ONE KNOWS*."

Although this verse had no author's signature, there is no doubt that it was contributed by Robin, as was "The Stream," which later in the year appeared in the magazine *Out West*.

His friend Dan Hammack wrote two plays for the senior program, and it is startling to find that Robin had so overcome his shyness and withdrawal in the two years at Occidental that he took part in both of them. Robin wrote the lyrics for the class song. And on June 15, 1905, graduating with ten others in Occidental's largest class up to that time, J. Robinson Jeffers received his Bachelor of Arts degree.

VI

ROBIN MEETS UNA

HAVING ACQUIRED his Bachelor of Arts degree, Robin decided to take his Master's degree in Letters. The University of Southern California offered a good course in literature, so Robin enrolled in the graduate school after a summer spent at Manhattan Beach with his family. At eighteen he was in possession of good health, a fine physique, and good looks; he had to his credit a European education, an intimate knowledge of the classics and several languages; a sensitive, imaginative mind, and a growing interest in writing verse. He had, during the past two years, made friends of boys his own age, although he still had to learn how to become friendly with girls. These had been constructive years for Robin, but he was now faced, in the larger university, with the necessity of defending his unique personality against the pressure of new friends who expected him to conform to their standards. He was not accepted with the ease which he had enjoyed at Occidental. Mental gifts were not considered as important as the ability to drink and to have a winning way with women. Robin's defense proved to be weak, and he accepted these new standards with a curiosity which soon developed into an enthusiasm. However, his school work did not suffer, and his record was a brilliant one.

Besides the seminar in Old English, which had been the compelling reason for his deciding to enroll at the University of Southern California, Robin entered classes of Spanish and Oratory; the latter he felt would be helpful in overcoming his shyness. The course in Old English was conducted by Dr. Dixon, a

Scotsman from the University of Edinburgh whose specialty was old Scottish ballads and early nineteenth-century poets. About a week after registration, Robin found that he had time on his program for another class and decided to take a refresher course in German. Miss M. G. Borthwick was conducting a class in Advanced German, with a quick reading of *Faust* and class discussion, so he added this course to his program.

Robin still had time to write verse, and in November the *University Courier*, the University of Southern California literary magazine, published his "The Steadfast Sky." By spring, two more poems had appeared, "Homeward" and "The Poultry Lover."

An illustration of his verse at this time is the poem "Homeward," which appeared in the *University Courier* on February 6, 1906.

> O the sun was on my right, leaning on
>   a hill of heather,
>   And the moon was on my left, hang-
>   ing on a hill of stone,
>   And between the two I walked, and
>   they watched me both together,
>   And they smiled upon me there as I
>   walked all alone.
>   For it's homeward I was going,
>   between the sun and moon,
>   And homeward to rest me at the
>   red hearthstone;
>   And my heart flew before tho' my
>   tired footsteps lagged
>   As I walked toward home all alone.
>
> O'er the hill upon my right poured a
>   fairy flood of fire
>   As a screen to hide the sun while he
>   sank from his throne;
>   O'er the hill upon my left the moon
>   was mounting higher,
>   And between them led the homepath
>   where I walked all alone.

Now the sky upon my right was like
    embers that smoulder
  When behind the broken ash angry
    red the heat is shown;
And the moon had sprung clear of the
    stone hill's rocky shoulder;
It was all alone in heaven, I on
    earth all alone.

Now when home was almost reached
    some few stars began to shimmer,
  Little peering friendly eyes o'er the
    skies haphazard thrown;
Yet a moment and I saw, near at hand,
    how the glimmer
Of my own warm hearthside beckoned
    to me plodding all alone.
For it's homeward I was going,
    between the sun and moon,
And homeward to rest me at the
    red hearthstone;
And my heart flew before tho' my
    tired footsteps lagged
As I walked toward home all
    alone.

Miss Borthwick's class had an interest other than German for Robin, as he had discovered pretty Una Call Kuster, Miss Borthwick's star pupil. Una, in turn, was curious about this brilliant young man in his loose tweed coat and stylish peg-topped trousers with their continental air.

Una was two years Robin's senior and had been happily married for three years to Theodore Kuster, a young Los Angeles lawyer. Una was tiny, wore high-waisted dresses, highlighted by a string of amber beads. Her heavy chestnut hair was worn in a big loop at the nape of her neck, and a big bow of ribbon graced the top of her head. Her features were delicate and her profile classic.

Una, Robin very soon discovered, appealed not only to the eye and to the mind but to the imagination. She was as many-faceted as a fine-cut gem, her color as rich, her value as dear. She was an exciting person, Una Kuster.

It was often said of Una that she was curious about people and interested in everyone. That was not quite true. She was discriminating, and her curiosity turned to interest only if people proved to have some quality of mind and of experience. She was impatient of mediocrity. Her capacity for absorbing people and knowledge was as great as her energy. Body and mind and heart were tireless and hungry, and seemingly never appeased.

Once Una had decided that a person was worth her time, she must know all about him, how he thought and what he knew. Then she must follow him, whether into the fields of literature, music, surgery, or mechanics—all equally interesting to her. She would ask her quick, intelligent questions, then give her complete, quiet attention to the answer, her dimple deepening with pleasure and encouragement. Her taste in response was faultless. She knew when to be serious, when to show her enjoyment with her infectious, warm laugh, when to chide, when to encourage.

Ted Kuster, her husband, adored her. They had married when she was seventeen, a student at the University of California at Berkeley. Their marriage was happy and complete, as they evidently had enough love, enough money, and enough friends, and both were intelligent and ambitious. Kuster approved of her returning to college for her Bachelor of Arts degree as long as her work would not disrupt their private life together; with her usual tact, Una spoke of her studies and experiences as little as possible. She was a good manager, and she excelled in both her studies and her home-keeping.

There was a compelling force back of Una, a drive which was certainly not actuated by an underprivileged environment. Until she came west to college, Una had lived with her mother and father, Isabelle and Harrison Call, in the small town of Mason, Michigan. With them also lived her Irish grandfather (her mother's father from Ballyminstra, Killinchy, County Down) who encouraged her in her love of music and first taught her to play the organ.

Rather oddly, Una had been named after her father's first wife, who had died. Una had older twin half-sisters, daughters of her father by the first Una.

The town of Mason placed great importance on "learning and knowing," and its schools adequately prepared Una in all the requisites of the University of California except in Greek. Unhesitatingly her family brought in a tutor to coach her.

Harry Call, Una's father, was a man of moderate circumstances who had brought up his children with "high ideals, and with the will and ambition to in turn make their contribution to a bettered world."[1]

Una had an unusual and dangerous combination of gifts: brains, beauty, and distinction. Because of these gifts she attracted both men and women to her, making a lasting impression on all who knew her and exerting a strong influence on most of them. There were few men who met Una who were not attracted to her. Una herself was conscious of their interest with almost naive wonder, occasionally testing her power with doubting hesitancy in mild flirtations.

This was the young woman, then, who had attracted Robin. It was not long before he was walking Una home from college, carrying her books like any other young man with his girl. That their interest in each other at this time was very deep is doubtful. When Nettie Carter, Una's neighbor and good friend, asked her about Robin, Una answered, "Oh, that's just a young man who attends my German class. He's a very gifted linguist and writes very immature verse."

This was the most that came of their friendship the first year. Robin completed his work in the graduate school in March and went abroad for the spring and summer. Una's only reminder of her friend was an occasional postcard from him.

In the meantime she was busy with her husband and their friends, and her books. Una loved books, and the friends who visited her home seldom came without bringing her one to add to her already extensive library. She also had as much enthusiasm for physical exercise as for mental, and she and Nettie Carter spent many happy hours on the golf course at the San Gabriel Country Club or swimming at Bimini Baths.

Then there were two young Englishmen whom the Kusters had met at the San Gabriel Country Club, Cyril Bretherton and

---

[1]*Ingham County News* editorial, September 20, 1923.

Harry Young. They often came to the house, and Cyril brought Housman's *A Shropshire Lad* to Una. Una's musical talents had given her a keen ear for poetry. She and her friend Esther Busby used to read aloud to each other, and it was Esther who, reading Yeats' *The Shadowy Waters* to Una, provoked her lasting interest in Yeats. Una often claimed that Yeats was "the greatest living poet."

In a letter concerning Esther Busby, Una wrote: "I did not instantly get enthusiastic but came to it. She *never* got completely entangled as I did so thoroughly in the Irish Renaissance."[2] Although their friendship languished between 1912 and 1920, it was renewed, and it was in 1920 that Esther Busby introduced Una to the works of Eugene O'Neill. Una also wrote: "We have always . . . had the most *thrilling* times together. We always talked all day and most of every night. A half of the time, perhaps, about literature, each trying to *force* our tastes on the other."[3]

Most important of these early friends of the Kusters was a young man of letters, an as-yet-unrecognized poet, Frederick Mortimer Clapp. He had been introduced to the Kusters by Carlton Parker, a professor whom Una had known at Berkeley. Parker, after a walking trip with Clapp in Europe, had persuaded him to come to California to give lectures on Russian literature and the early English dramatists under the auspices of the University of California Extension program. Attendance at these lectures developed in Una a great respect for Clapp and led to a lasting friendship between them. When he visited the Kusters' home, Clapp would arrive with armloads of books, including Baudelaire, Verlaine, Mallarmé, Dostoevsky, Tolstoi, Turgenev, and Gogol, and Una devoured them hungrily. He brought her Swinburne and Rossetti and read them to her. And it was Clapp who first talked to her of George Moore and Arthur Symons, and particularly of Moore's *Memoirs of My Dead Life*. When Clapp recognized the intensity of her interest, he gave her a copy of Moore's *The Lake* and planted the seed which was to grow into as absorbing an interest as Yeats.

[2]Letter from U. J. to M. B. B., July 31, 1943.
[3]*Ibid.*

As Fred Clapp's respect for Una grew, he read his own poems to her, and the delicate beautiful lines gave her the keenest delight. She gave him intelligent criticism and encouragement.

Ted Kuster shared Una's enthusiasm for these friends, but, because of the demands of his law practice, he had little leisure to read the books which meant so much to Una. He would, however, discuss entire law cases with her and listen with respect to her opinion.

In Switzerland, Robin lived at the Pension Tiefenau with his parents and, on April 27, 1906, he entered the University of Zurich, studying Einleitung in die Philosophie, Altere englische Literaturgeschichte, Histoire de la litérature française de 1840 a 1900, Dantes Leben und Werke, Spanische Romanzen Poesie, and Geschichte der Römischen Kaiserzeit. In September, when he had completed these courses, he returned to the United States despite the disappointment of his mother and father, who had hoped that he would remain abroad with them. Doctor Leadsworth, his mother's physician in California, had promised Robin that he could do some translating for him and, with this offer in mind, Robin was eager to return. He stopped off in North East briefly to visit his mother's relatives there.

Doctor Leadsworth had a quantity of German medical papers and journals which he wished Robin to translate, and for the next six months Robin worked on these. This work awakened in him an interest in medicine and, curious to know more about it, though not ambitious to become a practising physician, he entered the University of Southern California Medical School in September, 1907.

As a result of winning the highest grades in Physiology his first year in medical school, he became Dr. Lyman Stookey's assistant in the department for the next two years, also teaching Physiology in the dental clinic for a few months. Dr. Stookey had the highest regard for Robin's ability. The doctor had a younger brother, Byron, who was also a student in the medical school, an exceedingly handsome and brilliant young man who was later to become a famous nerve and brain surgeon. It was only natural that Robin and Byron should be drawn together. They became inseparable companions and members of the same fraternity. Stookey was the more sociable and polished of the two young men, but both were attractive to women, though women found Robin disappointingly slow in returning their interest.

According to his classmates, Robin, who had not indulged in drinking while at Occidental, now over-indulged. The excess may have been attributable to two or three things: a reaction to the restrictions of his home life; an effort to prove himself a good fellow; or a renewal of the old fight to overcome his shyness. His appearance suffered, and he became careless in his dress and slouched in posture. However, he still took time to write poems, most of them to girls in whom he was interested or with whom he imagined himself in love, and to Una whom he was beginning to seek out. The naturalist was now taking second place to the lover.

Una had received her Bachelor of Arts degree in 1908 and was now doing work in Liberal Arts at the university. When referring to Una, Robin spoke of her as "my proper young woman." But the university as a whole was aware of the growing friendship between Robin and Una and commended it, considering that Una was a steadying influence on this young man who wrote poems all night, fortified with a jug of wine, a packet of Bull Durham, and a sheaf of cigarette papers.

In a poem called "The Truce and the Peace,"[4] Robin told of his struggles during this period:

> All in a simple innocence I strove
> To give myself away to any power,
> Wasting on women's bodies wealth of love,
> Worshipping every sunrise mountain tower;
> Some failure mocked me still denying perfection,
> Parts of me might be spended not the whole,
> I sought of wine surrender and self-correction,
> I failed, I could not give away my soul.
> Again seeking to give myself I sought
> Outward in vain through all things, out
>   through God,
> And tried all heights, all gulfs, all dreams,
>   all thought.
> I found this wisdom on the wonderful road,
> The essential Me cannot be given away,
> The single Eye, God cased in blood-shot clay.'

[4] *Tamar and Other Poems.*

42

During the summer months the Kusters and the Norman Car-
ters both took houses at Hermosa Beach. Robin lived part of the
time at his fraternity house on the campus and part of the time at
Hermosa where he kept a room with Mrs. Melissa Nash.

According to Una, Mrs. Nash was a "kind and motherly soul
who liked having R. J. room with her, and board too sometimes.
She was much too indulgent with his irregular hours and untidy
ways (endless litters and scraps of paper!!). Once, for instance,
he locked his Airedale in his room and stayed away some hours
when she was away too, and the room was completely wrecked
beginning with his own typewriter. Of course he replaced everything, but she had the most admirable patience through it all."[5]

In the poem "At Playa Hermosa,"[6] Robin spoke of the peace
which he found by the sea:

> Here is not despair nor hope:
> Only gray waves rise and drop.
> Here against the level tides
> Strange and ominous peace abides. —
> What will Fate exact of me
> For this quiet by the sea?

Here was the son of his father speaking: the young man who
wanted peace, had found it by the sea, but doubted his right to
enjoy it unless paying Fate some tax.

Mrs. Carter's son worked in Kuster's office, and, after the two
men had gone into town for the day, Una and Nettie and Robin
would spend the day on the beach, swimming and walking. Robin was a powerful swimmer and would go out beyond the break-
ers, leaving the two women paddling around close to shore.

Despite the fact that Una and Robin were seeing each other
every day, they also exchanged innumerable letters. These testify
to the misery both were suffering over their illicit love. These two
letters were written by Robin to Una:[7]

"Una dearest — I did not *see* you last night but I *felt* your thought
and your presence plainly for I do not think that I imagined them only
and I lay wakeful and longed for you; — but for a little while I was a

[5]Letter from U. J. to M. B. B., May 8, 1935.

[6]*Flagons and Apples.*

[7]From R. J. letters in collection at Tor House.

43

little happy. How I desire your voice, your eyes; your lips — you — my very dearest. And today is black & tomorrow is black, — but the next day there is the hope of light, darling."

"Darling — I am used to unhappiness perhaps but not to such as is mine now — and yours. And how shall I know to deal with it? But I could bear it if it were mine alone — I do not know how I can bear it if you too suffer. Truly I am guilty — I could find it in my heart to wish you had never seen me. Perhaps I ought not to see you anymore. But, O, Una — not that — not that, Dearest, dearest — do not be so unhappy — for my sake do not — let me do the suffering, dearest."

There were also letters filled with his hopes and his ambitions:[8]

". . . you are the one shining thing in the world for me; and you have brightened all the rest.

"It seems strange to be hopeful again, and full of happy laughter. I've always considered recklessness as the one great virtue; but I see now that it must be positive and forward-looking recklessness, — not a desperate negative disregard of consequence. — The gay and laughing courage of D'Artagnan on his daffodil-colored hack; not the somber death-and-devil-defiance of Athos."

". . . Also, darling, we'll *have* wherewithal in the not very distant future. For I have just three ideas in my head: — you are the first; — the second is to write as good verse as possible; — and the third, to make money — I mean, plentiful money, — in our chosen profession. Don't doubt, sweetheart—and I know you don't—that I'm going to succeed in all three. I shall keep your love, star-of-hope, till the end of my life — and yours. — Second, I shall write, with you to help me, as good verse as any-one's living now. — And, third, we're going to have all the prosperity we shall need . . . .

"Keep this prophecy, Una-most-beautiful. Ten years from now we'll read it — and say, 'How true!' "

[8]*Ibid.*

VII

THEODOSIA

WHILE AT OCCIDENTAL, Robin had met and made friends with a young fellow student, Vera Brooke. While attending University of Southern California he occasionally took Vera on dates. She says that she marked Robin for "something outstanding," although she couldn't name just what. She found him definitely different from the other boys whom she knew. One day they went to Hermosa together, and Robin introduced her to Mrs. Nash and her cats. Mrs. Nash's cats were numerous and so coddled that they were absolutely helpless, having none of the self-sufficiency of the normal cat. But Mrs. Nash had a gift for indulgence, which included Robin, as she put up with his irregular hours and untidy ways and the vagaries of his Airedale dog, Paddy.

Vera made every effort to understand her handsome young friend, but his reticence and extended silences and abstractions made it difficult. One time Robin invited her to a fraternity dance. She went hopefully, but, as Robin had never learned to dance and neglected introducing his fraternity brothers to Vera, she spent the entire evening sitting with Robin, watching the others dance.

Despite his social shortcomings, Robin seemed to have a certain success with young ladies, and he himself has written, "Like other young men I had a number of love affairs before I was twenty-five—none of them contemplated marriage." One of these young women was a musician, Lenora Swift, who played and sang to Robin while he looked on admiringly.

Like any young poet, when Robin wrote a poem to a mythical "Helen," he would give a copy of it to each of the girls in whom he was interested at the time. It was natural that each of them should believe, or hope, that *she* was his "Helen." There is no doubt, now, that most of these early poems were written with Una in mind, and that Robin was merely reaching out for admiration when he made duplicate copies for "distribution."

Robin's family returned from Europe in the fall, and his father purchased a house in Los Angeles, at 1623 Shatto Street. The Manhattan Beach farm hadn't proved a lasting success for either the doctor or young Hamilton. Robin now gave up his "quiet by the sea" to live with his family in Los Angeles.

About three times a week Robin would join Una and Nettie Carter at Bimini Baths for a swim. These meetings were supplemented by an occasional dinner date, when Una and Robin would slip away alone to some out-of-the-way restaurant. Friends of the Kusters, seeing them, began gossiping, and word got back to Hazel Pinkham, one of Una's close friends. Hazel spoke to Una about it and reprimanded her for being indiscreet. But Una was always impatient of criticism and laughed off the advice.

Una had never told her husband of her friendship with Robin. When she had first met Robin, it hadn't seemed important to mention him to Ted, who took little interest in her college friendships. Now it would be difficult to confess that she had known Robin for four years without inviting him to her home. Ted would undoubtedly ask embarrassing questions, for inevitably Una and Robin were building up mutual interests and sharing experiences which created a secret world for them, secret because they had excluded Ted, and this very secrecy made it more intimate. When Robin telephoned Una at home, and Ted answered, Robin would ask for Theodosia. "Theodosia Fleming" was the name behind which she shielded her communications with Robin. If Una should answer the phone when Ted was home, she would simply answer, "wrong number." And still Una and Robin were trying to convince themselves that their feeling for each other was one of friendship, for Una wrote:

"I must not seem an idle or unhappy young woman eager to console some unhappy poet! I never even then liked *young* men very well. I was busy and had my occupation—my friends I loved and found amus-

46

ing. Life was opening out more richly before me every day. I was not emotionally satisfied but that was a vague thing in the background not analyzed. I lived in an incessant whirl of activity. *He* on the other hand had not the faintest wish to marry anyone. He caroused around with much interest tinged with an enjoyable poetic melancholy. He knew that he was coming into a legacy in January 1912 that would free him financially for some years and had a plan to go exploring with a party he had heard was going to South America. So without the wish of either of us our life was one of those fatal attractions that happen unplanned and undesired. We both hated for our families the unwelcome publicity of divorce. And I hated too to lose the respect and affection I had won with some difficulty from Teddie's difficult family to say nothing of Teddie who was and is most dear to me."[1]

By the spring of 1910, almost five years since they had first met in Miss Borthwick's class in Advanced German, their relationship had become so complicated that they were both in torment. Robin was not earning enough to support a wife, and, since he would not come into his inheritance from his Uncle John until 1912, marriage was out of the question. Robin decided it might help matters if he went away for awhile, so in August, 1910, when he had completed his semester in the medical school and Una had received her Master's degree in Liberal Arts, he left, accompanied by his parents, for the University of Washington to study Forestry.

Forestry seemed a far cry from medicine, but it was actually closer to Robin's real interests. He never would have been happy in a profession which kept him indoors, or which did not leave him enough leisure to write poetry, for by now he knew that he wanted to be a poet. He hoped that in forestry he might learn to reclaim the woods from the ravages of loggers and yet have time for writing.

In a letter which Una wrote to Robin when he left for Seattle, she cried:

". . . I do not see how I am to live, very dearest,—I cannot see anything ahead for many months but unending blankness—How can I tell you my utter love—my utter devotion. . . . I do not think that time or distance . . . can separate us any more. I am yours and I shall walk

[1]Letter from Una to M. B. B. August 16, 1935.

47

softly, all my days until we can take each other's hands and fare forth for those wild, vivid joys we two must know together. . . ."[2]

In October of 1910, Robin's mother wrote a letter to Minnie Pratt, describing their new life in Seattle:

"Of course, you know by this time that we are again torn up by the roots, and transplanted to Seattle soil. It is such a long story—the whys and wherefores—that it does not seem worth while to try to write it all out. We came back to Los Angeles fully expecting to stay there indefinitely, but we very soon discovered that Robin was restless and unhappy, and dissatisfied with the study of medicine, and he had to have a change of scene and occupation, and we had some anxious days and weeks; so much so, that I was not in a mood to write any letters or hardly to see anyone or go any place. But finally the study of Forestry was decided on in Seattle, where is one of the best, if not the best, school of Forestry in the U.S. It was not quite a sudden notion, for he has thought about forestry as a profession, off and on, for a good while. It is hard to say what he will make out of it; if he had a little less cleverness and a little better capacity for work, his future would look brighter. So he and the Dr. came up here, and I stayed in Los A. until I got the house rented.

". . . We felt that it was better, on various accounts, to come up here to make a home for Robin, as long as we could just as well as not. It was a little hard on Hamilton to change his school again, but he seems to like his school here, and he is getting along well. The Dr. thought a change of climate would do us all good. . . .

". . . We are living in a tiny four-room flat—the only place at all suitable to rent furnished near the University—five rooms really we have, for Robin's room is upstairs—a very nice corner room. We have disappearing beds, and are much more comfortable than I supposed we would be; only, of course, I have everything to do; and cooking nearly drives me wild. Really, I wonder that I get along as well as I do. I have to read myself a chapter on sinful pride now and then, for I do hate to live in a common apartment house with three front doors. . . ."[3]

Robin wrote lengthy letters to his friend Vera Brooke, who was at the University of California studying for her Master's degree in History. Each letter contained at least one, sometimes two,

[2]In collection at Tor House. August 12, 1910.

[3]This apartment was at 4215 Brooklyn Avenue, N.E., Seattle.

Annie Robinson Tuttle (Jeffers)

Birthplace of Robinson Jeffers

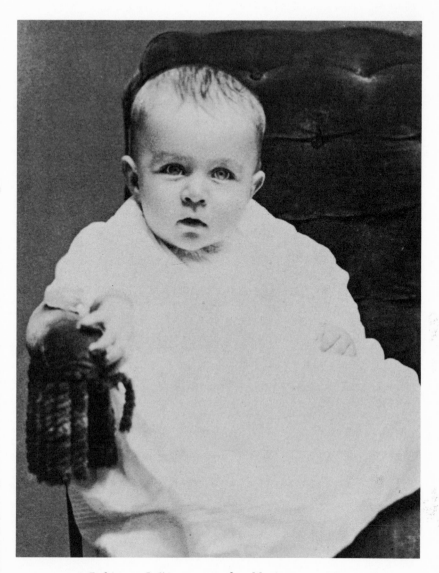

Robinson Jeffers, 7 months old, August, 1887

*Robinson Jeffers and mother. 13 months. February, 1888.
Taken at Pittsburgh*

Aunt Mary (Sis) Tuttle McCord, Robin's great aunt.
Taken at North East, Pa.

Robinson, 5 years old, January, 1892. Taken at Pittsburgh

Father, Mother, J.R.J., 1893. Taken at Pittsburgh

*Twin Hollows, Edgeworth, Pa. Hamilton Jeffers and mother,
about 1897*

poems which he had written and which he later included in his first volume of verse. But try as he would to find distraction, his thoughts continually returned to Una, and he wove her into his verses. One such poem, called "To Canidia"[4] confessed his bewitchment:

> Nay, is there need of witchcraft still,
> Witch-girl, to break my stronger will?
> Of strange enchantments, and of song
> In far pine-forests all night long?
> What use is there of woven charms?
> Have I not held you in my arms?
> And is there stronger spell than this?
> The burning memory of your kiss?
> Or mightier charm can you prepare
> Than the long wonder of your hair?
>
> But tho' the madness of desire
> Burn body and spirit as with fire,
> Tho' the wild longing never cease
> To seek out you and find out peace,
> I, being more strong than you, no more
> Will set my feet to seek your door.

And in a mood of melancholy he wrote "On the Lake:"[5]

> O weary firs along the shores,
> Why is your speech so sorrowful?
> O water voices sad and dull,
> What pain is yours?
>
> I grieve, and you should bring me cheer,
> Not mix strange sorrow with my own.
> Or do you also long for one
> Far, far from here?

Although at first he sent these poems to Una and wrote her long letters which she answered, they wrote to each other less and less, struggling toward a separation, until finally they ceased corresponding altogether. By spring they both felt hopeful that they had terminated a dangerous relationship.

[4]*Flagons and Apples.*
[5]*Ibid.*

That summer Robin returned to Southern California, determined not to see Una. He had been back in the city only about half an hour, waiting for a street car on a busy intersection, when a policeman halted traffic, and directly in front of him a large open roadster stopped. At the wheel sat Una. For a moment their startled eyes widened with dismay, then just before traffic moved on, they both smiled—little smiles of resignation, as if to acknowledge that Fate was stronger than they. The next morning Robin telephoned "Theodosia," and their affair flamed into new misery.

Robin was living with Mrs. Nash in Hermosa, and letters flew between the beach and Los Angeles, between their clandestine meetings. As early as June 9, Una wrote Robin:

". . . Dearest—dearest I love you so much today that I cannot contemplate the thousand ages that I must live until I see you again. . . ."

and

". . . one must be very strong to endure love, I think. . . ."[6]

The Jefferses did not return to Seattle in the fall, and by now there was no doubt of the seriousness of Una's and Robin's love affair. In December, Una wrote Robin:

"Dearest—so much the dearest in all the world. —it's only by the most super exercise of will that I keep my feet from running to you —as my heart does this morning. . . ."[7]

Robin took Una to Mount Lowe where they could discuss their problems without fear of being discovered. But rumors reached Kuster, and he went to Nettie Carter for confirmation. Nettie told him to talk with Una. Unhappily, Una admitted to her husband that she was deeply in love with Robin and was afraid that divorce was the only solution. Ted was frantic and insisted that Una's interest in Robin was only an infatuation. He begged her to take more time before contemplating so important a step and suggested a trip abroad, alone. Finally, and reluctantly, she agreed, promising not to see or write Robin for a year.

Recovering from his initial shock, Ted was kind and generous

[6]In collection at Tor House.
[7]Ibid.

and made all the arrangements for Una's trip. She left for Europe in April, 1912, and Ted went with her as far as Chicago. During the trip, they discussed their affairs soberly; Ted was confident that Una would recover her good sense and return to him.

In the meantime, Robin's family had moved again. Annie, in a letter to Minnie Pratt, written from her new home at 822 Garfield Avenue, Pasadena, said:

". . . I don't think we had taken this place when I wrote you last, but you may have heard about it from Alex. You know we have been looking around a little for an exchange of property, for the Dr. did not feel that he wanted to buy outright. Finally this place in Pasadena was offered, and we decided to take it. . . . It has large eucalytus trees on it, and two palms, and about two trees each of apricot, peach, plum, orange, walnut, nectarine, loquat, and I guess that's all, but it is plenty. The house needs some changes, and we were there one day last week with an architect to plan the remodeling: it can be done at a comparatively low cost, and I am rather glad the changes are necessary, for I like to have it all fresh. . . . Hamilton wants a dog, and over there we can have one. . . . It is a good thing that I am not particularly ambitious socially, as I should certainly be very envious, when I compare the new house I am going to have with Jennie's. Hers is elegant, and mine will be very ordinary, but the trees, etc., make up to me."

In other letters written to Minnie from 1910 to 1914,[8] Annie admits that she is weary of the doctor's restlessness. Alex Robinson had taken his Uncle John's place as the doctor's financial advisor, but when the family moved to California the doctor assumed the responsibility for his own investments. According to Alex, the doctor had neither experience nor wisdom in such matters and lost money on most of his transactions. This must have been of considerable worry to Annie. Certainly the photographs taken of her at this time show no hint of the "blithesome" young woman described by her family and friends in Sewickley. Rather, she looks humorless and stern.

Nor do her letters and diaries relieve this impression. They are colorless records of shopping tours, calls on friends, afternoon rides with the doctor, and an occasional concert or a lecture by a visiting missionary. There is no hint that she had any capacity

[8]Collection of letters given to M. B. B. by Robinson family.

for enjoyment or enthusiasm. This impression we have of an extremely dull woman is, however, constantly belied by Robin's classmates, who knew her at this time as always charming and hospitable, and by Una who found her beautiful and smiling.

Robin unhappily reconciled himself to Una's absence but was at a loss to know how to occupy himself until he met George Evans, his cousin from Ohio, who had spent so much time with Philena and John in Sewickley and who was now in California. Evans later wrote an account of their meeting and consequent summer experiences:

"In company with a younger University friend, Russell Coryell, I was living in Los Angeles. The two of us had banged our way west for a change and adventure, and were keeping bachelor's hall in a cellar room. We went occasionally on a Sunday evening to Pasadena to enjoy a good home lunch-supper at the McCords' who were cousins of my mother. . . . One Sunday evening, we met there, much to my delight, Cousin Annie Jeffers. With her to my surprise was Robin. I had lost touch entirely with him. I knew that he had attended a college in Southern California. I knew that he occasionally wrote verse. I had found some of it at one time in *Youth's Companion*, and remembered about it. If I had been warned that I was to see Robin again, I would have not been thrilled, for I would have expected to meet a young man a bit younger than myself who would act years older, a person with interests probably removed entirely from my own, nothing to bring us together except that we had seen each other years before. He would probably be homely, stooped, and boringly literary. What Russell and I found was a mighty good-looking fellow, tall, well set up, charming and quiet in manner, and full of fun. We took to him at once.

"Our stay in Los Angeles was about running out. Russell and I had spent the winter there. Russell got odd jobs and made money. I was engaged in writing and wasn't making any. We thought we'd try Santa Barbara, mainly because we liked the name of the place. On the Sunday evening when we met this new Jeffers person, we disclosed our plan of leaving Los Angeles, and in a burst of warmth toward him asked him to come along. He said in his very quiet way that he thought he would. The spontaneous friendliness of it won us outright. Here was another adventure to suit us down to the ground. . . .

"Before I left Los Angeles, Russell and I accepted a bid from Jeffers to join him and half a dozen friends of his on a day's sailing cruise out of San Pedro. The boys had rented a boat, and kindly let us in on the fun. It was fun. We had food along, and beer. We fished; we dived from the deck in the beautiful cold refreshing Pacific; we got sunburned, and we slept. Getting in after dark, we bade Jeff good-bye with the assurance that we were to see him later in Santa Barbara. All the boys who were his friends on the cruise called him 'Jeff' and nothing else. That was what he was to be to us.

"In Santa Barbara we lived for the summer in a vine-covered frame cottage up on the hill near the Mission, and with a view of the mountains and the sea, depending on which window you looked out of. I spent the whole summer writing a play which I still have in the attic. Russell, with his accustomed versatility at employment, worked first as a bell-boy in the Potter hotel, and later got a job on the local newspaper. Jeff wrote verses. We never asked him what he did with them. . . . He was as lazily busy as a poet needs to be. He would spend hours of a morning on the balcony over-looking the Mission, occasionally calling in to me in a voice low and pleasant to fill out a figure of speech or supply a rhyme.

"I had a dwindling bank account. Jeff always had a cheque-book in his suit case, and Russell always had ready cash. We kept our loose funds in a tin box to which we each had a key. Russell one evening dumped into it eighteen dollars for the days' tips at the hotel.

"Russell's hours at the hotel were staggered, and we often swam all afternoon in the ocean, or rode horseback on fairly good mounts hired from the stable. Sometimes we would lose ourselves on the mountain trails, and get back late enough to alarm the livery-stable keeper. At times we cooked our own meals; again for a period we would tramp into town, a mile or so away to a boarding house. Not infrequently we tapped the cash-box for enough to pay for the best meal the town offered—with wine. . . .

"I have the impression of Jeff reading several times from sheets of freshly written-upon paper, and doing it in a very low, quiet voice that was almost a rhythmic singing. We had no idea that he took any serious interest in poetic composition. What he read, at any rate, was good verse and not poetry in its fuller sense. The reason for this, as I now understand it, is that his life so far had been a pleasant and indulgent adventure. The love that later openly molded it—his life with Una—was yet fully to come. I recall that one morning he showed me her picture, and said that there was the woman he would marry.

"Once while riding with Jeff in Santa Barbara, I asked him, 'Have you any superstitions?' He said, 'Yes, one. If I'm having a good time, I later expect the opposite.' "[9]

[9]Letter to M. B. B., August 8, 1943.

In a letter addressed to Robin in 1941, Russel Coryell reminisces on that summer in 1912:

". . . I wonder if you remember the night we spent on Mrs. Hester's lawn, George having gone on up to the cottage and returned with blankets for us. He was crying in drunken melancholy as he came back because he was so humiliated to think that innocent little Padiesto[10] had seen him drunk. You comforted him in your best Latin by quoting, 'Forsan et haec olim meminisse juvabit! . . . How's your forty-five automatic? And do you still practice shooting at bottles along the waterfront from horseback? . . .'"

In the meantime, Una had settled in London. She communicated with her English friend, Harry Young, who was associated with his father's law firm in London, and who had agreed to be her banker. Harry, who was genuinely fond of Ted Kuster, disapproved of Una's contemplated divorce, but this did not prevent him from doing all he could to fill Una's stay in England with pleasant experiences and people. It was Harry's friend, Bert Gearing, an Englishwoman, with whom Una later went on a ten-day coach trip to Tintagel and the surrounding country. They got on well. Bert enjoyed Una's eager, gay personality and said that Una "made things happen." Una, in turn, found Bert's British travel habits comforting. Bert never complained, wanted to see everything, and was delighted with all she saw.

Percy Peacock, a friend of Hazel Pinkham's, came to call. Una saw him as a romantic, melancholy young man. He saw her as "young and pure and *so* beautiful," not at all the "neurotic, delinquent would-be-divorcee" he had feared to meet (as he later wrote Una). Percy brought England's past alive for Una. Enthusiastically they covered London mile by mile on walking tours, carefully planning each day's excursion; and, taking a train to the country, they would walk through the neighborhoods once haunted by Meredith, Carlyle, Whistler, Keats, and Shakespeare. Percy kept a little blue-bound copy of Shelley in his pocket, and from this he would read to Una. Back in London they would dance through the nights and be up early to visit the galleries by day. At the Fabian Society Una met the Sidney Webbs, George Bernard Shaw, St. John Ervine, and Millicent Murby.

[10]Paddy, Robin's Airedale dog.

Stirred by the memories of the tales told her by her Irish grand-father, Una wanted to see Ireland. Against the advice of all of her London friends, she took a trip alone through Ireland and Scotland. "People just don't travel in Ireland," they warned her. But Una did. With her usual luck she attracted the attention of two elderly gentlemen who adopted her as their particular responsibility and squired her in and out of the shabby Irish hotels and over the tortuous roads in rickety coaches and jaunting carts. Una went to Blarney Castle on a little train and wrote in her diary: "I remember best the yellow irises and the deep green meadow grass and buttercups around the castle."

In pouring rain, she visited her mother's family in Killinchy, "a pretty little place with many flowers." She visited Burns' cottage, the Walter Scott country, and Wordsworth's grave. She touched her fingers to her lips and blew a kiss to her beloved George Moore's manor house. Although Una never met George Moore, they later corresponded. On one occasion he wrote of her visit as he imagined it could have been: ". . . the story how near you were to visiting Moore Hall drew my mind back to years long past over and a number of pictures rose up before me: your carriage driving through the gates, up the winding avenue, and myself on the steps waiting to receive you. . . ."

Returning to London, she was persuaded by Millicent Murby and Gertrude Davis, two women whom she had met through Percy Peacock, to take a walking trip with them through the Austrian Tyrol. While there Percy wrote her tenderly:

". . . you have made London more beautiful for me than it ever was before. It is no good turning my head and looking for you here, you will not come up in your little grey suit. . . . What a lot of time we wasted in laughing when there were so many things to say, but somehow it seemed unnecessary to say them. Give my love to Millicent and Gertrude and take all you will for yourself. You will get many letters with this and all of them will be full of love for you. I gladly add my love to theirs. You cannot have too much, can you? Perhaps mine has a particular quality of its own."

Una sighed with pleasure and tucked Percy into her heart with her other loves.

After she and her friends parted, Una went to Italy and back to France. At times she thought longingly of Robin and regretfully of Ted and with confusion of Percy. But at Trafoi, in August, she had news from her husband. He had been granted an interlocutory decree! At the same time, she received a most disturbing letter from Hazel Pinkham, saying that Ted seemed to be falling in love with a plump young girl from Bakersfield, Edith Emmons, whom he was introducing as his "ward." He had also entered her in a fashionable school in Los Angeles. This was, to say the least, a shock to Una. In Ted's frequent letters to her during the four months of their separation he had made no reference to his "ward" or to a change of heart. He had expressed no intention of releasing her from her promise not to communicate with Robin, nor had he indicated that he was considering divorce proceedings. Una's immediate reaction was one of furious indignation, settling into a mood of frustration and depression.

She needed advice and decided to seek out Fred Clapp who, with his wife Maude, was now living in a hotel at Ouchy, near Lausanne. Sending them a wire that she was coming, she entrained for Lausanne, only to find upon her arrival that they had left for Italy the day before without having received her wire. Disappointed and disheartened, she went to Paris. Percy Peacock, having sensed her distress from her letters, was in Paris to meet her. Gratefully, Una placed herself in his hands. It was ineffable sweetness to have everything planned and to do only what she was told to do. She found Percy "dear and kind" and their hours together were spent happily, hand in hand, exploring old castles, feudal courtyards, romantic rivers, quaint villages. Their hours apart were spent thinking of each other. Her hurt vanity assuaged, even Robin faded momentarily from Una's mind.

However, when she returned to London with Percy, she decided to go home and straighten out her affairs, and Percy reluctantly agreed that she should. Again she had created a gay, new world for a man who had fallen in love with her.

VIII

"I AND MY LOVED ARE ONE"

"I arrived home from Europe in November, 1912, and went direct to the St. Francis Hotel in San Francisco. Teddie Kuster was there to meet me and stayed two days during which time we finally settled our affairs. . . . R. J. came the next day after Teddie left, and within a few hours we were *engaged*—an amusing thought to us. At first I thought I would go back to the University at Berkeley and begin work for my Doctorate in Philosophy—to put in the time until we could marry. I engaged rooms at a lovely place high up on Virginia Street. I actually moved over to Berkeley for several weeks and Robin went back south but we soon felt we were wasting time and decided to get away where we wouldn't bother any one so we hit upon a Seattle suburb—Madison Park, on the edge of the lake in the trees. So I went down to Los Angeles and visited Hazel and Robin's family for a few days, then we took the boat to Seattle . . . . We arranged to marry August 2—to give Teddie a day to get formalities of divorce complete on August 1 . . . ."[1]

Una had, of course, advised Robin of her reason for returning home so unexpectedly and had urged him to meet her in San Francisco. Here she found a rather formal letter awaiting her, in which he informed her not only of the date of his arrival but of the impending publication of his first book:

". . . I am having a book of verse brought out, under John S. McGroarty's supervision, the Grafton Publishing Co., who publish the *West Coast Magazine*. McGroarty (of the Mission Play, etc.) is become a good

[1]Letter from Una to M. B. B. September 11, 1935.

57

friend of mine, and praises my productions in an exaggerated and satisfactory manner,—as he might, being friend, and publisher's reader, and Irishman. The book should be out by Christmas.

"Also I have an Ayrdale terrier pup, who looks as much like Bernard Shaw as is possible for a dog. . . ."

After Robin's reunion with Una in San Francisco, he had not returned immediately south, but had proceeded by boat to Seattle to look into the possibilities of resuming his studies in Forestry at the University of Washington. While there, he first got the idea of trying to persuade Una to join him, and they had considerable correspondence on the subject. He also advised her that an exaggerated version of their affair had even reached as far as Seattle, that his fraternity brothers believed that he had gone off to Europe with "another man's wife," and that he had had a difficult time persuading them that it was not true.

After Robin had made arrangements for his return to the University in January, he returned to his family's home in Pasadena.

Annie, in her letters to Minnie Pratt, pointedly avoids reference to her son's troubled affair of the heart, but, in a letter dated December 12, 1912, she does tell her, with well-controlled pride, of the publication of Robin's first book of poems:

". . . Robin has just come back from a delightful trip to San Francisco and then on up by boat to Seattle. He likes the country up North. The dear boy, as you know, is really interested in nothing but literature and he writes this and that all the time, verses a good deal of the time, and he has just had a dainty little volume of verses printed. It makes me proud to see his name on a title page, though I do not know much about poetry. The Dr.'s comment is that he will do a great deal better later on. Robin has some friends in literary work, who say nice things about his talent. Of course it remains to be seen whether it ever comes to anything or not. This little first effort are mainly love poems, and some of them are real dainty, as even I can feel . . . ."[2]

Flagons and Apples was published at Robin's own expense. In an article written for *The Colophon* in 1932, he recalls:

"I am willing to tell the history of my first book, though it is not clear why it should interest anyone; certainly it does not interest me. In 1912

[2]In collection of letters at Tor House.

I came into possession of a little money,[3] a little more than was immediately required, a novel experience. I had written verses, like almost everybody, and had not offered them to magazines, but it occurred to me that now I could afford to get them printed. For the purpose I made the acquaintance of an older author of verses who was somehow interested in a printing-shop called the Grafton Publishing Company. I asked him to luncheon, drank with him, and showed him my typewritten poems. I believe he really thought well of them, although it seems to me now an impossible generosity. It was arranged that they should be made into a book; I was very willing to pay for the manufacture of five hundred copies, and took away my manuscript to arrange it for the printer.

"This was in Los Angeles; I lived rather solitary at one of the beaches twenty miles distant, and was too young for my age, and drank a good deal when I came to town. At Redondo, on my way home in the evening, I left the electric car to visit a bar-room frequented by longshoremen friends of mine. I stayed there until the cars stopped running, and had to walk the three miles home. For several hours I had thought nothing about my verses, which only interested part of my mind, for I had no confidence in them. It was not until the next morning that I looked for the bundle of manuscript which had been under my arm, but it must have been laid down somewhere, and was not to be found, either at home or in Redondo. The loss was not serious in any sense; not even serious for the moment, because I have always had an excellent memory for trifles, and every line and rhyme was lodged in my head, only needing to be typewritten again.

"A name had to be found for the book, and discovering that all the verses were more or less amatory, I thought sadly of the conversations reported in George Moore's *Confessions of a Young Man*, which I had lately read. 'My dear Dayne, you always write about love; the subject is nauseating.'—'So it is; but Beaudelaire wrote about love and lovers; his best poem—' 'True, *mais il s'agissait d'une charogne*—there was a carrion in it, and that elevates the tone considerably.' But I had no *charogne* in my little verses, and was never witty, and could only think of the line in the Song of Songs, 'Stay me with flagons, comfort me with apples, for I am sick of love.' So the small book was called *Flagons and Apples*, a title much too big for it.

"Something was said at the printing-shop about sending out review copies; but my interest in the book was waning, the irrational need of

[3]Hamilton Jeffers told me that the bequest of $9,500 was made to Robin as his "grandpa's" namesake (John Robinson). He had not received a similar bequest.

publication seemed to be satisfied by the printing and nothing further was done.

"Soon after this, life became more interesting than anybody's book; I went away to Seattle and left my 480 volumes in the printer's cellar. Twenty I had taken; I gave away three or four, and later burned the rest. I cannot remember how much time passed before a letter from the printer reached me in Seattle, asking what he should do with the volumes left on his hands. I told him to have them pulped, I remember thinking that perhaps their substance would save a young forest tree from the paper-mills. But the honesty of the printer wanted to cut my loss; he sold the whole edition to a second-hand book shop, for twenty cents apiece, I cannot imagine how it was accomplished, and sent me the check. Holmes's Book-store—or was it Dawson's?[4]—remained of course unable to resell their bargain; I have lately heard that they were reduced to giving away the volumes, and would broadcast them to be scrambled for, at auction of other books. . . ."

The passive quality of Robin's nature was very evident. Some spur, in this case his rarely exercised personal gratification, had moved Robin to give his poems to a printer. Quickly, apologetically, it denied itself almost at conception. He was satisfied to see his poems in print and tried to destroy, almost wholly, the evidence. His initiative was a tool of the inner man almost entirely. The outer man was normally, or, for all we know, more than normally, interested in girls, but he couldn't express this interest, being incapable, as with Vera, of aggressive action. He needed a Una, a woman mature enough and sensitive enough to understand his desires, and forceful enough to spur him into putting them into action. Una's influence lay, not only in her drive, but in her beauty and in her intelligence. She was the rare, the perfect mate for him.

The "older author" with whom Robin had made friends was a man by the name of Willard Huntington Wright, who was a book reviewer for the *Los Angeles Times*. (After 1925, Wright was identified with the Philo Vance mystery stories under the pseudonym of S. S. Van Dine.) Wright instructed Robin to compose his own review, which, after editing, he would print. However, Robin wrote Una that Wright had made only a few verbal

[4]It was Holmes's Book Store, although referred to as Jones's Book Store in a letter from R. J. to Donald Friede, March 9, 1926.

changes to make it sound more like his own style, these being " . . . not lascivious, be it noted, but psychologic." At this time Wright was an editor of *Town Topics*, and chief editor of *The Smart Set* and editor and contributor to *Truth*. Although Wright urged Robin to accompany him to New York and promised him work on one of the publications, Robin felt that it would take him too far from Una and declined.

In December, 1912, Robin started writing a lyrical novel which he had discussed with Una in San Francisco. The title he had selected was *Man Maker*. He wrote Una, on December 8:

"The heroine (Nona McLeod) falls in love several times: and makes each of her victims amount to something worth while—even, now and then, in spite of themselves . . . . It's a good theme; but, since it's a little *popular* I'll have to drop in a suspicion of burlesque, so that people won't be quite sure whether I'm in earnest or not. 'Irony', somebody says, 'is the final achievement of art.'—but not too much irony, nor too evident . . . ."

Robin wrote several chapters during the winter months, but his heart wasn't in it, and nothing came of it. He was also putting together another group of poems which he intended publishing under the title *Songs and Heroes*, but nothing came of this project either, though some of these poems may have appeared later in *Californians*.

Robin sent one copy of *Flagons and Apples* to Una at Berkeley, inscribing on the flyleaf:

"To my little Una, my dearest,
Who is very responsible for this
book but not to blame for it.
R.J."

Others who received copies from the author were Daniel Hammack, Vera Brooke, Robert Cleland, and Lenora Swift.

In December Robin wrote Una of the joys they could experience together if she would join him in Seattle:

"But you and I will be canoeing this winter on Lake Washington, dearest, and wandering loose, and kissing in the wet woods. We'll be out mornings in the white mist calling to each other; and we'll sit under the roots of a wide fallen tree, in a place I know on the lake, where the clay is red and there are tall green ferns, and little pools of water between the young pine-trees back of it . . . . And then, O my dearest—the little cottage we'll have, near the lake shore, among great red cedar-trunks, where we'll hear the lake water rippling against the roots of the cedars, that are like the bent elbows and knees of some monstrous ante-deluvian. And squirrels and little birds will play on our doorstep . . . . so that for us Adam will never have fallen, nor Pandora opened the forbidden casket.

"I will be Naysha, and you a more beautiful Deirdre, we living among the far Alban woods and not ever looking backward to Eire."

The lovers wrote of other things than love, often discussing at length the books which they were reading at the time. In answer to a letter which Una had written praising the Greek dramatists, Robin answered:

". . . But then I don't care much for Euripides, Una, nor for any Greek drama—save in a spirit of pure dilettantism—except the Prometheus—Even *that* has its *longueurs*.

"But the Greek lyrics are the *thing*. Archilochus—Sappho—Alcaeus —so the good pedants have handed us down just a few miserable patches of their old magnificence. A pedant or grammarian, I think, is the worst possible judge of literature—except the general public."

Years of travel and frequent changes of residence had developed in Robin a restlessness as chronic as his father's, and he chided Una for assuming that they could settle down for any length of time:

". . . You know very well that two people like ourselves could never stay seven years in the same place—even in a wonderful woodland with our wonderful love . . . ."

Robin, disliking both Los Angeles and Pasadena, escaped to Hermosa Beach for two or three days at a time, every other week, staying with Mrs. Nash, writing Una, "I feel like a cat who has come to a clean place between mudpuddles. . . . Cities are odious."

Although Robin had confessed his love of Una to his mother, he had not yet had the courage to tell his father. In her letters, Una continued to urge him to get it over with. Finally, on December 21, Robin wrote Una:

"I just had interview with our father—it's *our* father now, as well as *our* mother, dearest—because everything went well, and he appears quite reasonably content . . . . he was most kind and even a little enthusiastic . . . . Before our interview ended he was telling me that I must persuade you to leave Berkeley, and study at the University of Washington while I'm there. . . . And he said not a word against you for being divorced. . . ."

Even so, it was with some trepidation that Una went south in January, 1913, to meet Robin's father and mother. The Los Angeles papers had played up her divorce from Ted Kuster with headlines and pictures, as a divorce in 1913 was indeed considered a scandal. Kuster had secured the interlocutory degree in Los Angeles in July, 1912, from Judge Willis, at which time the *Daily Times* and the *Evening Herald* made much of it. Then on February 28, 1913, headlines (name of paper cut off Una's clipping) shouted, "Love's Gentle Alchemy to Weld Broken Lives," accompanied by photographs of Una, Kuster, and his bride-to-be Edith Emmons. On March 1, 1913, the *Los Angeles Times* carried Una's and Robin's pictures with headlines "Two Points of the Eternal Triangle" and "Parents Wash Hands of It." Robin's poem "On the Cliff" was boxed in large print.

Una was completely unprepared for the cordial reception which she received from the Jefferses. The doctor treated her with a gentle reserve which held no trace of criticism. Annie's generous heart immediately embraced the apprehensive Una and put her at her ease. Sis, who still made her home with the Jefferses, joined them in accepting Una into the family with warm affection.

Una was enchanted with Annie's beauty; her hair was graying but her eyes were as full of sparkle as ever, and her dark eyebrows set off with distinction both hair and eyes. She dressed her slender figure with taste. Una began called her "Belle Mère," which term of endearment she continued to use as long as Annie lived. The doctor always remained courteously aloof from the fun that Annie, Sis, Una, and Robin shared, and Una never felt quite at ease with him. Hamilton, Robin's brother, was seldom home, as he was studying at the Throop Polytechnic Institute (which was to become, in 1920, the California Institute of Technology) and was soon to go north to the University of California, for he was deeply absorbed in the study of astronomy.

Una was impressed by the formal courtesy with which Robin's family treated each other. They were reluctant to encroach on each other's privacy with either questions or criticisms. Although

63

the family was deeply religious and never missed Sunday services, the doctor preferred to worship without them and went to another church.

At the completion of her visit in the South, Una and Robin took the boat to Seattle to wait out the six months before they could marry. They found rooms in a house on Laurel Shade Avenue in Madison Park, on Lake Washington. They bought a canoe and spent many happy hours drifting on the water as a respite from their studies. Other times they walked in the woods and countryside, with Billie, Una's English bull dog, puffing along at their heels. Robin was completing his work in the Department of Forestry, and Una had enrolled in the Department of Education.

About July, Percy Peacock wrote Una that he was in the United States, and, since she had promised him that when he came West she and Robin would meet him at Lake Louise, she felt that she must make every effort to do so. He didn't reach Lake Louise until the end of July, and, by then, Annie had arrived in Seattle to be with them when they were married on August second. So Robin remained with his mother, and Una went alone to meet Percy. It seemed crowding fate, but now Una's heart was steady in its decision, and Percy was to hear little but of Una's happiness, her love for Robin, and their plans for the future. This time Una's farewell to Percy held no such doubts or confused hopes as when she had said good-bye to him in England the year before.

Annie accompanied Una and Robin to Tacoma where they had decided to be married to avoid the embarrassment of making explanations to Robin's fraternity brothers. Annie and Una had retired early the night before the wedding, but Robin was sleepless with happy anticipation and, after a late walk about the town, sat down to write the good news to Mrs. Nash:

"Dear Mrs. Nash:

Tomorrow we'll be mailing you the announcement of our wedding, and I suppose you'll receive it at the same time as this letter. It hardly seems possible that we are really going to be married tomorrow; so great a happiness is almost incredible. But it is true. This morning we left Seattle and came to Tacoma, and this afternoon we went to the court house here and got the marriage license. My mother, as Una has told you, has been with us in Seattle for the last three weeks; she is staying with us now, and will start for California early tomorrow afternoon, soon after the ceremony is performed. We are very glad that she is going to be here to see us married, and I think that she has very much enjoyed her stay in the North. I wish you too could be here, my foster-mother.

"You'll be surprised, I'm sure, to hear that Una and I intend going to Europe this winter. Una enjoys England and her English friends so much that I think it will give her great happiness to go there again and to live there for a year or two. And I shall be able to work as well there as in America—perhaps better. At any rate, the experience will be helpful to me, and I look forward to it with great pleasure. We'll be back to visit California after a year, I think; but probably a good deal of our future life will be spent in England and on the Continent.

"Our plan is to remain in Seattle until the middle of September; then to go to Los Angeles—and Hermosa—for almost three weeks. After that we'll go straight to Europe, stopping only a few days in Michigan, where Una's parents live. And perhaps for a few days in New York.

"So we'll see you, Mrs. Nash, in September; and I'm looking forward with more pleasure than I can tell you to staying a fortnight in Hermosa. You have always been so good to me, and I have a son's affection for you—how anxious I am to see you and talk to you!

"It is almost midnight, and I shall have to close this letter—the last I shall write before my marriage. I'll write again very soon, and more fully, about our plans and our experiences. Thank you ever so much for your sweet letter which I received yesterday morning.

"Goodnight, my dear Mrs. Nash,

Robin"[5]

Shortly after eleven o'clock the next morning, Una and Robin were married by the Reverend Hugh Mitchelmore in the study of the Tacoma Presbyterian Church.

After Annie returned to Pasadena, she wrote her blessings to Una:

". . . I want to assure you again that whenever you can come to us you will be welcome for just as long as you can stay. Dr. Jeffers and I both rejoice that our boy is so happy with you and that you seem to be able to encourage and bring out his best self & his best work. We wish for you both abiding happiness in each other—success & joy—Best love for you both. . . ."

[5]Copy of letter in Tor House collection.

And the doctor wrote to his son:

"My dear boy Robin, It was very thoughtful & kind of you to write me that beautiful letter in the immediate prospect of your marriage. The thought & sentiment it contained, together with the circumstances under which it was written, really touched my heart. And now my purpose in writing you, besides thanking you for your letter, is to present to you & to your beloved Una my hearty congratulations & my best wishes for your prosperity & happiness in all the picture that lies before you.

"From what your mother tells me of Una I feel that you have brought us as a daughter one whom we can welcome with parental affection. May she & you ever prove worthy of each other . . . ."

Although they must certainly have had misgivings when their son fell in love with a married woman, they were sincere in their acceptance of her. The warmth which Una felt as a guest in their home was not simulated; despite their innate courtesy, they were too forthright to have been more than formally polite to a young woman whose clandestine meetings with their son had brought about her own divorce. Had their years abroad made them more tolerant and less conventional than the average preacher's family, their acceptance of Una might not have been so surprising, but, from Annie's diary written during her European travels, it is evident that their friends there were cut from the same cloth as those in America: religious, conventional, and provincial. They had returned to America unchanged by the morals or customs of the Europeans. So it is obvious that they were either desperate about their son, or that Una's charms were as persuasive with them as with everyone else whom she met. Certainly they had great faith in Una's power to bring happiness to Robin.

Robin and Una stayed on in Seattle until September and then went south to spend a few weeks in Pasadena with Robin's parents. They were happily, deeply in love, with their dreams realized. Rising early, Robin would slip out for a walk, leaving his beautiful bride asleep in the big, old bed on the sleeping porch. Picking a small nosegay of dew-dipped flowers for his love, he would place them on her breakfast tray with a little note of tender words.

They found and rented a small house in La Jolla called "Breezy

Nest." They knew few people there, being content in each other's company, walking, keeping house, and reading from Swinburne.

Ted Kuster, now married to his young ward, Edith, also came to La Jolla for a few months, and the two couples would sometimes take excursions together into the hills. Robin and Kuster seemed to accept each other amicably enough, and Edith's devotion to Una was nothing short of adoration. She asked and accepted Una's advice on the care of Ted, establishing a situation that proved highly amusing to the friends of the two couples.

Their plan to go abroad in October was set aside with the discovery that Una was with child. Robin's tenderness for his "little Una" grew with her pregnancy, and she seemed to become even more precious to him. They remained in La Jolla until a month before their child was expected and then moved to a flat near Good Samaritan Hospital in Los Angeles, where Una was to be confined.

On May 5, 1914, Una's and Robin's first child was born, a ten-pound baby girl, Maeve. This child, born for another world, lived but one day. Robin wrote in the poem, "The Year of Mourning:"[6]

> Out of bland May the fair and firstling
> fruit
> Was reft in sudden dark . . .

As soon as Una was well enough, Robin moved her to his family's house in Pasadena for her convalescence. Una showed her fortitude by insisting that Annie and Sis go to North East for a visit with their relatives there and leave her to take care of the doctor. This wasn't an easy assignment as he was extremely difficult to please. He was predisposed against vitamins and considered fruit, butter, eggs, and milk as poisonous. He appeared to live on thin, dry toast followed by cups and cups of boiling water, sometimes topping off this repast with a quantity of large English walnuts, and, of course, indigestion. Discouraged as she was by her father-in-law's taciturnity and her own grief over the loss of her child, her natural sparkle had a struggle for existence. But Robin's love sustained her, and on August second they celebrated their first wedding anniversary.

[6]*Californians.*

67

IX

"WE HAD FOUND OUR PLACE"

RUMORS OF WAR, which were confirmed in September, 1914, necessitated Robin's and Una's giving up their plans to live in England, and they turned their thoughts to finding a home in California. Fred Clapp had told them of a little village called Carmel, near the old historical town of Monterey. As neither of them was familiar with it, they decided to take a trip north to visit it. Carmel had originally been discovered in 1602 when Sebastián Vizcaíno, the Spanish navigator, searching for a harbor free of pirates, landed in Monterey Bay. He left no imprint, except the name "Carmel." It wasn't until 1771 that Father Junípero Serra established a mission there and a small settlement of Spanish people.

Carmel, as the Jefferses saw it, was a small village with an unpaved main street called "Ocean Avenue," leading down to a white sand beach and a sparkling sea, a few small shops, a post office, and a scattering of houses. From El Camino Real to the ocean, the view was unbroken by anything but a succession of rolling, white sand dunes. By night there were no street lights, no flashlights; the homes were lighted, for the most part, by kerosene lamps or candles. Late strollers used a contrived miner's lamp of coffee-can and candle, to light their way. A bulletin board near the post office carried the news of the day: dates of important events, occasional political-campaign pamphlets, and a list of lost-and-found articles. There were few automobiles, as most persons kept a saddle horse. An eight-horse team made the run between Monterey and Carmel, as well as Goold's auto-stage which met the train at Monterey.

Milk was delivered to the neighborhood "milk shrines" instead of at individual back doors. The local butcher ruled his customers' menus with a heavy cleaver, giving them not what they wanted but what he needed to dispose of. Newcomers to town were appraised by Mrs. Yard, the librarian, who measured out three hundred and fifty books a month from the small library cottage. The Manzanita motion-picture theatre charged 5 and 10 cents for admission, except on Saturdays and Sundays when it was raised to 10 and 20 cents. There were four hotels and four churches.

The permanent resident population of about 350 persons was joined in the summer months by professors and their families from Stanford University and the University of California. There were a number of artists and writers among the permanent residents, including Frederick Bechdolt, Jimmy Hopper, Alice McGowan, Grace McGowan Cooke, Mary Austin, Harry Leon Wilson, Charlotte Kellogg, Arnold Genthe, Frederick Clapp, Ira Remsen, George Sterling, and David Starr Jordan.

The dominant interest of the citizens was the theatre and in 1914 three movements started. The production of Mary Austin's *The Arrow Maker* at the out-door Forest Theatre was the most important event of the summer.

That season William Chase conducted the first school of painting at the Carmel Club of Arts and Crafts, a gesture which was the beginning of the summer art classes that were to advertise to the world the beauties of Point Lobos and the Carmel coast.

It was this little village, with its blue sea, its pine forests, and its fearsome, ragged coast-range mountains, to which Robin and Una Jeffers came that September in 1914. Here they found their "Dream of the Future."[1]

> Faithful and loved, you know when at first
> we came
> Out of the too-bright land, from a shore
> without trees,
> Though mighty of rocks, and clothed with
> the same blue wave, —

[1]*Californians.*

69

You know how our hearts were moved at
    looking down
From the high peninsular yoke; the breath
    of the morning
Hung in the pines; and this, we felt, was
    our home;
This, the narrow bay; the promontories;
The islands, each one rock; the capes beyond,
To the left, of Lobos, and yonder of Pescadero.
We were glad: we had found our place . . . .

They rented a small cabin which was set in a grove of eucalyptus and pine trees, at Fourth and Monteverde Streets. White plaster chinked the living room walls; the tables, chairs, and benches were fashioned out of small birch logs, unpainted and rough; rag rugs only partially covered the floors. Una settled down to housekeeping and Robin to writing. They interrupted their chores only for daily excursions along the beach to forage for the driftwood that kept their little cabin warm and snug against the cold fogs of morning and evening. Billie, Una's English bull, enjoyed these walks as much as Una and Robin. They always made some interesting discovery: a new color in the sea, the beauty of a storm rising on the horizon, or even the surprise of meeting other people on the beach. Robin wrote of one of these jaunts:

"Only three houses could be seen from the Carmel beach when we first walked there; a chimney of one, a gable-end of another, but the third stood out distinctly. It was small, steep-roofed, pleasant to look at, but its extraordinary quality was its changeful aliveness. Windows would appear where there was none before, and then vanish again; the color of the paint would change overnight; the shape of the roof would change, then a dormer would blossom through it; and all this was the more mysterious because we never saw anyone at work. I suppose the owner's time for carpentering did not tally with ours for walking. . . ."[2]

And Una, too, wrote of their first years in Carmel:

"So began our happy life in Carmel, full and over-full of joy from the first. For a long time we knew no one, but we were busy from morn-

[2]*The Carmel Pine Cone.* May 3, 1935.

ing till night, anyway. Robin was writing poetry, his reputation yet to make; I was studying certain aspects of late 18th century England and receiving from the State Library at Sacramento, through the little village library, priceless packages of old and rare books on my subject. There was housework, and continual woodchopping to fill the maw of the great fireplace in our drafty cabin. We bought simple textbooks on flowers, shells, birds, and stars, and used them. We explored the village street by street, followed the traces of the moccasin trail through the forest, and dreamed around the crumbling walls about the old mission. When we walked up from the shore at sunset scarfs of smoke drifting up from hidden chimneys foretold our own happy supper and evening by the fire. It was pleasant to sniff the air and recognize the pungent scent of eucalyptus, the faint, somehow nostalgic quality of burning oak, the gunpowdery smell of driftwood, redwood like ripe apricots, and keener than all, the tonic resin of pitch pine.

"One dark night the fire-bell clanged wildly and we stumbled down the canyon toward a blazing shed. Overhanging pine trees began to crackle. It seemed as if the whole forest would soon be on fire. Men ran to and fro; on top of a roof a slender man with flashing black eyes fought the flames like a demon—our first sight of Bob Leidig battling his chosen foe. Timmie Clapp advanced into the circle looking very old with a tiny candle-lantern in his hand. His wife had delayed to pack her bag, wary from many experiences with conflagrations in Constantinople.

"The big adventure of our first winter was a trip down the coast on the horse stage with Corbett Grimes, who carried the mail and occasional passengers three times a week. He picked us up at 7:00 in the morning at Ocean and San Carlos, and set us down at Big Sur Post Office after dark, a long day but not long enough. This was the first of a thousand pilgrimages, that we, and later our twin sons with us, have made down the coast and into the back country, where with books and maps and local gossip we have tried to piece together a fairly complete picture of this region: its treasures of natural beauty and vivid human life have been inexhaustible."[3]

One of the most amusing incidents which befell them was the evening they met Jaime. Walking along the beach they saw a man with two dogs coming briskly towards them. The day before, Una had received a letter from Ted Kuster describing two Irish wolfhounds he had just purchased. Now she asked, "Aren't

[3]Article in *The Carmel Pine Cone*, January 10, 1941.

those dogs Irish wolfhounds, Robin?" Interested and curious, she begged, "Please, let's stop the man, Robin, and ask him about the dogs." The man was friendly and responded to their introduction by saying that his name was "Jaime."[4] They discussed dogs for awhile, and then Jaime pointed to a brown parcel under his arm and asked, "See this package? It contains an exceptionally fine porterhouse steak. It would be most kind of you both if you would come home with me and help me dispose of it."

Enchanted with this amusing and friendly little man, Una turned to Robin and put her hand on his arm pleading, "Let's go, darling, shall we?" Raising his eyebrows in defense against such rashness, Robin cleared his throat preparatory to making a protest, but already he found himself being propelled along by his unpredictable wife and the stranger, Jaime.

At Jaime's cabin they met his very young wife who was in the kitchen daintily and gingerly cleaning spinach. A few minutes after they arrived, she pitched the whole thing out of the back door, calmly joined them in the front room, and stated flatly, "Nothing in the world is worth that much trouble."

Jaime asked Una, "Can you cook?"

"Yes, anything," she answered.

"Good. If you will fix some potatoes, we can have potatoes and steak."

Una worked fast, and in no time she had the potatoes peeled and on to boil. But Jaime had already started cooking the steak. When it was finished, he asked Una accusingly, "Aren't your potatoes cooked yet?" Guiltly she admitted that they weren't. "Well, then," Jaime announced, "we shall have just steak for dinner."

They sat down at the table, and Jaime started to serve the steak. It looked and smelled delicious, and Una and Robin were glad that it was a large steak so that there was plenty for all. But suddenly Jaime, turning from his guests to the two wolfhounds, tossed the steak to the dogs, saying, "It would be a pity if *they* were to go hungry."

Whether the man was temperamental or crazy, Robin hoped that this experience would teach his wife not to pick up strangers on the beach!

[4]Una never identified him with a surname.

The Jefferses were happily surprised the day they met the Clapps walking along the beach. Due to the Clapps' reluctance to intrude on Robin's already generally-known preference for solitude, they had not advised Una of their presence in town. Now Una was delighted to find that they were intending to spend the winter there. Clapp had just completed a course of lectures for the University of California's summer school, and, since Maud was curious about this little village of which he had so often spoken with such affection, they had decided to take a house there. The house, which was being built by the tragedienne Hedwiga Reicher, was not quite completed, so for the present they were staying at La Playa Hotel. Una invited them to dinner at the log cabin the next week. As they parted to go their separate ways, Maud remarked to Fred, "What a dear little thing she is, and what fine eyes she has."

Maud, who was finding it a little difficult to adjust to the lax ways of the Carmelites, was pleasantly surprised to find Una, the night they dined with her and Robin, dressed in a black velvet dress which, with its low square-cut neck, set off the beauty of her creamy throat and bosom. Her hair, wrapped around her small head in two long braids, shone in the candlelight. The dinner she cooked was delicious and was served without fuss, with little break in the lively conversation—lively, that is, for the Clapps and Una. Robin sat quietly watching Una and marvelling at her beauty and her ability to make conversation so easily and charmingly.

Although the Clapps saw Robin often that winter and in the years to come, they never felt completely at ease with him. The men respected each other as poets, yet never discussed their craft when together.

Actually Clapp came as close to being an intimate friend as anyone Robin knew after his marriage to Una. There were many persons in the years to come who played an important though brief role in the life of Jeffers, but he lacked the need and the gift for encouraging friendships. How ironic that Robin, whose own youth had been distorted by his father's obsession for closing himself off from human contacts, was himself just such a recluse. More and more Una was protecting him from "intrusions," even sharing her own friends with him sparingly. It is inconceivable to think of Jeffers telephoning or writing to a friend to invite him to meet him for lunch, or for a drink at a bar, or even to go for a walk. Nor did he attend sporting events or go to movies or indulge in any other activities in which most men take a normal, if not avid, interest. He followed world events through the mediums of newspapers and magazines.

Just before Christmas, on December 20, 1914, Dr. Jeffers, who was then seventy-eight years old, died at his home in Pasadena. Una later wrote me an account of the circumstances of his death:

"Robin and I were called south when Dr. J. had a seizure early one morning. We think it must have been a stroke. He was downstairs cooking breakfast. Belle-Mère heard the noise of a fall and then silence. She found him unconscious with his head within a few feet of the gas grate he had just lighted. He died about two days after we arrived. Never regained consciousness. I stayed there at 822 for at least three weeks. I had a different impression then of the relationship of the Dr. and Belle-Mère than I had before for she was simply *sunk* with the loss of him. I cannot even remember the Christmas part. I have no recollection of it at all. Hamilton was there. I believe that he was at that time a student at Berkeley. He was born in 1893 so would have been 21. He went to Cal. Tech. for awhile after graduating from Pasadena High. I believe we stayed until great-aunt Mary hurried back from the east to be with Belle-Mère again. Robin and Hamilton betrayed no grief at all. They were the exact poker-faces that Garth and Donnan are (and it upsets most people to understand them)."[5]

At the time of his death, Dr. Jeffers' estate had diminished to only a fraction of what it had amounted to when he arrived in California. Hamilton wrote me:

"His will provided for the estate to be divided into three trust funds, about equal in size, one for my mother and one each for Robin and myself. I do not remember what the income was at that time, but I think each of us received somewhat less than $2000. annually."

Despite his inability to show his grief, Robin was deeply moved by this second loss within the year, as is apparent in the poem "The Year of Mourning":[6]

[5]Letter from U. J. to M. B. B., July 25, 1945.
[6]*Californians.*

... What twofold suffering
One dark-starred year may bring!
Out of bland May the fair and firstling fruit
Was reft in sudden dark; and now the root
Is hewn; fallen the strength!
. . . . .
Thou more than friend, thou dearer, art denied
All music of lament: thou hast the tones
Of a mere broken sobbing—lo, thy son's.

During that first year, the only other Carmelites whom the Jefferses saw frequently were the Fred Bechdolts. Fred was a writer of serials, and his wife was an invalid. The Jefferses had met the Bechdolts as a result of their curiosity about the chalk-stone chimney of their house in the forest. Robin and Una were already discussing the building of their own house in Carmel and were interested in this local chalkstone, so one night they followed the Bechdolts home from a walk to inquire about it. After this first meeting they became good friends and saw each other often. Robin's first social appearance in Carmel was at a barbecue at the Bechdolts. Roast pig, wine, old-fashioned cha-rades, and old songs filled a happy, easy evening.

But distractions were few and widely spaced, and Robin was amazed to find how his stack of completed poems was growing. By the end of the summer, he had more than enough to make up a good-sized book. Una encouraged him to submit them to a pub-lisher, so he began the tedious task of editing them. He had little confidence in himself but drew strength from Una's faith. Later, he wrote of some of the mental hell holes he fell into at this time:

"We used to walk in the Del Monte Forest in the days when it was uninhabited. Near the place where we climbed a fence to enter the woods there was a deep ravine, bridged by the water-main that ran from the dam up the Carmel Valley to the reservoir lake back of Mon-terey. A wooden trestle supported the big pipe where it crossed the gorge, and this was our bridge into the farther woods; but we had to scramble carefully, for wild bees hived halfway over, in the timbers against the pipe. And it was harder coming back. I had to make two crossings then, one to carry the dog, and one with the firewood that we brought home from the forest.

"This was twenty-one years ago, and I am thinking of a bitter meditation that worked in my head one day while I returned from the woods and was making my two crossings by the pipe-line. It had occurred to me that I was already a year older than Keats when he died, and I too had written many verses, but they were all worthless. I had imitated and imitated, and that was all.

"I have never been ambitious, but it seemed unpleasant just the same to have accomplished nothing, but exactly nothing, along the only course that permanently interested me. There are times when one forgets for a moment that life's value is life, any further accomplishment is of very little importance comparatively. This was one of those times and I can still taste its special bitterness; I was still quite young at twenty-seven.

"When I had set down the dog and went back over our bridge for the bundle of firewood my thoughts began to be more practical, not more pleasant. This originality, without which a writer of verses is only a verse-writer, is there any way to attain it? The more advanced contemporary poets were attaining it by going farther and farther along the way that perhaps Mallarmé's aging dream had shown them, divorcing poetry from reason and ideas, bringing it nearer to music, finally to astonish the world with what would look like pure nonsense and would be pure poetry. No doubt these lucky writers were imitating each other, instead of imitating Shelley and Milton as I had done—but no, not all of them, someone must be setting the pace, going farther than anyone had dared to go before. Ezra Pound perhaps? Whoever it was, was *original*.

"Perhaps this was the means to attain originality: to make a guess which way literature is going, and go there first. Read carefully your contemporaries, chart their line of advance, then hurry and do what they are going to do next year. And if they drew their inspiration from France, I could read French as well as any of them.

"(This was not all quite seriously thought, partly I was just tormenting myself. But a young man is such a fool in his meditations, at least I was; let me say for shame's sake that I have not considered 'trends' since turning thirty, nor been competitive either.)

"But now, as I smelled the wild honey midway the trestle and meditated the direction of modern poetry, my discouragement blackened. It seemed to me that Mallarmé and his followers, renouncing intelligibility in order to concentrate the music of poetry, had turned off the road into a narrowing lane. Their successors could only make further renunciations; ideas had gone, now meter had gone, imagery would have to go; then recognizable emotions would have to go; perhaps at last even words might have to go or give up their meaning, nothing be left but musical syllables. Every advance required the elimination of some aspect of reality, and what could it profit me to know the direction of modern poetry if I did not like the direction? It was too much like putting out your eyes to cultivate the sense of hearing, or cutting off the right hand to develop the left. These austerities were not for me; originality by amputation was too painful for me.

"But—I thought—everything has been said already; there seems to be only this way to go on. Unless one should do like the Chinese with their heavy past; eliminate one's own words from the poem, use quotations from books as the elder poets used imagery from life and nature, make something new by putting together a mosaic of the old. A more promising kind of amputation; one or two noble things might be done that way, but not more, for the trick would pall on Western ears; and not by me, who never could bear the atmosphere of libraries since I escaped from my studious father's control.

"I laid down the bundle of sticks and stood sadly by our bridge-head. The sea-fog was coming up the ravine, fingering through the pines, the air smelled of the sea and pine-resin and yerba buena, my girl and my dog were with me—and I was standing there like a poor God-forsaken man-of-letters, making my final decision not to become a 'modern.' I did not want to become slight and fantastic, abstract and unintelligible.

"I was doomed to go on imitating dead men, unless some impossible wind should blow me emotions or ideas, or a point of view, or even mere rhythms, that had not occurred to them. There was nothing to do about it.

"We climbed the fence and went home through the evening-lighted trees. I must have been a charming companion that afternoon.

"This book began to be written three or four years later. I was past my green-sickness by that time, and did not stop to think whether the verses were original or followed a tendency, or would find a reader. Nor have I ever considered whether they deserved to find one."[7]

[7]From "Introduction" to Modern Library edition of *Roan Stallion, Tamar and Other Poems*, 1935.

INFLUENCES

EARLY IN THE YEAR OF 1916 Robin finished editing his poems and sent them off to the Macmillan Company. He had little confidence that they would accept the work of an unknown poet, so was agreeably surprised to receive word from them that they would publish his work in the fall under the title *Californians*. On October 11, 1916, this second book of Jeffers' poems made its appearance, causing scarcely a ripple in literary circles. As Robin himself said, ". . . it found no readers." His first poem had been published in 1903, thirteen years previously, so he read with pleasure the mention of *Californians* in the *Anthology of Magazine Verse for 1916 and Yearbook of American Poetry*. It commented briefly: ". . . California is now to have its part in the poetry revival. Robinson Jeffers is a new poet, a man whose name is as yet unknown, but whose work is of such outstanding character that once he is read he is sure of acceptance."

And, within the year, four more reviews appeared, in *The Nation*, the *Overland Monthly*, *The Literary Digest*, and the *Springfield Republican*. ". . . such passionate devotion," wrote the latter, "to rivers and stars and eucalyptus trees as Mr. Jeffers seems to have is certainly impressive. Even in itself it is a subject for a great deal of meditation. But when it is so splendidly illustrated and set forth as it is here, one must be inspired by it. Mr. Jeffers' point of view is enviable in itself; presented as he presents it, it is our own for the mere reading." Of the four reviews, this was the most generous in its praise.

The Literary Digest briefly called attention to the poem "He Has Fallen in Love with the Mountains" as "the most notable poem" in the volume. And the *Overland Monthly*, a California-published magazine, gave the opinion that the development of Jeffers' artistic temperament was probably due to "the landscape and atmosphere of California." O. W. Firkin's review in *The Nation* was the most perceptive. He claimed that "there is something mildly symbolic in the fact that Mr. Jeffers' localism should have thrust its roots so piercingly into the soil that breeds Sequoias—has Mr. Jeffers the patience and humility which will loose his evident force from its no less obvious encumbrances? All turns on the answer to that question...."

The poems in *Californians* were written in formal meter. Jeffers had not yet found his way in the original verse forms which he later adopted. Although the verses are rather immature and are shaded by his preoccupation with other poets (Swinburne, Coleridge, Shakespeare, and particularly Wordsworth and Shelley), they do have originality, a quality that is already unmistakably Jeffers' He said that the poems from 1912 to 1916 "were only preparatory exercises, to say the best for them...." As to his ability to "loose his evident force from its ... obvious encumbrances," let him answer this:

"By this time I was nearing thirty, and still a whole series of accidents was required to stir my lazy energies to the point of writing verse that seemed to be—whether good or bad—at least my own voice.

"... it became evident to me that poetry—if it was to survive at all—must reclaim some of the power and reality that it was so hastily surrendering to prose. The modern French poetry of that time, and the most 'modern' of the English poetry, seemed to me thoroughly defeatist, as if poetry were in terror of prose, and desperately trying to save its soul from the victor by giving up its body. It was becoming slight and fantastic, abstract, unreal, eccentric; and was not even saving its soul, for these are generally anti-poetic qualities. It must reclaim substance and sense, and physical and psychological reality. This feeling has been basic in my mind since then. It led me to write narrative poetry, and to draw subjects from contemporary life; to present aspects of life that modern poetry had generally avoided; and to attempt the expression of philosophic and scientific ideas in verse. It was not in my mind to open new fields for poetry, but only to reclaim old freedom.

"Still it was obvious that poetry and prose are different things; their

79

provinces overlap, but must not be confused. Prose, of course, is free of all fields; it seemed to me, reading poetry and trying to write it, that poetry is bound to concern itself chiefly with permanent things and the permanent aspects of life. That was perhaps the great distinction between them, as regards subject and material. Prose can discuss matters of the moment; poetry must deal with things that a reader two thousand years away could understand and be moved by. This excludes much of the circumstances of modern life, especially in the cities. Fashions, forms of machinery, the more complex social, financial, political adjustments, and so forth, are all ephemeral, exceptional; they exist but will never exist again. Poetry must concern itself with (relatively) permanent things. These have poetic value; the ephemeral has only news value.

"Another formative principal came to me from a phrase of Nietzsche's: 'The poets? The poets lie too much.' I was nineteen when the phrase stuck in my mind; a dozen years passed before it worked effectively, and I decided not to tell lies in verse. Not to feign any emotion that I did not feel; not to pretend to believe in optimism or pessimism, or unreversible progress; not to say anything because it was popular, or generally accepted, or fashionable in intellectual circles, unless I myself believed it; and not to believe easily. These negatives limit the field; I am not recommending them but for my own occasions.

"Here are the principles that conditioned the verse in this book before it was written; but it would not have been written at all except for certain accidents that changed and directed my life. (Some kind of verse I should have written, of course, but not this kind.) The first of these accidents was my meeting with the woman to whom this book is dedicated, and her influence, constant since that time. My nature is cold and undiscriminating; she excited and focused it, gave it eyes and nerves and sympathies. She never saw any of my poems until they were finished and typed, yet by her presence and conversation she has co-authored every one of them. Sometimes I think there must be some value in them, if only for that reason. She is more like a woman in a Scotch ballad, passionate, untamed and rather heroic—or like a falcon —than like an ordinary person.

"A second piece of pure accident brought us to the Monterey coast mountains, where for the first time in my life I could see people living —amid magnificent unspoiled scenery—essentially as they did in the Idylls, or the Sagas, or in Homer's Ithaca. Here was life purged of its ephemeral accretions. Men were riding after cattle, or plowing the headlands, hovered by white sea-gulls, as they have done for thousands of years, and will for thousands of years to come. Here was contempo-

Annie Jeffers, Robin, Hamilton, 1900

Farmhouse by Chateau de Vidy near Lausanne, 1900, where Robin went to school. In the yard was a linden tree under which Napoleon was supposed to have rested. Robin tells of an enormous poplar, which he used to climb and the smell of it made him sick, and of the walled vineyard stretching down to the lake

John Robinson Jeffers, 12 years old, January, 1899.
Taken at Pittsburgh, Pa.

Una. A.B. degree cap and gown. March, 1908

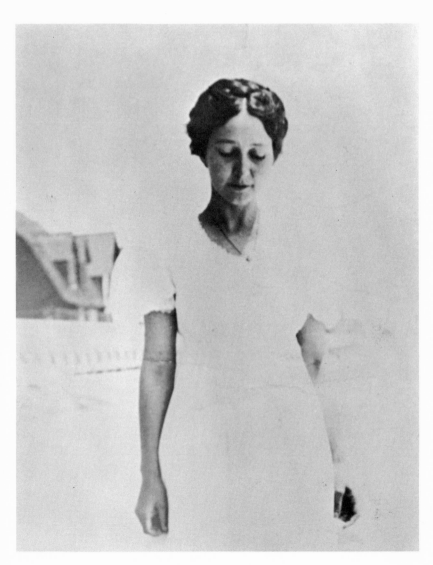

Terminal Island. Una. 1908

Robin Jeffers. Hermosa Beach, January, 1912

Robin, Great Aunt Mary, Una, Billie, Belle Mère.
Log Cabin, Carmel, 1915

Cherokee and Banksia roses on sleeping porch at Robin's father's house, 822 Garfield Avenue, Pasadena, April, 1914

rary life that was also permanent life; and not shut from the modern world but conscious of it and related to it; capable of expressing its spirit, but unencumbered by the mass of poetically irrelevant details and complexities that make a civilization. . . ."[1]

Influences on Jeffers' poetry continued to form, and, aside from the first thrill on the acceptance of his poems, he was more interested and concerned over Una's pregnancy. Although Una felt particularly well and strong, she was urged by Robin to accept his mother's invitation to close their cabin and move to the Garfield house in Pasadena, where she would be free of household cares and could await the arrival of their child under the loving eyes of Annie and Sis. She finally gave in, and, in the last week of June, Robin drove her south in their new Ford. In a letter I received from Una in 1943, she told me of this adventure:

". . . we came to a place where the road was being remade. If there had been a *detour* sign we had missed it. It was late p.m. and we hated to retrace our way some unknown distance. At the same time there was a drop of some four feet in front of us between the old road and the new. We thought it too big a bump for *me* . . . . We solved it by going to the edge, stopping the engine, getting out and pushing 'Emily' (the car) over by itself. We felt very mean doing it.

"Then we expected to stop the night at an old adobe Inn at Jolon . . . . We had Billie, our white bull dog, along. They refused to let him inside the hotel. We knew how he'd yell if we put him in the barn as was suggested. Our car was an open one so we couldn't lock him in that, so we pushed on. There were no hotels, night fell and the roads were terrible. At last we drew up beside a hayfield, climbed under the wire fence and spent the night in a hay cock. . . . It was a very uncomfortable night. We were full of straw and grass. But the stars were wonderful and there was a very long shooting star — marvelous."

Annie and Sis sewed happily on a layette for the expected baby, while Robin took Una on long slow rides in the country. Una also spent peaceful hours in the back garden, under the fruit trees. One of the neighbors owned a goat, and every day he brought a bottle of its milk to Una. Once he said to her, "An expectant mother who drinks goat's milk will have twins, you know." Una laughed and admitted that she hadn't known it, but

[1]From "Foreword" to *The Selected Poetry of Robinson Jeffers.*

if she did have twins she would remember that she had the goat's milk to thank for them.

On November 9th, 1916, attended by Dr. Titian Coffey, Una gave birth to twin boys. Donnan weighed five pounds and seven ounces and Garth weighed seven pounds and two ounces. Una explained in a letter she wrote me July 25, 1943, that Dr. Coffey:

". . . acknowledged an error in judgment in the case of Maeve. He should have done a Caesarean section. I was tremendously large. He had diagnosed twins—thought he could detect two foetal heart beats—at that time they were not using Xray to look-see about babies. So many people said I was foolish to trust him a second time but we did not think so. He was extremely unhappy about the loss of Maeve and we thought he would get us a live baby if it could be done. He took wonderful care of me—and as it turned out, both boys had to have surgical help. . . . I had no trouble of any kind."

Adele Bechdolt, who came down from Carmel to see Una soon after she had moved from the hospital to Pasadena, found her lying in a bed which looked very large because Una was so very small. Adele looked around for the twins, and Una pointed to a large highboy on one side of the room. There they were, on top of the chest, lying side by side. One was tiny and very dark, and beautiful. The other was fair and very boyish-looking. Adele observed, "But they are so tiny, and they don't look at all like twins."

It was necessary for Robin to return to Carmel to find a larger house for his new family. With twins, Una would need help, for a time at least. He found and rented the Tretheway cottage, a frame house in the pine-forest not far from their little log cabin. Since Dr. Coffey was eager for Una to keep the babies in the south under his supervision as long as possible, Una remained in Pasadena. The nurse who had attended her in the hospital stayed with her for six weeks and was then replaced by a practical nurse. Annie and Sis were also willing helpers and were busy duplicating a layette for the unexpected twin. So Una and the babies had plenty of care and loving attention.

When, in March, Una felt strong enough to return to Carmel, Robin, with a high heart, went south to bring her and the twins home—Una had been away from Carmel over seven months.

Fifield, who had done sewing and mending for Una when she was married to Kuster, and who now, because of failing eye-sight, could no longer sew, was free to help Una with the twins. She accompanied them to Carmel and remained until the boys were nearly two years old.

The war was moving grimly to encompass all nations. The people of Russia were in a state of revolt. In March, 1917, the Czar abdicated, and a special government was set up under Prince Lvov. Germany announced the renewal of unrestricted submarine warfare which forced the United States, on April 6, to declare war on Germany. These events were proving deeply disturbing to Robin. He discussed with Una his desire to enlist in his country's service. Una refused her consent, feeling that Robin's duty was to the twins and herself. Like many another young man, he suddenly became aware of the fuller meaning of marriage, his responsibility to his wife and children who were dependent on him for support. It was difficult to fold his patriotic impulses and put them away in deference to his domestic obligations. He knew that the little he contributed financially was negligible, and that Una's stand was unfair. This battle of loyalties reacted on his nervous system and made him so irritable that Una was at her wit's end to please him, but she did not relent. She finally wrote Annie and asked her to take him home for a while. Annie, with good sense, refused, explaining that she couldn't cope with his moods. Robin's brilliance and taciturnity made even those closest to him feel as ill at ease as if he were a moody stranger.

His writings attest to his dissatisfaction at this time, as we have seen. However, when I suggested to Una that Robin had been unhappy with his writing in 1917, she wrote:

"He says he hasn't the faintest recollection of it. We both remember he had days of unrest because he thought he ought to go to war—and there I was with two babies! but he hadn't a bother in the world that he remembers about his work."[2]

After further discussion with Robin she wrote me again the following month:

[2]Letter from U. J. to M. B. B., July 31, 1943.

"He has an honest indifference about getting things straight about himself. For instance your idea about his suffering during his early verses in Carmel, I said that looking back over our more than thirty years together it seems to me he was during our 1914-1915-early 16 years here more simply and completely happy and at ease than I ever knew him at any other time and he said 'yes, that is true' —and added 'Moreover, you know I felt confident about my verses and really very pleased with them!' So—I said—'Well, what shall I tell Melba?' and he said, 'What does it matter —one way or the other. She will have some interesting theory. It will serve very well!'

"Well, what can one do with that kind of person? At any rate I can check tangible facts, and dates for you. And he remembers few of them."

My original "theory," taken from Jeffers' own admission of discontent written in 1935, less than ten years before this correspondence, only points up the fact that it just was not worth Jeffers' while to argue with Una—or Melba! He could indeed pose problems for a biographer.

Una searched for other ways of distracting Robin; she planned more trips of exploration, she sent him out more often for driftwood, she gave him more chores around the house. Then she began looking for new subjects which might hold his attention, and toward the end of the year she started a notebook on the stars and planets with which she and Robin were becoming familiar. From time to time both she and Robin made entries in this book.

Una noted: "Our latitude is about 36.5 N. The twenty brightest stars are called First Magnitude Stars. Five are too far south to be seen in our position here." This note of Una's was followed by one of Robin's, "Zodiacal light—false dawn—observed a November night from the pine-crested hilltop above Oliver's ranch. Had been asleep a half hour, the cold east wind awakened me. Stars shining brightly; filmy cone-shaped light came up from the east along the line of the ecliptic, reaching for more than half way to its highest point. The Cone's Point was rounded. After some minutes it seemed to lose form and diffuse itself, and shortly the dawn began."

Undoubtedly Una had rekindled an interest in astronomy which Robin had enjoyed during his school years. His later poems often contained allusions to the stars and the positions of the planets, and he came to judge the seasons by the heavens rather than by the thermometer.

But such activities were only diversions to a man with the mental and physical energies of Jeffers. There was nothing concrete enough to which his thoughts could attach themselves or to which they could cling. So Una began campaigning for a home for the children and herself. She and Robin looked at possible building sites, even discussed and drew up plans for their house. However, nothing came of it at that time, as further considerations convinced them both that the price of property and construction was prohibitive, and they would have to wait until after the war.

In spite of such distractions, Robin finally decided to enlist and, accordingly, applied for training in the balloon corps since he was over-age for training in the air corps. He had not been called to duty when the war ended. "Robin continued, however, with his verse-making, while waiting to be called into service—writing at night, mostly. He was up until all hours and then slept all morning. Tretheway cottage was built on a hillside and there was a room underneath the big living room which Mrs. Tretheway had used as a store room. We cleaned this out and pushed her trunks and boxes back into a corner and Robin had a table down there where he worked—when he did—in the daytime."[3]

In some personal notes he had made, Robin explained his attitude towards the war and his desire to participate:

"As to my motives in offering (rather late) to become a soldier: I did feel a duty to protect the country that had protected me and my few possessions, and should probably feel it again if the occasion should come. On the other hand I felt a duty to stay home and help take care of year-old sons; we were (and are) too poor to keep servants. Yet not so poor that the family could properly be called dependent on my (non-existent) earnings; indeed I'd likely have been drafted if the war had lasted much longer. I had no conscientious objection to fighting; it seems to me a natural condition of the race. But I was never deluded with ideas of a noble and crusading war; it seems to me an unavoidable spectacular madness. I never felt hatred of the Germans; nor imagined the U.S. in much danger; for I thought of the war as a foreign war, and

[3]Letter from Una to M. B. B. July 25, 1943.

that its best apology was that it was preventive of future changes, in case of a decisive victory in which we had no share.

"So that throughout the call for troops my mind was perplexed and at conflict with itself. I felt quite sure that this conflict emotionally realized the external world for me and made much of the difference between my verses before the war and my verses since."[4]

There were other pencilled notes[5] among his papers on the subject of war. Often speaking of himself in the third person, one note states:

"He regards war with horror and disgust but believes it to be inevitable—and claims that he sees, at a certain level of contemplation, the tragic and the spectacular beauty of war, as of a storm or other natural disaster."

And in another note he says: "The only war that is morally defensible is a war of defense."

The Armistice was declared in November, 1918. In the poem "The Truce and the Peace,"[6] Jeffers wrote:

> . . . God built our peace and plastered it
> with wars,
> Those frescoes fade, flake off, peace
> remains firm. . . .

At last, early in the spring of 1919, the Jefferses purchased a parcel of land at Mission Point. This had been one of their favorite picnic spots, and they had grown to think of it as their own; it was truly at the very "continent's end," and in a poem by that name Robin describes the site:

> . . . I gazing at the boundaries of granite
> and spray, the established sea-marks,
> felt behind me
> Mountain and plain, the immense breadth of
> the continent, before me the mass and
> doubled stretch of water.

---

[4]Among collection at Tor House. Jeffers could not recall if these notes had been made in answer to a questionnaire, or letter, or if they had even been transmitted.

[5]Tor House collection. Transcribed by M. B. B.

[6]*Tamar and Other Poems.*

Una's story of this memorable event was written for *The Carmel Pine Cone* (January 10, 1941):

"In 1919 we built Tor House on a knoll where stones jutting out of the treeless moor reminded us of tors on Dartmoor. Our favorite walk had been along the grass grown track that wound around the Point. At that time there were no houses, except the Reamer's and Driftwood Cottage, beyond Philip Wilson's at 14th and San Antonio; instead acres of poppies and many colored wild flowers spread out like a millefleurs tapestry, and golden-breasted meadow larks sang enchantingly from every lupin bush. Philip Wilson had laid out a golf course here and although I never saw anyone playing, for years to come we dug up an occasional ball in our garden. Horses grazed at will across the moor and whinnied wildly on windy nights, and sometimes Andrew Stewart's herd of dairy cows wandered across from the Mission farm and rubbed against the Altar Stone. A withered old Chinaman came regularly to pull edible seaweed from the rocks. He would spread it out to dry on the cliff and later totter away with it in two baskets swinging from either end of a pole balanced on his shoulders.

"Whales drifted by, spouting high and dolphins curved from the water; we seldom see them now, nor the curious thin weasels full of sly menace among the stones. On cold moonlit nights coyotes' voices came down on the valley wind—once several of them raged and yelled like maniacs in our very courtyard.

"All about us here was pulsing life and motion—flighting birds and pounding waves and cloud shadows fleeing across grasses bent and woven by the winds. There was a special night wind from the valley that wuthered unhindered around our exposed little house—now it seldom wins through to us and we miss its banshee wail."

Work on Tor House started. The Jefferses had decided to use granite rather than the perishable chalkstone, and engaged a contractor named Murphy, and the stone mason Pierson of Monterey. Heavy granite boulders were lifted from the beach to the construction site via a chute. Jeffers has often been given the credit for building the stone house, but this legend lost verity in a letter which Una wrote to Sydney S. Alberts and which is quoted in his bibliography of Jeffers:

". . . The anxiety of these years (and the children) seemed to bring to maturity a mind which hadn't made itself really face things until then. It was then, too, he did his first manual labor. We had bought the land on the cliff here outside the village in spring 1919 and had let the contract for a small stone house (finished early August 1919). It was far outside the village and was going so slowly we decided to try to get the contractor to hire R.J. so that he could keep an eye on the men. R. J. hadn't any skill of any kind so he did the hardest and plainest job (at $4.00 a day, I think), mixed mortar and carried the hod to the master mason. It was thus he learned to handle stone, and the craft of mason, which led to years of building (garage, tower, walls, etc.). These things I have mentioned were all disciplinary,—and he had never encountered discipline really before."

As Jeffers worked, he drew verse images from his daily experience: from watching the flight of a gull or hawk, or from seeing the shadows lengthen on the Santa Lucian hills, or the kelp change the color of the sea, or from the stone masons themselves. Once the poet William Rose Benét asked him what his favorite poem was of those he had written, and he said, ". . . the choice will have to depend on associations, not poetical quality. The brief poem that comes to my mind is called 'To the Stone-Cutters'. When I was building the walls of our house we wanted carvings of unicorn and hawk, my wife's favorite animal and mine, to build into the stone work, and we persuaded the old man who used to carve tombstones in Monterey to make them for us. His and our preoccupation with the stones made me think of writing the verses and they are chosen rather for love of old stones and old Scotch stone masons than for any more arguable reason."

TO THE STONE-CUTTERS[7]

Stone-cutters fighting time with marble, you
    foredefeated
Challengers of oblivion
Eat cynical earnings, knowing rock splits,
    records fall down,
The square-limbed Roman letters
Scale in the thaws, wear in the rain. The
    poet as well
Builds his monument mockingly;
For man will be blotted out, the blithe earth
    die, the brave sun

[7]*Ibid.*

Die blind, his heart blackening:
Yet stones have stood for a thousand years, and
      pained thoughts found
The honey peace in old poems.

As to the books that Jeffers read and their influence on his thinking and writing, there has been much conjecture. He said that, as a youth, one of his favorite books was Milton's *Samson Agonistes*, and another one was Plutarch's *Lives*. At fifteen, while in Zurich, he read Nietzsche's *Thus Spake Zarathustra*, but made no claim as to its influence on his own thinking. He also had a fondness for a few books of the Old Testament. Through Una, he was introduced to the work of George Moore, Yeats, and to Arthur Symons' *Essays*. Una had such a passion for Moore and Yeats that one might say that throughout his marriage they shared his home.

Though much of his philosophy has been attributed to the influence of Freud and Jung, Jeffers claimed that what he knew of their philosophy was second-hand; that he hadn't read them. Nor had he ever read Schopenhauer, though he had "read much that derives from his thought; as well as some of the ancient literature—Hebrew, Greek, Chinese, Christian—that in thought it derives from, or is parallel to."[8] He also claimed to know nothing of Santayana's philosophy. Nor was he, according to pencilled notes preparatory to answering questions on the subject, "conscious of 'the debt to D. H. Lawrence.' Can't remember reading any of his work before 1930. . . ." In another of his notes, which I transcribed but of which he could not recall the recipient, he says:

"Horace's pleasant, bourgeois wisdom is not especially attractive to me, but I have had two or three of his odes in my memory for thirty years, and still say them to myself for pleasure in the sound of the verses and their flawless architecture. I don't know that he has had any influence on my writing, except perhaps unconsciously a little, and that was a matter of intention rather than persuasion."

In a letter in answer to questions from Mr. William Hubbell of Kentucky, written in 1939, he says:

[8]Answer to letter from Elizabeth Bauer. 1935.

"I cannot tell you what is my favorite work of fiction. It depends on what I read at the moment. For mere greatness it would probably be the 'Karamazov Brothers'—for pleasure and aesthetic enjoyment it would be one of Thomas Hardy's, 'The Woodlands' or 'Far from the Madding Crowd.' And my favorite chapter of fiction would come from one of these latter books—some description of Gabriel Oak or Giles Winterborne and their activities."

The student of Jeffers' poetry can certainly find the influence of his reading, particularly of the Greek myths, books of astronomy and botany, but it is, as he himself would have said, "intentional."

XI

TOR HOUSE

A barren foreland, without a fountain without
    a tree,
Bulks of monument granite push up from the
    brow of the hill,
Monstrous blocks break through for a broad-
    beaked prow in the sea,
Winds blow over, the waters below never are
    still . . .
  There are only simple things here,
  Three great people my dear,
  The earth's old hard strength,
  The keen air's messenger powers,
  The coiled sea's moving length,
  Immense neighbors of ours.
I will build a stone house for young life
    and rock walls for the seedlings of love,
Ribs of rock around a hot soft heart, crannies
    in granite for the roots of flowers;
Waves wrestling below, winds ranging above,
Braggarts, go by, the old earth is our friend,
    touch nothing of ours.[1]

On the wall by Una's bed under the sloping attic roof of Tor
House, Jeffers wrote this unfinished poem soon after they moved

[1]*Robinson Jeffers and the Sea,* by M. B. B.

into their new home on August 15, 1919, six years after their marriage.

Tor House had been fashioned after an old Tudor barn that Una had seen and admired in Surrey, England. There was a low-ceil-inged living room, a front bedroom (for guests), bath, and kitchen. Upstairs, under the eaves, was one large room encircling the chimney-vent in the center of the room. In four niches were the four beds, one for each of the Jefferses. By the east window overlooking the courtyard (still in the planning stage) was Jeffers' desk and the heavy old chair made, some sixty years be-fore, from a plank taken from the ruins of the mission. This room was heated by a Franklin stove that Una had brought from Michigan. When the west window was open, the pound of the surf filled the attic room, echoing back and forth from wall to wall.

Steep steps led down to the friendly redwood living room. At the far end of the room windows looked out on the sea. Crowded between these windows and the north wall was Una's grand piano, looking oddly overbearing in its simple surroundings. There were two windows on the south side of the room, and, be-tween the easterly of these and the heavy front door, Una had placed her mahogany bureau. Here she kept her clothes, and before its stately beauty Una stood to brush and braid her lovely long hair. Next to the bureau stood the little melodeon on which Una played her Gaelic tunes. Shelves to the left of the front door held books dear to both Una and Robin. Here were Una's beloved Yeats and Moore, alongside of Swinburne, Mallarmé, Synge, Flaubert, O'Neill, the Greek dramatists, and the English classics. A tiny nook next to the shelves contained Una's desk, and here, with the light streaming through the window over her shoulder, she was to write those delightful, chatty letters which have made it possible for so many friends to share the daily life of Tor House.

Between the nook and the stairs which led up to the loft was the door to the little kitchen. Here over the dish-washing, Una and Robin took time, then and all through their marriage, to keep acquainted with each other's opinions on things, people, and world events.

There was no telephone at Tor House, no electricity, no heat other than that furnished by the Franklin stove in the loft and the stone fireplaces in the living- and bedrooms. Kerosene lamps gave them light and threw deep shadows against the Chinese-red muslin curtains.

Each morning, after breakfast, Jeffers would go up to the loft where he would write laboriously until Una called him to lunch. Most of his work was done as he paced back and forth, thinking out a line or an idea. Back at his desk, he wrote the line down on an odd scrap of paper; then reference books were pored over to prove the fitness of each word for its task. There was no pleasure in this kind of writing. It was toil—and exhausting. After lunch he would go down to the beach and roll up boulders for the garage that he was adding to the house. He had learned enough from the stone mason and the builder to continue alone. And as he worked with his stones, his mind labored over ideas for his poems. He would work until Una would call to him to stop for the day. Then the family, including Billie the dog, would walk along the beach, or into the hills, or take a drive down the coast.

As Jeffers worked at his rock-laying or watered his cypresses, the neighbors or idly curious would stop by to watch or chat. James M. Hopper, short-story writer who had just returned from overseas as foreign-correspondent for *Collier's*, often stopped by on his walks to check Jeffers' progress and to exchange gossip with Una for a glass of homemade wine. One of Hopper's first books, *9009*, was written in collaboration with Frederick Bechdolt, the Carmelite whom the Jefferses met when they first arrived in Carmel. The book was published by the McClure Company and caused quite a stir. Besides several novels, Hopper published over four hundred short stories. His correspondence with George Sterling (over fifty letters) is now in the Bancroft Library.

One day when Jeffers was down the hill back of the garage, mixing mortar, a young woman appeared. She seemed to have sprung from the ground. He glanced up and then went on with his work. She spoke, saying she had come there because she wanted to meet the poet and talk with him. He answered that he was too busy to talk just then. Well, she asked, might she just watch him for awhile? Yes, she might watch if she wished, but he couldn't talk when he did stone work; that was his time to think. So he worked, and she watched. He filled two buckets with mortar and carried them up the hill. She followed. She watched him lay the mortar and set the stones; she followed him back down the hill, and watched him refill the buckets, and again carry them up. All this in silence, until he looked up and asked gently, "Aren't you tired standing there watching me?" "Yes, I am tired standing," she answered, taking his question not as a polite dismissal but as an invitation to come nearer and be seated. Another long silence, and then coaxingly she asked, "Aren't there some people you like better than others?" "Yes," he said, "There are." He turned his back to her and continued with his mortar-mixing in a preoccupied silence. The woman watched, her silence stirred only occasionally with an impatient sigh. Then the poet stood up from his work and, facing the woman, protested, "Really, you disturb my thought. Would you mind going, now?" Springing to her feet, the woman set off down the hill, but first she snapped, "If you ever run out of stones, use yourself. You are a man of stone!"

Jeffers cherished his solitude. It was enough to have Una and the twins, who were now four years old and following their father about his work like busy shadows, each with his little wheelbarrow loaded with small stones, making piles alongside their father's huge boulders. In their little red caps and red sweaters they were the only spots of color on the bleak landscape. There were also the four goats and the bantam chickens and rooster. A few friends were, of course, welcomed by Jeffers, but they were considerate of his working hours and his silences. The Clapps were frequent visitors at Tor House, as was Nettie Carter who would come up from Los Angeles to spend a few days with her beloved Una. George Evans brought his wife and baby daughter for a visit while he was teaching in the English department at Stanford University. Ted and Edith Kusters' warm reception as guests at Tor House caused considerable discussion amongst the Carmelites, who were fully acquainted with the story of Jeffers' courtship. There was much speculation as to whether Kuster was still in love with Una. Tongues wagged anew when they heard that Edith and Ted Kuster were planning a separation. Jeffers had better watch out that Kuster didn't win Una back! And then they learned that a young girl by the name of Ruth was staying at Tor House and that she was to become Kuster's wife. The discovery that Kuster had bought the property next to Tor House and was going to build a house on it was further proof to them of Kuster's fixation. Work on the house began at once and—of all things—it was a stone house, too! When Kuster married Ruth, the Carmelites decided that this was done deliberately to put them off. Oblivious of or indifferent to this gossip, the Jefferses and Kusters continued to enjoy their pleasant relationship.

Full as the days had become, the nights settled into a comfortable and pleasant leisure. Due to the difficulty of finding anyone who would stay out on the isolated Point at night with the twins, the Jefferses seldom accepted invitations for the evening. Jeffers was as unsociable as his father before him and was only too happy to have an excuse to remain at home. But for Una, who was truly an extrovert and enjoyed stimulating conversation, to forego willingly and happily such social contacts was proof of her love for her husband and their twin sons, and her contentment with her life as she found it.

After dinner, the dishes done and the twins in bed, Jeffers would sometimes read to Una until the day's work caught up with them, and they wearily and sleepily climbed the stairs to bed. There were times, however, when their peace was disturbed. One night, after they all were asleep, a crash of broken glass awakened them. Taking his gun, Jeffers descended the narrow stairs, followed by Una. They found that the glass near the handle of one of the living room windows had been shattered with a force which had carried it clear across the room. Una was terrified. They listened and were sure they could hear movements outside. Una whispered timidly that there just couldn't be two men, there must be a gang! She insisted that Jeffers stay on guard by the window and she would go up and protect the children.

After Una returned upstairs her imagination began working and she thought, "Suppose those desperados kill Robin. How shall I protect the babies alone?" They had but one gun which Robin had downstairs. She rummaged around the attic for possible weapons and finally assembled a battery of three old flat irons which she placed at the head of the stairs. She felt sure that with these she could stun the intruders so that they would fall back down the stairs if they tried to storm the attic.

The night wore on, and Una occasionally called to Robin from her post at the top of the stairs, to reassure herself that he was still alive. His movements in the chair by the window were comforting, and she finally decided it was quiet enough for her to climb into bed. Lying awake, straining her ears, she thought after a time that Robin had ceased to make any movement. Creeping to the stairway, she spoke to him but received no answer. "There," she said to herself, "they've killed him and I'm left alone to protect my babies!" She peered fearfully down the hatch to view the situation and found that Robin, the defender, was asleep in his chair!

For some time after this incident they were on the alert for prowlers. It isn't possible to exaggerate the loneliness and isolation of their Point, especially on winter nights. They investigated every strange sound. One night, after Una and the children were asleep, Jeffers heard a noise outside. Not wishing to disturb Una for fear of frightening her, he slipped cautiously out of bed and crept downstairs. A few minutes later Una awakened and was quite sure that she could hear someone moving around in the living room. She decided that she would deal with this emergency herself and not disturb Robin, so she took her gun—they now had two—and, slipping out of bed, she crept to the stairs. Concealed by the darkness she called out boldly, "Stop, or I'll shoot." Robin made haste to identify himself. Poor Una was horrified at what she might have done and dissolved in tears, crying, "Oh, Robin darling, I might have shot you." The twins, awakened by the commotion, sat up in their beds and asked reasonably, "What would Father do if Mother shot Father?" And Father answered, "Shoot back."

As enduring as the granite of Tor House, is the poem which Jeffers wrote a few years later:

> If you should look for this place after a
>   handful of lifetimes:
> Perhaps of my planted forest a few
> May stand yet, dark-leaved Australians or the
>   coast cypress, haggard
> With storm-drift; but fire and the axe are devils.
> Look for foundations of sea-worn granite, my
>   fingers had the art

To make stone love stone, you will find some remnant.
But if you should look in your idleness after ten
    thousand years:
It is the granite knoll on the granite
And lava tongue in the midst of the bay, by the
    mouth of the Carmel
River-valley, these four will remain
In the change of names. You will know it by the
    wild sea-fragrance of wind
Though the ocean may have climbed or retired a little;
You will know it by the valley inland that our sun
    and our moon were born from
Before the poles changed; and Orion in December
Evenings was strung in the throat of the valley
    like a lamp-lighted bridge.
Come in the morning you will see white gulls
Weaving a dance over blue water, the wane of the
    moon
Their dance-companion, a ghost walking
By daylight, but wider and whiter than any bird in
    the world.
My ghost you needn't look for; it is probably
Here, but a dark one, deep in the granite, not
    dancing on wind
With the mad wings and the day moon.[2]

The Jefferses busy in their own little world at the continent's end, were hardly aware that 1920 had brought changes to the village of Carmel. According to the villagers, the paving of their main street was the evil which was responsible for many of the ensuing changes. The hazardous adventure of driving down the erratic ruts of Ocean Avenue was forever gone—pavement had smoothed out all of the uncertainties.

The town had divided itself into various small cliques and groups by differences of interest and opinion. Mary Austin had her following and the MacGowan-Cookes their group; the theatre cliques kept to their stormy niches; and Ruth Kuster and her young crowd gambled the nights away at fan-tan and mah-jongg. "Rem" Remsen, son of Ira Remsen, president emeritus of

[2]*Cawdor and Other Poems.*

Johns Hopkins, had his little coterie of literati who, following dinner at Holiday House, gathered to hear him read his latest drama. George Sterling, California's unofficial "poet laureate," whose home was in San Francisco, was a frequent visitor, bringing gay friends from the Bay City to join with his Carmelite friends in night picnics on Point Lobos where they cooked mussels and drank red wine.

But from these cliques the Jefferses kept aloof. In 1920 Jeffers had completed the building of the garage. Una, knowing that her husband's hands must be kept busy, had further plans for him; she wanted a tower. She had loved the medieval round towers of Ireland, and now she would have one of her own. It was to consist of a room for Una, a "dungeon" for the twins, with a "secret passage" connecting the two, and a high turret from which they could look across the Pacific towards distant worlds.

So work on the tower started. And while Jeffers worked he planned the verses he would write today and tomorrow. There was no room for the incidents which crowd the mind of the average man. He was impatient of things which intruded on the time he had set aside for his work, and of irrelevancies. He had work to accomplish and all too few years, he felt, in which to accomplish it. Yet alone, he was powerless to protect himself from distractions. It was Una who could be depended upon to see that at the end of the day he had put in a satisfactory number of hours making verse, laying stones, watering trees, walking and exploring. Even the shortest walk was an adventure to the Jefferses; kelp on the beach, colored shells, a stranger in the distance (preferably in the distance)—all were exciting experiences worthy of the deepest attention and scrutiny. Certainly the ghost of Robin's early restlessness had been successfully laid, and he was deeply content with a life which was limited to Tor House and its environs. In a letter which he had written to Una in 1912 he had prophesied grandly that in ten years time he and Una would be rich on what he made at his writing. They were, instead, very poor, but that they were still very much in love could not be argued, and that Jeffers was well on his way to writing "as good verse as any-one's living now" (another youthful declaration) was also true.

Annie had been seriously ill for the past several months, and Una and Robin went south as often as possible to be with her, writing to her daily when away from her. It was a blessed relief from pain when she died in March, 1921. Una went south to help Sis dispose of the property and Annie's effects. Una preserved letters, papers, and diaries that she felt might have some importance, and from these we have gained a familiarity with Jeffers' youth and his family. Jeffers himself would never have troubled to keep anything, since he placed no value on personal mementos.

Work on the tower was progressing. Jeffers had rigged up a pulley that hoisted the boulders to their position. One day the rope that held him and prevented him from sailing off into space with the gulls broke loose, and he had a bad fall, but he never mentioned it. He was still the "Spartan." Una wrote me of Jeffers' extreme deliberation: "Only thus could he have managed without hurt to himself the enormous boulders of the tower. He used until near the top a long inclined plane, such as the old Egyptians used to roll up the great stones."

Ella Winter, Lincoln Steffens' wife, described Robin at that time in an article which she wrote for the December 12, 1928, edition of *The Carmelite*:

"The same figure was watched by indifferent and then increasingly curious neighbors . . . as it hauled great granite boulders from the beach and rolled them up an inclined plane, higher and higher in the course of the five or six years that Robinson Jeffers took to build his Hawk Tower. Early Carmelites recall how in those days they first wondered, and then ceased to wonder, as the phenomenon took on the slow unchangeability of the cliffs and the ocean and the herons flying. You cannot wonder all of six years.

"And so Robinson Jeffers came to be accepted in his home surroundings as one with the nature he loves so well, as permanent and unperishable . . ."

Lincoln Steffens had been closely associated with the liberal and radical movements in America and was well known for his exposé of municipal corruption while serving as editor of *McClure's Magazine* at the turn of the century. His wife, Ella Winter, had the wandering instincts of a journalist and was an extreme radical. Una wrote Albert Bender, "I've been talking to a man who saw Ella Winter in Moscow. She isn't altogether contented! but refuses to see any but the ideal side of the Russian situation. And stands firmly on the necessity of a career!"

Though Una found them both very stimulating, neither she nor Robin were ever influenced by their political philosophies, remaining staunch Republicans throughout their later years.

At this time the favorite pastime of the Jefferses was picnicking with their friends—usually the Steffens, the Flavins, the visiting Clapps and Sara and Erskine Wood who lived in Los Gatos. Una wrote of them, "I love Sara and Erskine . . . they are so real and sincere and warmhearted besides having such keen and alert minds. . . ."[3] Una also had great respect for Sara's poetry (she wrote under the name of Sara Bard Field).

The Clapps had returned from a trip to the Orient, and not until they saw Jeffers hanging from the tower, fashioning posterity in granite, working at exactly the same chore as when they left Carmel four years before, did they realize that time had as little meaning to a man like Jeffers as it had to the Chinese.

Una told an amusing incident in connection with Jeffers' work on the tower. She said that during the time it was being built, the Carmelite Monastery of Our Lady and St. Therese was being built near by, and the workmen had shown great curiosity about the activity at the Point. Shortly after the tower was completed, Jeffers noticed that some patches of cement had fallen from the roof above the oriel window and was working out a strategy for reaching it to make repairs. Because it was a dangerous place with no foothold, Una begged him to leave it alone. However, one day he secretly took a long rope and attached it to a huge iron ring in the turret wall and let himself down over the edge to re-cement the damage. The workmen at the monastery saw him disappear over the edge and came running, certain that the lunatic, having completed his insane project, was committing suicide. They were greatly embarrassed when they found Jeffers serenely cleaning away mortar.

The tower was completed by the end of 1924, and the last of the gift-stones cemented in—"a bit of the Chinese wall from

[3]Letter to Albert Bender, February, 1932.

Kalgan, a piece of the Great Pyramid of Cheops, a carved head from Ang-Kor, Indo-China, a bit of lava from Vesuvius and from Kilaurea, green Commera marble from Ireland, a bit of Cornish Stone cross, marble from Hadrian's villa, etc."[4]

Over the little fireplace is a quotation from Virgil: "They make their own dreams for themselves." How appropriate! Una not only made her dreams but realized them. Her husband, fashionably dressed during his college years, now wore short-sleeved, open-collar shirts, khaki trousers, puttees, and rough boots. It has been suggested that Una planned his clothes so that he would resemble her idol, Yeats. Una had also been enchanted with Irish towers. She now had a tower of her own, even if it wasn't round. It was a make-believe world that Una had created and would continue to enhance, and which would later be attributed to the "strangeness" of her poet-husband.

On January 1, 1925, Garth, then 8½ years old, made a note in his diary that the occasion had been celebrated with a fine old bottle of Scotch that Uncle Teddie Kuster had brought, and that much excitement had attended the moving of Una's melodeon up to her tower room.

Hawk Tower was habitable, but it was some time before Una's little room achieved its warm character, made so by the smoothness of the oak walls trimmed with the lovely carvings made by Garth and Donnan; by the sun coming in the Gothic windows; by the cooing of the doves that peered in from their perch on the comfortably wide sills. These doves had found feeding more liberal at Tor House than at the mission, so had boldly moved in with the Jefferses. There were so many of them that they fought over their positions on the ledge. They became terrified if a hawk flew over. Once a hawk stunned one of the pigeons, picked it up in its talons, and was about to fly away with it when Jeffers opened the door of the house. Frightened, the hawk dropped the pigeon near the house and flew off. Jeffers watched over the pigeon until it revived and retreated to safety. Soon the hawk returned, looking greatly surprised and indignant that the pigeon wasn't where he had dropped it. He circled until he had located his prey. This was too much for Jeffers. He again opened the door

[4]From Una's notes. Undated. In M. M. B. collection.

and frightened off the hawk, and remained on guard until the hawk gave up the hunt.

Later (May, 1934), Una wrote a description of Hawk Tower for the *London Poetry Review*:

"The Tower is joined to Tor House by the courtyard wall and they stand firm set against the strong winds that come sweeping across the Pacific at certain seasons of the year.

"I am writing from my little oaken sitting room on the second floor where at one end an oriel window juts seaward, at the other a spinet with piles of old Gaelic ballads stands beside an open fire.

"If I climb the winding stair two stories higher I can look from the top of the turret southward and see beyond the river mouth and Point Lobos wisps of cloud caught in the gentle folds of the Santa Lucia Mountains; northward lies the village with the Del Monte forest beyond, and to the east the fertile Carmel Valley with the old amber-colored Spanish Mission where its founder Father Serra sleeps, at its foot.

"Hawk Tower rose out of our dreams of old Irish towers but we have seen in the eyes of our friends as we have so often climbed to the turret with them in the last dozen years, that in many hearts is the mirage of some symbolic tower—citadel, belfry or beacon light."[5]

[5]First paragraph of article omitted.

XII

RECOGNITION

ALTHOUGH JEFFERS had been steadily writing poems since the publication of *Californians* in 1916, compiling them and sending them off to various publishers, he could arouse no interest in his work. In 1920 he had submitted a group of poems to The Macmillan Company, but they rejected them as lacking "the grace and charm" of his earlier work, conceding however that Jeffers' "genius is evident throughout, both in respect to style and philosophy." In 1922, when Jimmy Hopper went to New York, Una entrusted a packet of Robin's poems to him in hopes that he might interest a publisher in them. Jimmy read the poems on the train going east, and, although his knowledge of poetry was limited, he was struck by the power of the words and the depth of Jeffers' philosophy. On arriving in New York he showed them to the critic Van Wyck Brooks, who complained that they were "too dirty." Jimmy then showed them to Boni & Liveright, who rejected them. Edwin Bjorkman, although no critic of poetry, read them and claimed, "It is the real thing, I believe, and there is something big about the man." But Jimmy was unsuccessful in marketing them and returned them to Una apologetically.[1]

In 1920 when Jeffers completed the narrative poem, "Tamar," he was too discouraged to show it to a publisher, and buried it in a drawer. However, writing of it later he said,

". . . I saw a little advertisement by a New York printer, Peter G.

[1]From interview with Hopper, by M. B. B. 1935.

Boyle, in the book-review section of *The New York Times*. Boyle has since then retired from his business. The advertisement offered printing, not publishing, and my mind reverted to my folly of 1912, yet with differences. This time I had no extra money burning my pocket; on the other hand, it seemed to me that the verses were not merely negligible, like the old ones, but had some singularity, whether they were good or not. Perhaps, if they were printed, someone might look at them sometime—*habent sua fata libelli*—little books have such queer destinies. Boyle read *Tamar and Other Poems*, and set a price on the printing, one that I knew was very moderate. He added some praise of 'Tamar' that seemed to me excessive, but I learned later than he was sincerely enthusiastic about it. After several months of hesitation I told him to print, but only five hundred copies, not the thousand that he advised.

"Publishing was not in the bargain, but Peter Boyle was generous, and did his utmost as a publisher. He sent review copies in all directions, at his own expense of time and postage; but quite in vain, no one would notice the book. Suddenly he despaired, and shipped me 450 copies in a big packing-box, across the continent. I stowed them under the eaves in the attic.

"Meanwhile, the Book Club of California was preparing an anthology of verse by California writers, afterwards called *Continent's End*. George Sterling, James Rorty and Genevieve Taggard were the editors. Someone, having perhaps heard of my Macmillan volume, told them that I also wrote verses; and a letter came from Rorty asking me to contribute. I sent some pages of verse; and when *Tamar* was printed I mailed a copy to Rorty because of our correspondence, and one to George Sterling because he had lived in Carmel before my time, and knew the scene of my stories.

"Rorty was only temporarily in California; when he returned to the East he persuaded Mark Van Doren to read *Tamar*. Soon a review of the book by Rorty appeared in the *Herald-Tribune* "Books," Mark Van Doren wrote about it in *The Nation*, and Babette Deutsch in *The New Republic*.

"I received a telegram from Peter Boyle saying that people wanted to buy *Tamar* and he had none to sell; then the big packing-box, as big as a coffin, was dragged out from under the eaves and shipped back to New York. As it emptied, Boyle proposed to print a second edition, but on second thought he decided that a more established publisher might be to my advantage. He offered the book to Boni and Liveright, and it was reprinted in my *Roan Stallion* volume. It pleases me to think of Boyle's honesty and good will, and of the active generosity of Rorty,

Mark Van Doren, George Sterling and some others, to a writer at that time perfectly unknown to them.

"To close the story, it appears that the Los Angeles book-shop which so recklessly bought the edition of *Flagon and Apples* had not been able to dispose of it, even by giving it away at auctions. There were still copies in the cellar; after *Tamar* was spoken of they were dug out and sold for more than they had cost. So now it has become impossible for me to buy them up and drown them, as I should like to."[2]

Peter Boyle had been deeply distressed over his inability to arouse the public to the importance of *Tamar* and had written Jeffers shortly before returning the books to him:

"In New York at the present time there has been a great 'to-do' about unclean books and a bill passed by the N.Y. Legislature, which is very severe, and some of my friends have advised me to be careful, as the puritanical mind is something only the devil himself understands. However, I am not letting that worry me as it would be a mighty good 'ad' for our book. *Tamar* is a beautiful book, and only a fool could see evil in it."[3]

And later he reported that all the publishers with whom he had tried to place the book, hoping for a wider circulation for it, had had the same reaction. They were convinced that the clean book laws would smother it in the East. In November of 1924, Albert & Charles Boni, Publishers, had refused its publication; in December, Seltzer also turned it down; and in January, Boni & Liveright wrote Boyle: ". . . there is a certain intensity and ruggedness to these poems of narrative passion, but we do not feel that they contain sufficient beauty."

There were precedents for the timidity of publishers. Walt Whitman had also been forced to pay for the publication of his poems, to write his own reviews, and to bear the scorn and ridicule of his contemporaries. Whitman, like Jeffers, had introduced a philosophy which was at variance with the accepted literary and moral conventions of the day. Nor could either of their poetic forms be catalogued. The literary public had shuddered over the nonconformity of the Imagists. Who would be daring enough to assert that this was poetry?

[2]*The Colophon*, Part 10, May 1932. Article entitled "First Book."
[3]Letter in collection at Tor House.

In *Tamar* Jeffers had created a new narrative style, fiercely dramatic and tragic. He had created his own rhythms, long and flowing lines balanced against short, tight lines. Of this poem he has since said, ". . . the poem seems nearer to my mind than many later things."[4]

Despite its fury and violence, Jeffers' poem has dignity and fine descriptive passages; it is intense, good narrative; it has beauty. It also has flaws and a philosophy which could easily be interpreted as negative. It was a book to invite criticism. That James Rorty and Mark Van Doren recognized its authenticity is a tribute to them as well as to its author.

Shortly after Liveright's rejection, the reviews of Rorty (*New York Herald Tribune*) and Van Doren (*The Nation*) wiped the film from Liveright's editorial glasses, and they decided that the beauty of Jeffers' poetry was sufficient to warrant their publication of his book. They wired him:

AT EDITORIAL MEETING TODAY WE VOTED UNANIMOUSLY TO PUBLISH WITH YOUR APPROVAL ONE VOLUME THIS FALL CONTAINING ALL POEMS IN TAMAR AND ROAN STALLION FOR THREE DOLLARS. OFFER TEN PERCENT ON FIRST THREE THOUSAND AND FIFTEEN PERCENT THEREAFTER. CATALOGUE ABOUT GOING TO PRESS SO PLEASE WIRE ANSWER AND POSSIBLE NAME FOR VOLUME.

HORACE LIVERIGHT

It is evident that the reviews of *Tamar* had been written by men whose opinions carried authority. Their approbation gave Jeffers the break he had awaited for thirteen years, since the privately printed publication of his first little book of verse, *Flagons and Apples*. The patience which he and Una had shown was remarkable, but just how much further could it have been stretched?

The following unpublished preface Jeffers had written in August, 1923, intending to include it in the book *Tamar*. It gives us a rare document of his mature thinking at this period:

"Poetry has been regarded as a refuge from life, where dreams may heal the wounds of reality; and as an ornament of life; and, as a diversion, mere troubadour amusement; and poetry has been in fact refuge

[4]From pencilled notes for a letter.

and ornament and diversion, but poetry in its higher condition is none of these; not a refuge but an intensification, not an ornament but essential, not a diversion but an incitement. As presenting the universal beauty poetry is an incitement to life; an incitement to contemplation, because it serves to open our intelligence and senses to that beauty.

"The poetry that means to be amusing, or ornamental, or a refuge, has its own licenses; it may play the clown or the dreamer, it may chatter like a fashionable person, or mince out bits of life for its own enjoyment, like a dilletante. Its one condition is to be what it sets out to be, amusing, or ornamental, or a refuge. But the higher form of poetry has laws, many of them too basic to be conscious; there are three to be spoken of because they are so much ignored; this poetry must be rhythmic, and must deal with permanent things, and must avoid affectation.

"The superfluousness of imitative poetry is quite recognized nowadays (in principle) by everyone who thinks on the subject; and this is a gain; but a second-rate mind is sure to confuse eccentricity with originality; its one way of saying something new is to deform what it has to say; like the bobbed fox it sets a fashion for third-rate minds; and these are inevitably imitative, only now they follow a bad model instead of a good one. Here, I believe, is the origin of those extraordinary affectations which distinguish so much of what is called modern poetry. But this is not a disease of adults; and all there is to say further on the subject is that one's clearest thinking is not certain enough, nor one's most natural choice of words appropriate enough, for the passionate presentment of beauty which is poetry's function. If we alter thought or expression for any of the hundred reasons: in order to seem original, or to seem sophisticated, or to conform to a fashion, or to startle the citizenry, or because we fancy ourselves decadent, or merely to avoid commonplace: for whatever reason we alter them, for that reason they are made false. They have fled from reality.

"As to the necessity of dealing with permanent things I have spoken in the verses called 'Point Joe', in this volume; and need but add that permanence is only another aspect of reality; a railroad, for example, is not real as a mountain is; it is actual, in its fantastic way, for a century or two; but it is not real; in most of the human past and most of the human future it is not existent. (Novelty is in itself no bar to poetic quality; permanence is the condition. An airplane is as poetic as a plow or a ship; it is not existent in the human past except as a most ancient of dreams, but it is existent, in some form or other, in all the human future. It is a real thing, not a temporary expedient, but the incarnation of metal and tissue of a permanent human faculty.) Most of our inventions are mere expedients, or the possible essential in them remains hidden; and here is what makes the life of modern cities barren of poetry; it is not a lasting life; and it is lived among unrealities. A life immensely fantastic is not poetic; and what is romantic is not usually poetic, though people think it is.

"This poetry must be rhythmic. By rhythm I do not mean the dissolved and unequal cadences of good prose, nor the capricious divisions of what is called free verse, (both these being sometimes figuratively spoken of as rhythmic), but a movement as regular as meter, or as the tides. A tidal recurrence, whether of quantity or accent, or of both, or of syllables and rhyme as in French verse, or of syllables and rhyme and tone as in Chinese verse, or of phrase and thought as in old Hebrew verse, has always been the simplest and inevitably one of the qualities of poetry. A reason is not far to seek. Recurrence, regular enough to be rhythmic, is the inevitable quality of life, and of life's environment. Prose belongs rather to that indoor world where lamplight abolishes the returns of day and night, and we forget the seasons. Human caprice, the volatile and superficial part of us, can only live sheltered. Poetry does not live in that world but in all the larger, and poetry cannot speak without remembering the turns of the sun and moon, and the rhythm of the ocean, and the recurrence of human generations, the returning waves of life and death. Our daily talk is prose; we do not often talk about real things, even when we live with them; but about fictitious things; expedients, manners, past times, and aspects of personality that are not real because they are superficial and exceptional.

"So we are brought a third time to the question of reality. It is the distinction of all the higher sort of poetry that it deals in the manner of reality with real things; not with abstract qualities; but not either with fantasies nor pretences, nor with things actual indeed, but so temporary and exceptional that they are not to be counted among realities.

"The two earliest of the longer poems in this volume were written six years ago; the manner and versification of the story about Myrtle Cartwright, and the Theocritan echoes of 'Fauna', do not much please me now; but the latter is retained for a geographical sort of richness that closes it, and the other because it is part of a series and seems useful to the purpose of the series; to make apparent the essential beauty in conditions and events of life that from the ordinary point of view appear merely painful, or wicked, or comical."[5]

While Jeffers was brooding his way through his poems, Una was faithfully caring for her husband's and children's needs,

[5]In collection at Tor House.

shopping for them, cooking for them, washing for them, ironing for them, besides living frugally and without the stimulating and admiring companionship to which she had been accustomed before her marriage to Jeffers. Familiar as she was with the great poets, she must have been hard put, in the early years, to encourage her husband to write his mediocre poems. But how great must her pride have been when he came into his own, for she had the knowledge to evaluate truly his "new voice."

Her part in the making of these poems was important, for it was she who brought home incidents about the coast people which stirred Jeffers to weave his stories around them. For instance in *Tamar*, there is the incident of Verdugo's burning which was inspired by a report Una had heard on one of her trips to the post office. One of the Allen girls (the Allens owned Point Lobos) told of an experience she and her sister had had the day before when they were riding their horses home from the village. They had seen smoke rising near the schoolhouse and had ridden over to investigate the cause. As they approached, it seemed that the shack next door to it was burning, but as they rode nearer they found that a bonfire had been lighted near the building and around it stood several sober-faced Mexicans. About to ride away, one of the Allen sisters was startled to see human legs protruding from the fire. She screamed and pointed, and then the sisters demanded an explanation from the men. Without hesitation they were told that an argument between two of the men had resulted in one of them being stabbed and killed. To avoid the cost of a burial they had simply tossed him onto the fire to burn.

Jeffers was completely absorbed in his family, his stonework, and in the production of enduring poetry fashioned from a vocabulary replete with scientific and classical origins, sensitive, deeply philosophical, singular, and honest. There was nothing dainty about this verse, nothing frivolous or slight. Its force and virility were gripping. The boy whom Una had married had developed into a man, physically and mentally powerful, who was capable of living up to the great things which she demanded of him.

When the telegram from Horace Liveright arrived at Tor House, Una's satisfaction was even more intense than was Robin's. She laughed on reading the reviews of the book, as the critics scrambled for synonyms and antonyms with which to describe their new "discovery."

Outwardly, however, the Jefferses seemed singularly unmoved by all this stir. When friends or family wrote their congratulations, Jeffers' answer was typical of him: "We feel none of the percussion down here." They had other, more immediate concerns. Garth wrote in his journal, "Father and we were in the chicken pen when one of the goslings swallowed a feather and was choking on it when father caught it up and pulled the feather out."

During the twelve years of their marriage and their ten years in Carmel, legends about the Jefferses were growing. Certainly Jeffers' strange ways gave the villagers an ever-fascinating subject for conversation. Then, with recognition of his poetry, outsiders came to Carmel with questions, and every neighbor became an authority on the Jefferses. With each telling, the story became more colorful. Jeffers, who enjoyed his wine and needed its friendly encouragement for those evenings which must be spent in the company of strangers, was accused of habitual indulgence; if he was shy with strangers it was set down as intentional rudeness; if he appeared to enjoy the conversation of one of the local women, it was discussed until it was told as a love affair which had been called to a halt only when Una had scratched the face of the lady in question. It is difficult to match this picture with the one of Jeffers' preoccupation with his poetry, his stonework, his family; his concern over trees, animals, and birds; his ever-increasing search for the secrets of nature. He lived his life in quiet dignity.

Jeffers' inscription in Una's copy of *Tamar* shows with what he was most concerned:

> "Dearest Una, I loved you then, all that
> was in me, I love you a great deal more
> these twelve years. Let's go on.
> Robin
> Tor House, September 1924

The anthology *Continent's End*, published by The Book Club of California, made its appearance in June, 1925. The man responsible for promoting the book was the club's secretary, Albert Bender, God's gift to San Francisco's impecunious writers and artists. He had also been instrumental in selecting the interesting trio of editors—Sterling, Taggard, and Rorty, all of whom he knew personally. At the time *Tamar* was published, Bender had not met Jeffers, but shortly before its distribution Bender wrote the poet to ask for a copy of *Tamar* and then again to thank him for autographing the book. This was the inception of the extensive correspondence between the two men which is now in the possession of the Occidental College library.

Tamar's acceptance was the forerunner of the fame that came to Jeffers with the publication of *Roan Stallion, Tamar and Other Poems* by Boni & Liveright. The book appeared toward the end of 1925 and created enough controversy to arouse the interest of many who might never otherwise have read the book. It was reviewed by Frank Ernest Hill, himself a poet, in *The New York Sun*. Hill found the poetry vital, and said, ". . . nothing since Whitman has had as vigorous a beat as these rough lyrics. . . ," but he claimed that what Jeffers had written "is not yet great," that his greatest fault was one of craftsmanship. On January 3, 1926, *The New York Times Book Review* gave a full page to a review of Thomas Hardy and Robinson Jeffers, written by Percy A. Hutchison, lauding the work of the new poet and prophesying a successful future. *The San Francisco Call*, January 2, made a news item of the rise of this "great new poet" with a headline spread and pictures of the poet and Hawk Tower. The two outstanding literary magazines, *The Saturday Review of Literature*, January 16, and the June issue of *Poetry*, also carried good reviews of the book. When before, or since, has a new literary star received such an overture? This was history in itself.

In *Roan Stallion*, Jeffers continues the technique, established in *Tamar*, of reaching high emotion through pain rather than pleasure—the negative moralist startling us to a consciousness of our civilization's disintegration, tracing it with the broad, black, downward-pointing curve of perversion. His mysticism becomes combustible in California's confusion of Christian religion with her own native superstitions. Jeffers' philosophy was taking shape in this poem which loosened the teeth of the conservatives and stirred the literati into anxious awareness.

111

In his foreword to his *Selected Poetry*, Jeffers tells how the idea for *Roan Stallion* came to him:

"... *Roan Stallion* originated from an abandoned cabin that we discovered in a roadless hollow of the hills. When later we asked about its history no one was able to tell us anything except that the place had been abandoned ever since its owner was killed by a stallion.

"This is the only one of my poems of which I can remember clearly the moment of conception. I had just finished 'Tower Beyond Tragedy' and was looking about for another subject—which was to be contemporary, because I repented of using a Greek story when there were so many new ones at hand. I was quarrying granite under the seacliff to build our house with, and slacking on the job sat down on a wet rock to look at the sunset and think about my next poem. The stallion and the desolate cabin came to mind; then immediately, for persons of the drama, came the Indian woman and her white husband, real persons whom I had often seen driving through our village in a ramshackle buggy. The episode of the woman swimming her horse through a storm-swollen ford at night came also; it was part of her actual history. . . . So that when I stood up and began to handle stones again, the poem had already made itself in my mind."

Jeffers offers a further explanation of the theme in a letter written on November 5, 1944, though there was no indication on his pencilled draft as to whom the letter had been sent.

"... A poem like any other event is to be understood by each person in his own way. The writer's interpretation has no particular authority. Personally I think the woman fell in love with the stallion because there was no one else she could fall in love with: and then because the love was physically impractical and the stallion seemed infinitely superior to any man she had known she identified him half-consciously with God. First with the God she had heard religious stories about, the Conception and so forth; and then with a more real God—not a human invention but the energy that is the universe. She was glad to sacrifice her husband to him—for whatever the man was worth. But at the end she slipped back into ordinary life, 'obscure human fidelity'—an animal had killed a man—she must kill the animal. Though the animal was also God. As to Christine's fetching the rifle—it was obviously because she saw her father in trouble and knew that was the only way to save him . . . ."

Of the many other poems in this volume, some short and some narrative, it is probably "The Tower Beyond Tragedy" that has become the best known, though many of the shorter poems have been included in anthologies. Hedwiga Reicher, the actress, was the inspiration for the poem, according to Jeffers' foreword in his *Selected Poetry*.

"'The Tower Beyond Tragedy' was suggested to me by the imposing personality of a Jewish actress who was our guest for a day or two. She was less than successful on the stage, being too tall, and tragic in the old-fashioned manner; but when she stood up in our little room under the low ceiling and recited a tragic ballad—'Edward, Edward'—for a few people gathered there, the experience made me want to build a heroic poem to match her formidable voice and rather colossal beauty. I thought these would be absurdly out of place in any contemporary story, so I looked back toward the feet of Aeschylus, and cast this woman for the part of Cassandra in my poem."

Hedwiga Reicher had visited Tor House about 1923 and again in 1938. Una said that she was a goddess in stature and mien and a most interesting woman as well.

The story of "The Tower Beyond Tragedy" has often been referred to as the story of Electra. It is, but it is more than that; it is also the story of Clytemnestra, Agamemnon, and Cassandra. The story of Electra forms the second part of the play when the action and theme revolve around Electra, Clytemnestra, and Orestes. This is a fine dramatic poem, well suited to the stage. Its first reading, however, was at a private party given by Harry Laffler on Telegraph Hill in San Francisco. George Sterling, according to Lillian Bos Ross who attended the party, "reached inside his coat pocket and produced some very worn-looking yellow second-sheets of a manuscript of a play which he told us was not yet published. . . ." He parcelled pages out amongst the guests and since there was only one script, there was a rather confused over-lapping of "parts," but it did not prevent Sterling from insisting that the reading be carried through to the end of the play. Benjamin De Casseres, who was present, was so impressed by the beauty of the poem that he demanded a repetition of some of the lines and later wrote to Jeffers and visited him at Tor House, after having secured an introduction through Donald Friede. In answer to Friede's letter asking him about De Casseres' doing a piece of writing, Jeffers wrote:

"I'd be delighted to have De Casseres write the pamphlet you speak of, if you really think it's worth while. He sent me a note from Hollywood about *Tamar*, and when he was in Carmel a month or two later I drove him around a bit of the coast in our Ford and was well repaid by his conversation and enthusiasm. He has written brilliant things. . . ."[6]

The result of this was an article in the November 1927 issue of *The Bookman*, by De Casseres, "Robinson Jeffers: Tragic Terror." The following year, 1928, it was privately printed in pamphlet form by J. S. Mayfield, Austin, Texas.

When "The Tower Beyond Tragedy" appeared in the *Roan Stallion* edition in 1925, a young Harvard student, Lincoln Kirstein, of Northampton, Massachusetts, reading the play, had an immediate desire to see it staged and set to work moulding small clay figures for the cast. He completed his models and his small "theatre" in January, 1926, and staged the first production of the Jeffers tragedy.

Jeffers claimed to have "stripped the rhyme tassels" from his verse; however, attention should be called to the poem "Fauna," in this same volume, for its conventional form and rhymed lines. The variety in structure of the verses in this volume proves that Jeffers was still experimenting with the metrics of his poems.

The success of the *Roan Stallion* book brought Jeffers recognition from many sources, and it also brought interruptions to his routine. In a letter to Albert Bender, dated June 6, 1926, he said in part:

". . . And a man here began yesterday to paint a full-length life-sized portrait of me! so the coming week promises to be as occupied as usual. In between I do some stonework and water several hundred lately planted pines and cypresses. 'Even in a palace life may be led well,' Marcus Aurelius said—even in Carmel you can be busy!"

The portrait to which Jeffers referred was a full-length one of him standing, with his arms crossed. It was painted by the artist Rem Remsen.

[6]February 19, 1925.

XIII

JEFFERS DEFENDS HIS PHILOSOPHY

THE NEXT FIFTEEN YEARS of Jeffers' life proved to be his most fruitful. He had an enthusiastic publisher and a growing audience. That early hour of self-doubt had been replaced by one of confidence. Donald Friede, a member of the firm of Boni & Liveright, had been appointed liaison correspondent between his firm and the poet. Many letters passed between Jeffers and Friede[1] during the next two years, and from these letters as well as from letters that Jeffers wrote to Bender[1] over the same period it is evident that the poet was writing under considerable pressure, trying to meet publication dates, a new and not too pleasant experience for him.

In April, 1926, in one of Jeffers' first letters to Friede, he described the long narrative poem that he had been writing for the past year or more, "Point Alma Venus." But shortly after this he wrote to say that he was dissatisfied with the poem, that ". . . every story that ever occurred to me had got wound up into this one poem, and it was too long, too complicated, and from the attempt at compression, neither clear not true. . . ." He regretted disappointing the publishers but promised a poem for spring publication. The work of a year set aside! But his integrity left no other course open to him as he had promised himself to "tell no lies" in his poems. So he began work on the long narrative poem "The Women at Point Sur."

[1]Copies in M. B. B. collection.

115

Una wrote me that " 'Give Your Heart to the Hawks' was a *phrase* in his mind for some years before he wrote the poem named that, and before he in any way thought of the plot of it. Contrary to his custom he spoke of this phrase. He doesn't think so, but it is possible he had planned and written a little on the proposed poem—but discarded the early plans for it."

He discarded the poem "Point Alma Venus" but used the clean verso sheets of the typescript for other poems. For this reason many portions as well as versions of this poem are still extant and show that characters, situations, and pieces of plot were incorporated into "Give Your Heart to the Hawks."

In December Jeffers wrote Friede, ". . . I've been so busy trying to get your book towards completion. . . ." And in a letter to Bender in January he complained, ". . . I am in a horrid pressure of work just now, having promised to finish a long story in verse by February, and it will be wonderful if I can keep the promise but I'm trying to . . ." On January 25, 1927, he wrote Friede:

"This thing that I am working on grows in spite of me, and to omit anything to bring it to a quick conclusion would quite spoil it. So I must just go on thirty lines a day to the end. This is to warn you that the manuscript will be two or three weeks late in spite of my best intentions. Sometime next month it will be finished, I hope early in the month, and nobody will be so pleased as I when that day arrives. It goes on seven days to the week, and I'd like to be at something else.

"I'm awfully sorry to be the fortnight late, but if 'Tamar' was any good I think this will be better and perhaps you'll find it worth waiting for. I'll never promise anything again until it's finished. 52 lines this morning (26th)."

Finally, on February 9, 1926, ten months after Jeffers had started to write the poem, it was completed, and he wrote the good news to his publishers:

"The thing was finished three or four days ago; I am typing it (nobody else could) and shall send it on in a week or less. Thanks for your benevolent patience.

"I understood the importance of doing it well as possible, especially since the theme and dimensions make it—for a poem of this century— rather like a dinosaur in a deerpark. —I think it will do.

"Men of various capacity—like you and Ezra Pound—fascinate me all the more because music, art, mathematics, are perfectly opaque to me. Probably music and art and mathematics are none the worse for it.

Yours,

Robinson Jeffers

"I see (through the bore of copying) that 'The Women at Point Sur' is a bit longer than 'Tamar.' But don't let that alarm you; if it's as long as a novel it's as interesting as a good novel, besides being—I dare say—the Faust of this generation."

Although Jeffers was so frankly favorably inclined towards this poem of his, its intent was almost universally misunderstood. Upon its publication on June 30, 1927, *The Women at Point Sur* was widely reviewed and controversy over the book flared into hot words, as critics were swept from their safe moorings by this Jeffers tidal wave. Protests stormed the tower. Critics who had claimed the "discovery" of Jeffers now groaned over his "failure." Genevieve Taggard, who had claimed that Jeffers had potentialities which "would make him an enormous figure in our literature" was bitter in her disappointment over the "terrific death which he is now experiencing." She prophesied: "Here is the annihilation of Robinson Jeffers." Percy Hutchison thought that "perhaps the critics turned Mr. Jeffers' head. And, perhaps, which would be sad indeed, his poetic genius is spent and the white flame is no longer at his command." Babette Deutsch scolded: "What is lacking here is a sterner self-discipline, a more reticent expressiveness. Then might pity flower out of horror. Then might a hard grain of wisdom be left in the clenched fist of desperation. . . ." And James Rorty shook his pen at Jeffers: "For better or worse, it is metaphysical. And I for one think the flags should be hung at half mast every time a first rate artist turns metaphysical . . . ."[2]

But not until Jeffers read what Mark Van Doren had to say about the book did he offer an explanation in the story's defense. In part, Mr. Van Doren had written: *"The Women at Point Sur* is unbearable enough. I have read it with thrills of pleasure at its power and beauty, and I shall read everything else Mr. Jeffers writes. But I may be brought to wonder whether there is need of

[2]All reviews in "Scrap Book" at Tor House.

117

his trying further in this direction. He seems to be knocking his head to pieces against the night."

So finally a defense was wrung out of Jeffers, and he wrote to Rorty:

"You were right evidently about the need of an explanation. I have just read Mark Van Doren's article, and if he, a first rate critic and a poet and a good friend of my work, quite misunderstands the book, it is very likely that no one else will understand it at present.

"You remember a couple of letters ago I spoke of morality—perhaps I said old-fashioned morality—implied in Point Sur. Tamar seemed to my later thought to have a tendency to romanticise unmoral freedom, and it was evident a good many people took it that way. That way lies destruction, of course, often for the individual but always for the social organism, and one of the later intentions of this Point Sur was to indicate the destruction and strip everything but its natural ugliness from the unmorality. Barclay incited people to 'be your desires. . .flame. . . enter freedom.' The remnant of his sanity—if that was the image of himself that he met on the hilltop—asks him whether it was for love of mankind that he is 'pouring poison into the little vessels?' He is forced to admit that if the motive seems love, the act is an act of hatred.

"Another intention, this time a primary one, was to show in action the danger of that Roan Stallion idea of 'Breaking out of humanity,' misinterpreted in the mind of a fool or a lunatic. (I take the idea to be what you expressed in 'the heart is a thing to be broken,' carried a little farther perhaps.) It is not anti-social, because it has nothing to do with society, but just as Ibsen in the Wild Duck made a warning against his own idea in the hands of a fool, so Point Sur was meant to be a warning; but at the same time a reassertion.

"Van Doren's criticism assures me that I was quite successful in this intention and in the one about morality; only I proved my points so perfectly that he thinks—and therefore other intelligent people will think—that they are proved against me and in spite of me. So I have written in these two respects well but not wisely. For the rest of the book was meant to be:

"1) An attempt to uncenter the human mind from itself. There is no health for the individual whose attention is taken up with his own mind and processes; equally there is no health for the society that is always introverted on its own members, as ours becomes more and more, the interest engaged inward in love and hatred, companionship and competition. These are necessary, of course, but as they absorb all the interest they become fatal. All past cultures have died of introversion at

118

last, and so will this one, but the individual can be free of the net, in his mind. It is a matter of 'transvaluing values', to use the phrase of somebody that local people accuse me quite falsely of deriving from. I have often used incest as a symbol to express these introversions, and used it too often.

"2) The book was meant to be a tragedy, that is an exhibition of essential elements by the burning away through pain and ruin of inertia and the unessential.

"3) A valid study in psychology; the study valid; the psychology morbid, sketching the growth of a whole system of emotional delusion from a 'private impurity' that was quite hidden from consciousness until insanity brought it to the surface.

"4) Therefore a partial and fragmentary study of the origin of religions; which have been necessary to society in the past, and I think necessary whether we like it or not, yet they derive from a 'private impurity' of some kind in their originators.

"5) A satire on human self-importance; referring back to (1).

"6) A judgment of the tendencies of our civilization, which has very evidently turned the corner down hill. 'Powers increase and power perishes.' Our literature, as I said in answer to the New Masses questionnaire, is not especially decadent (because in general it is not especially anything); but our civilization has begun to be.

"(Some of you think that you can save society; I think it is impossible, and that you only hasten the process of decadence. Of course as a matter of right and justice, I sympathize with radicalism; and in any case I don't oppose it; from an abstract point of view there is no reason that I know of for propping and prolonging the period of decadence. Perhaps the more rapid it is, the more rapid comes the new start.)

"There were more intentions, but these are the chief ones that can readily be said in prose. Too many intentions. I believe they all carry over to an intelligent reader, as results though not as intentions, but no doubt I was asking him to hold too many things in mind at once. I had concentrated my energies for a long while on perceptions and expression, and forgot that the reader could not concentrate so long nor so intensely, nor from the same detached and inclusive viewpoint."[3]

Jeffers still believed in the poem's poetic integrity but was now willing to admit to its "grave faults." Never again was any poem of his to display sex-extravagances in such broad proportions.

[3]Also quoted in Sydney S. Alberts' *A Bibliography of the Works of Robinson Jeffers*.

119

Rorty's answer to Jeffers showed a sincere endeavor to understand his philosophy:

"I ran into a chap last night who seemed to understand you better than I do—better than any of your critics I have read so far. His name is James Mahoney—a southerner who was with me in the ambulance camp at Allentown during the war. Now a student and intermittent fiction writer—a diabolically clever chap. He had read Roan Stallion and thought it the most important work being done in America; pointed out its relation to William Blake. I myself begin to understand, or think I do, the repeated attack on the single theme of 'breaking through'—the only perception that matters I suppose from your point of view. I even get a notion why you have to repeat the incest material . . . . I write myself because I have been wanting an occasion to send you greetings —I was a bit uncomfortable about that review, which I suspect was a little stupid in asking you to be things which you neither are nor need to be."[4]

Jeffers also tried to explain his intent in a letter to Albert Bender written in August, 1927:

"The book concludes a train of thought that began with Tamar; it was meant to complete the ideas but also to indicate the dangers and abuses of them, which it does pretty thoroughly. Just as Ibsen wrote the Wild Duck to show how his ideas could be perverted by a fool: I set a lunatic to work with the same object in mind. It puzzles people; but will be understood eventually."[5]

Jeffers had been the victim of several small annoyances caused by his publishers. He repeatedly had to remind them that his royalty checks were overdue, and upon the publication of *The Women at Point Sur* he had to ask them to send him a copy of the book which had already been distributed to book sellers. Donald Friede had even sent his own copy to Jeffers to be autographed.

Friede had asked Jeffers for the manuscripts of "Roan Stallion," "The Tower Beyond Tragedy," and "The Women at Point Sur." Attaching no importance to them, Jeffers willingly obliged him, writing of the first two, "They are smeared and illegible and quite worthless, but perfectly yours if you want them." In answer

[4]In Tor House Collection.
[5]Copy in M. B. B. Collection.

to Friede's request for the "Tamar" manuscript, Jeffers answered that he had burned it after the book was printed. About "The Women at Point Sur" manuscript, Jeffers wrote Friede: "If you want the pencil manuscript sufficiently, I'll send it as soon as we get a proof; keeping it here till then to guard against the loss of the other. I'd hate to have to write the thing from memory." Later, Una wrote Friede that the manuscript was on its way to him, "which Robin is giving you with his best wishes." Una wrote me later that Friede had sold it to John Hay Whitney. He also sold the manuscript of "Roan Stallion" and some of Jeffers' letters which he had taken with him when he severed connections with Boni & Liveright. Una was very distressed when she learned of this but later made her peace with Friede.

Despite his critics, Jeffers was not "through," for the year 1928 saw the publication of three books under his name. It was also the ninth anniversary of Tor House. Besides the house, the garage, and Hawk Tower, Jeffers had completed work on the stone wall which formed a courtyard east of the house. Jimmy Hopper claimed that the wall was symbolical of Jeffers' desire to shut out the world. It wasn't only symbolical, it was practical, because by now his private world was constantly invaded by visitors eager to meet this man who was making literary history.

Una was often criticized because she zealously protected her husband against constant interruptions. What her critics didn't understand was that Jeffers was powerless to retreat when he found himself cornered by the curious; he was reluctant to offend them; so he was only too happy to rely completely on Una's firmness. If his hours of writing were intruded upon it depressed him. At last they hung a little gray board on each of the two gates to inform casual callers that there were to be "No Visitors Until After 4 O'clock." Four o'clock might find the Jefferses well up the beach or back in the hills.

Jeffers wrote the poem "Ninth Anniversary" (unpublished) to commemorate their homemaking, which Una later sent to me to be used in this book.

> Only a fortnight out of nine years has found
>   me afield
> From the ocean-cliff where I perched my house,

And long before that I lived in hearing of the
    long voice
And thunder of the shore: yet to this hour
I never look west but shaken with a joyful
    shock of astonishment,
By dark nor by day: there the most glorious
Creature on earth shines in the nights or glit-
    ters in the suns,
Or feels of its stone in the blind fog,
Or shakes its hair in the storms: I never wake
    in my bed
But surprised with pleasure to hear it speaking.
An east wind brings me the smell of the river,
    all the others carry
The sea-fragrances, the salt and the sea-wings.
— What, did my blood before me live inland
    always? — Admire
One's next neighbor after nine years?

The Carmelite, one of Carmel's two weekly newspapers, devoted its December 12, 1928, issue to Robinson Jeffers. Among
the contributors who paid homage to the poet were Carl Sandburg, Edgar Lee Masters, Lincoln Steffens, Sara Bard Field,
Charles Erskine Scott Wood, Ella Winter, James Rorty. Here we
may read what Jeffers' contemporaries thought of him. To quote
Rorty:

"I think Jeffers is one of the best poets alive and have said so at various times . . . . This in spite of the fact that I don't share his philosophy
—am in fact convinced that it embodies distortions which, for example,
prevented me from getting any genuine tragic purgation out of 'The
Women At Point Sur.' What of it? He writes with greater poetic intensity than any other living poet I have read."

Edgar Lee Masters wrote:

"If I were writing a poem about Jeffers I might draw a picture of
some of those evenings I spent at his house in Carmel in July of 1926,
when George Sterling was along, and Gaylord Wilshire (whom I nick-
named Quex) and when while Quex talked about London, and an English writer named Shaw, and Sterling heckled Quex, Jeffers sat by
smoking and chuckling, while Mrs. Jeffers made no attempt to restrain

a mirth which equally captured the fun of the occasion. Or I might write a poem about our tree planting (it wouldn't be in the manner of Bryant's planting an apple tree). I don't know what kind of trees they were; but one was set out in honor of me and one in honor of Quex. Sterling I believe had won his tree before this time. That was a humorous hour too, full of mischievous irony. One could see it in Jeffers' eyes, as with bared arms he dug the holes and planted the roots. Well, here's to the powerful young Jeffers, alive with health, and of sanest vision, qualities so necessary to handle and to treat sick and bewildered humanity. He took up his abode by the sea, where he could walk like the priest Chryses along the shore of the many-tongued waters, and get their rhythms. And he went back to the Greeks to brighten his eyes for contemplation of the American scene, the wisest things—that an American poet could do. All of which means that I believe in Cawdor without having seen it; and hope for America's appreciation of it—without being sure of that for the present."

Sara Bard Field wrote:

"I am still dazed from contact with certain blind souls who cry 'unmoral' 'obscene' 'destructive' after reading Jeffers' poetry. No poet has ever come to us with cleaner hands or purer heart. He has attacked the poison, as he sees it, at the root of life, not with sugar coated pills but as a great physician and surgeon—with aloes and wormwood, with sharp knives laying open the repulsive sore that the heart of humanity may be made clean as the bitter waters by which he lives, clean as the Carmel Coast . . . ."

Charles Erskine Scott Wood stated:

"I think Jeffers the largest of our living poets, the greatest English poet of today . . . . My reason for placing him as I do—the greatest of our poets—is not a reason at all, but an emotion. I feel instinctively—that he is a great original, and originality is our most precious jewel. . . .

"I do not know of anyone else so little imitative—so dramatically imaginative. So much the bard, the seer, the poet."

Sandburg wrote:

"Often I have the feeling that Jeffers is more than an equal of Balboa, for he too has discovered the Pacific Ocean. And to discover something as big as the Pacific Ocean, after others have discovered it, requires eyesight and navigation ability requisite to the business of being a poet."

Steffens wrote of "Jeffers the Neighbor," and his wife, Ella Winter, gave a vivid picture of the life at Tor House—Jeffers, Una, and their twin sons.

The first of Jeffers' three books to be published in 1928 was *Poems*, a small book of lyric poems, some of them reprints, printed by The Grabhorn Press for The Book Club of California, with an introduction by Benjamin H. Lehman, of the University of California. Dr. Lehman, whose opinion carried authority, was one of Jeffers' earliest champions on the west coast. Influential in educational and literary circles, he introduced and defended Jeffers' poetry. Later, when he married the distinguished actress Judith Anderson, he fired her with his enthusiasm, and she, in her turn, recognizing Jeffers' talent for drama, became one of the outstanding influences in the poet's career.

In quoting from Jeffers' poem "Night" at the conclusion of his Introduction to the book, Lehman states: "This is poetry, every line of it, poetry, authentic and powerful, brooded in a mind informed with the neutral universe, heard by an ear sensitive to rhythms current in the world, vocal on a tongue that uses the speech of living man." The slim volume also includes a fine Ansel Adams portrait of Jeffers.

The second book to be published that year was a pamphlet privately printed by John S. Mayfield. It contained the short poem *An Artist*. Mayfield, of Austin, Texas, had also printed *Robinson Jeffers: Tragic Terror*, the portrait of Jeffers by De Casseres. De Casseres has also written an article for this book, describing his "discovery" of Jeffers ("A great tragic poet, a genius of the first magnitude had swum into my ken") and his subsequent visit to Tor House. He says: "I could find out nothing about his methods of work, his ideas or his dreams. . . . A simple man who has spent fourteen years getting rid of the machinery of civilization. My final vision of Robinson Jeffers is a fusion of Saint Francis of Assisi, Thoreau, and the Eumenides." Mr. Mayfield also quotes a letter from Havelock Ellis in which he writes: "I can only say that I have great regard and admiration for Jeffers. So far as I know, he is the strongest poet to come out of America in recent times."

A note by Jeffers explaining the conception of the poem is also included:

"Reading recently for the first time Oscar Wilde's *The Soul of Man Under Socialism* I was impressed by some paragraphs about the independence of the artist; and I think that a certain (not more than emotional) sympathy with what was said lay at the origin of these verses, they were written during the next two days. The poem seems to carry that independence to its logical conclusion."

The third book to be published in 1928 was the long narrative poem, *Cawdor*—third and last of the trilogy which began with *Tamar*. Jeffers explained the alliance:

"The events of the principal poem in this book, Cawdor, may be thought of as being already ancient history on this future-ridden coast; they end under the comet of 1910. I think of Cawdor as making a third with Tamar and The Women at Point Sur; but as if in Tamar human affairs had been seen looking westward, against the ocean; in Point Sur looking upward, minimized to ridicule against the stars; in Cawdor looking eastward, against the earth, reclaiming a little dignity from that association.

"The soil that I dig up here to plant trees or lay foundation-stones is full of Indian leavings, sea-shells and flint scrapers; and the crack-voiced churchbells that we hear in the evening were hung in their tower when this was Spanish country. Where not only generations but races too drizzle away so fast, one wonders the more urgently what it is for, and whether this beautiful earth is amused or sorry at the procession of her possessors. Probably these wonders are the theme for most of the book."[6]

When *Cawdor* was released to the public, it was received with far less protest than *The Women at Point Sur*. Some reviewers regretted its "darkness and pessimism"; others considered it a "magnum opus"; but all conceded that Jeffers was a titan among American poets.

In France, Eugène Jolas, editor of the French magazine *Transition* had translated "Roan Stallion" and it was published in part in *Anthologie de la Nouvelle Poésie Américaine* in April, 1928. There was a limited edition of 100 copies released simultaneously with a trade edition of 500 copies. The latter subsequently had five reprintings of 500 copies each. The interest of readers in

[6]Sydney S. Alberts' *A Bibliography of the Works of Robinson Jeffers.*

this anthology was obviously far beyond the expectations of the publishers.

In 1928, the twins, Garth and Donnan, entered the eighth grade of the Sunset Public School in Carmel. They were now eleven years old. Donnan says that their mother taught them various subjects that she was interested in, "from quite an early age—Latin (which she tried to start us at when we were four, I think, but then gave up when we proved too uninterested, and started again when we were six or seven), reading, writing, composition, etc. She also sent us at quite an early age to a small school for instruction in other matters in which she was not so interested such as arithmetic, geography and history." The small school of fifteen or twenty children was operated by a Miss Stark and Miss Williams and was referred to by their mother as "a dame school." They went there for about three years and then something happened to Miss Stark, and after that they were tutored by Miss Williams. Their education had also been supplemented by their father who read to them every evening.

XIV

CAN JEFFERS BE DISTRACTED?

JEFFERS was now forty-one years old, and he and Una had been living in Carmel for fourteen years. During that time he had been no farther away than Pasadena. He didn't even own a hat or a town suit. He had written Albert Bender in April, 1927:

"I'm set here like a stone in cement. There are many reasons, but I suppose they come down in the end to preserving our serenity and getting my work done, if possible. A natural lover of mankind, like Markham or yourself, can meet many people and enjoy it; but for me to see more than two or three in an evening would mean a month's quarrel with the whole race. A giant like Markham can travel about and get his work done too, but I have to stay home. He is a great man, and I wish you would offer him my admiration and most cordial good wishes. . . ."

However, for the past year the Jefferses had been discussing the possibility of a trip to the British Isles. Jeffers was reluctant to leave Tor House or to upset his daily routine, and he had a deep prejudice against the discomforts of travel, but Una felt it would be a good change for all of them, and when a gift from Albert Bender made the trip financially possible, they tentatively set their departure for the late spring or early summer of 1929.

Until the success of *Medea* twenty years later, Una gratefully and joyously accepted the generous gifts of close friends to provide her family with the luxuries they couldn't possibly afford on Robin's slim earnings from the sale of his books of poetry, and

127

the small income from his trust fund. It was an embarrassment to Robin but he had resigned himself to leave such decisions to Una.

Jeffers had two long poems in the making, to be included in one volume—"Dear Judas" and "The Loving Shepherdess"—which had to be completed and in his publisher's hands before he could sail. Once again he was writing under pressure. By January, Una had tickets purchased to sail from Montreal to Belfast on June 14, and now that their departure was definite, she was alive with excitement, and her eyes shone like the stars she loved so well. She wrote to Bender:

"I think by day and dream by night of Ireland—not that my deep love for Tor House ever fails—but there is somehow an allegiance to that island in my very soul and I think Robin and the boys are going to find something that belongs to them there too. . . ."

Preparations for the trip included a shopping tour to San Francisco which Una described in another letter to Bender:

"We rushed to town yesterday and back last night—all our hours spent in hectic shopping. I felt very discouraged last night. Crowds and noise and all the terrible hustle about living in a city had reduced Robin to utter misery.

"My one hope of making this trip a success is to speedily get him into a quiet glen in Ireland and stay for a time—the train I hate to contemplate. One says to oneself, 'Is it right to keep so away from the whirl of things that the mere sight of them is painful?' and one must answer if truthful that much of that whirl is utterly unnecessary—the useless trouble about complicated living—clothes, motion pictures, needless supplies of all kinds and amusements! I don't think I shall try to change Robin for the good of his soul! All the sea and land are his. . . ."

Friends recognized the enormity of the occasion and Tor House resounded with echoes of loving adieus. Bender came down from San Francisco to make sure that they had everything they needed for their journey. Even Hamilton, Robin's brother, descended from his roost at Lick Observatory on Mount Hamilton to say good-bye. Dr. Ben Lehman came from the University of California to add his farewells to those of Charles Erskine Scott Wood, the elderly poet, and his wife, Sara Bard Field. And the Jefferses'

Carmel friends, Lincoln Steffens and his wife Ella Winter, Mollie and John O'Shea the artist, Noel Sullivan, and Ellen O'Sullivan—all gave farewell parties or came by Tor House with gifts, causing a round of gaiety that was difficult for Jeffers but great fun for Una.

Jeffers lived through the festivities, as well as the long train ride to Montreal, and the boat trip to Belfast. Through friends, Una arranged to rent a small cottage at Knocknacarry, County Antrim, in a wild section of Ireland with beautiful scenery; so upon their arrival in Belfast, they bought a second-hand Ford and drove directly to their little house. In August, Una wrote Bender: ". . . Robin didn't settle down to writing for several weeks —but now he is occupied at least half the day at his desk and is happy and full of plans I can see. . . :' The cottage was small and had no room where Robin could write in privacy, but he had made a work-table of an old washstand in one of the bedrooms.

On August 26, Jeffers sent a card to Horace Liveright saying,

"We've been in every county in Ireland except one, and it seems to me in almost all the hotels and church yards and pigmarkets. And twice to George Moore's ancestral home which was wrecked in 1921 and stands a very beautiful ruin by its lake, and twice to Yeats' feudal tower that he wrote the poem about. Neither is inhabited at present; we've been visiting places not people. After September 19 our address will be Kerry Vot Cottage—Britwell Salome, Watlington, Oxfordshire."

In a letter to Houston Martin of the University of Pennsylvania in February, 1934, Jeffers wrote:

". . . A. E. Housman seems to me enviable among modern poets, for many reasons. His work is lyrical without self-implication—he does not give himself away—it has a classic quality, though not bound up with any fashion or school, therefore exempt from declining with any. The carefully limited range of his work has enabled him to give only of his best, and escape the temptations of mediocrity; and has preserved his sensitiveness, so that no one knows more clearly than he what is poetry and what is not. He has never overworked his vein, nor thought of poetry as a profession.

". . . 'On Wenlock Edge' was especially present to our minds when we were in Shropshire a few weeks ago, and looked for and found Wenlock Edge and the Wrekin and Unicorn. That is another assurance of Mr. Housman's abiding fame: —that it is anchored in the firm earth, in beautiful tangible country and the names of quiet places. . . ."[1]

In September they toured to the northernmost corner of Scotland and then traveled on to England, staying a fortnight in London at the home of Mrs. Denis O'Sullivan, a relative of Carmel friends, later moving to her daughter's cottage at Oxfordshire, which Una described in a letter to Bender:

". . . This is a rambling up and down old house of nine rooms but we live mostly in the big kitchen-sitting room which has an enormous fireplace at one end with copper and brass pots about it. At the other a big dresser with gay Breton china. The walls are white panelled and the floor red bricks. Robin works all morning in the tiny Drawing-Room which has a good fireplace and two long French windows opening into the garden and all the morning sunshine comes in. Robin is writing constantly at something these days down here—He had to autograph the unbound sheets of the special edition of his 'Dear Judas' last week. Such a business as it was to get them repacked and remailed to the satisfaction of the Post Master! and British rules. . . ."

The poems that Jeffers was writing at this time made up a book called *Descent to the Dead*, to be published by Random House in December, 1931. In these short poems he caught the elegiac mood of the Isles with their cairns and graves and ghosts. He concluded the poem, "Ghosts in England" with the lines:

> And on the Welsh
>   borders
> Were dead men skipping and fleering behind
>   all the hedges. An island of ghosts.
>   They seemed merry, and to feel
> No pity for the great pillar of empire settling
>   to a fall, the pride and the power slowly
>   dissolving.

On December 10 the Jefferses sailed for home, on the Canadian Pacific's *S.S. Duchess of Bedford*, and from the ship Jeffers wrote Albert Bender:

[1]Pencilled draft in Tor House Collection.

130

"We are on our way home, and shall be there I think by New Year's. Ireland was best, and it was like coming home to come back to it before we sailed. Northern Scotland we loved intensely too, and the moors and sea-rocks of Cornwall were very fine. We loved our travel, and are most grateful to you for your share in it.

"The days were becoming too short to see new places, and the weather too bad for wandering in Scotland, or we'd have stayed longer.

"We drove up rapidly from Oxfordshire through Shropshire and Wales and Carlisle into Scotland, through Gretna Green and Carlyle's village Ecclefechan, where he was born and sits on the hill in bronze. We took a boat from Stranraer to Ireland during 'the greatest storm within living memory'—the papers called it—and may I say that we were all sea-sick for an hour—the passage took three—we crossed before breakfast.

"We spent four or five delightful days seeing northern Ireland again, and sailed from Belfast for New York.

"The storm was still going on, or had revived, and our ship made slow progress the first two or three days, but we didn't mind. Its motion is not so excitable as a channel steamer's. There is only a handful of passengers, and most of these were sick at first, so that we have had the big ship to ourselves. It is the one Ramsay McDonald went home on. Night before last the ship unexpectedly stopped for an hour to steady it while they operated on our poor cabin-steward for sudden appendicitis.

"We've told no one in New York the name of our steamer, not wishing to be met, and haven't yet made up our mind to call on anyone. We shall only stay a day or so, and then go to visit Una's family in Michigan for a few days, then home by New Orleans and Los Angeles. Then I'll begin building a round tower of something, and in a few days you'll come and see us. Una and the boys send their love to you. . . ."

The four Jefferses stayed in New York only long enough to arrange for transportation to Michigan. Jimmy Hopper happened to see them as they were trying to get all their belongings to the train, and offered his services. Una, in her handsome military cape, was engineering things, while Jeffers and the two boys docilely carried out her suggestions. There were so many odd packages that Jimmy was entrusted with a huge stone from Yeats' tower to carry. When each had the luggage assigned to him, Una led the way to the station, the four men silently tagging along behind her, single file, even as young Robin had trailed behind his father on the way to the station at Edgeworth, years ago.

The first reviews of *Dear Judas and Other Poems* were appearing in the newspapers and magazines: *Time*, *The New York Times*, *The New York Herald Tribune*, the *San Francisco Chronicle*, *The Saturday Review of Literature*, and most of the newspapers in large cities across the States. Of the two long poems in the book, almost without exception the reviews favored "The Loving Shepherdess." Here was a new Jeffers, gentler, simpler, more acceptable, yet none the less powerful. To Sydney S. Alberts Jeffers wrote:

"The story of 'The Loving Shepherdess' was suggested by a footnote in one of the novels of Walter Scott, which I was reading aloud to our sons. I cannot remember which novel it was. The note tells about a half-insane girl who wandered up and down Scotland with a dwindling flock of sheep, that perished one by one. . . . It is the story of one who has committed self-sacrifice . . . . a saint, I suppose, going up to a natural martyrdom, aureoled with such embellishments as the mind of time permits. Incapable of taking thought for herself, she wanders the length of the coast that has been usually the scene of my verses. I am going away for a year, and have perhaps lingered on that account a little wistfully over my home hills, before looking at others. . . ."

Of "Dear Judas," the title poem, Jeffers wrote Sydney S. Alberts:

"There is some relationship of thought between the two longer poems of the book; the shepherdess in the one, and Judas and Jesus in the other, each embodying different aspects of love: nearly pure, therefore undefiled but quite inefficient in the first; pitying in the second; possessive in the third. [It was written] with the thought of presenting the only divine figure still living in the minds of people of our race, as the hero of a tragedy. The Japanese Nō plays, in which the action is performed by ghosts revisiting the scenes of their passions, no doubt influenced my conception."

The reviews of the book were kind, with the exception of one by Yvor Winters, who wrote a scathing and vindictive criticism for the magazine *Poetry*,[2] claiming that Jeffers' "aims are badly thought out and essentially trivial."

[2]February, 1930.

The Hogarth Press published the English edition of *Dear Judas* and it received a cool review by Humbert Wolfe, one of the most impressive of the English poetry critics. The review appeared in the London *Observer*, and said in part:

"We begin with Mr. Robinson Jeffers whose considerable reputation has as yet found no echo over here. This is in part due to the inordinate length at which he writes. Few could be found who could honestly pretend to have read through *The Roan Stallion* and *Cawdor*, his previous publications in the Hogarth series. But that is only part of the reason. The other part is a doubt whether what Mr. Jeffers writes is poetry at all. His work has a queer, dragging monotony that suggests muttering in a corner rather than speaking right out. Moreover, his form —particularly in *Dear Judas*—is often so loose that it is difficult to recognize it as poetry. Nevertheless, he has a real quality that will reward those who have patience to read him through. He has the power of investing ordinary emotions and events with significance. He writes in simple language because he sees and understands directly and simply. It is this directness and simplicity which makes his study of the betrayal of Jesus so quietly effective. He has chosen a form which has an affinity with the rhythm of the Gospels, but which never descends into the archaic or the purely derivative. When Christ speaks He speaks with a beautiful authority, and Judas is given the benefit of the immortal doubt. It is particularly interesting to compare this sketch with D. H. Lawrence's picture in *The Man Who Died*. Jeffers is definitely better because he does not seek to impose his mind upon that of Jesus. The work may not be poetry, but there is no doubt of its significance."

It is doubtful if *Dear Judas* can be successfully used as a theatre piece, since it lacks a steep enough pitch to or from the climactic aim. It is more a piece of characterization, through rationalization, than a piece with plot or action. It does achieve some motion through the development of the characterizations, but it would be difficult to sustain the interest of an audience through the long soliloquies; one follows another with a minimum of action and dialogue separating them.

In *The New York Herald Tribune* (January 12, 1930) Babette Deutsch reviewed *Dear Judas*. She said, in part:

"The previous work of Robinson Jeffers has worn savagery like an angry brand on its forehead. In this most recent book . . . the fierceness is still present, but self-contained and exalted. It is as though the poet started out hot set to kill whatever was mean, sapless and ugly in its stupid ease, and having handled the world before him brutally enough had retired to some desert or mountain cavern for a season, returning armed with peace, like an older, a contemplative Cain. The man has not changed, except to grow in wisdom and the tenderness which is its issue. His fiery energies have not diminished; they burn with a less petulant flame. . . ."

In a pencilled draft of a letter to Frederic Carpenter (November, 1933) in the Tor House Collection, Jeffers explains the purpose of this poem:

". . . When I spoke in my letter to you of Jesus as having 'fallen in love outward' I was thinking of 'love the Lord thy God with all thy soul'—however it is worded—'and thy neighbor as thyself'—(which might mean *greatly*, or might mean *hardly at all*, the self and the neighbor being recognized as wholly unimportant, and human love swallowed up in divine love). But when I wrote 'Dear Judas' I was thinking of Jesus as a subject for tragedy—the Greeks had many demigods; we have only that one—and the subject of tragedy cannot be a perfect person. The perfect man could have no conflict in his mind, and could feel no misfortune; could not even have felt the agony in the garden or the despair on the cross that the evangelists impute to him. However, the two points of view are not contradictory. Mystical vision may be only a momentary experience; one may have it, and then have only a fading remembrance of it, and become a very imperfect person after all. It seems to me that the *having had it* is somewhere indicated in the poem.

"I don't remember altogether what Lazarus said in my verses, but it seems to me that he represented only the clear negations and detachment of death, had nothing to do with love. . . ."

With the publication of *Dear Judas* there began a controversy about Jeffers' "godlessness" which continued throughout his life. Students, teachers, ministers, priests, wrote asking him for a statement of Faith. Obviously they weren't familiar with the body of his work as Jeffers admonishes us repeatedly to "look to God." Jeffers' religious beliefs were not founded on emotionalism but on a solid knowledge of the history of religions and their influence on the individual. In 1940 Jeffers wrote a dissertation on the impact of religion on civilization for the Phi Beta Kappa scholarship society which conferred upon him an honorary membership. Quoting from this may clear up some of the questions about his thinking. After presenting two other thoughts, Jeffers continues to say:

"The third of these ideas is the one I wish particularly to present; because perhaps it may be new to you, whether or not acceptable. It is the idea that the most characteristic qualities of our civilization are produced by the discordance between its people and its religion; this discordance causing a constant state of strain, which generates great energies and many confusions.

"Other races that have attained to high culture—the Greeks for instance, or the Egyptians or Chinese—grew up with their religions; these were at least partly indigenous, and were moulded to the natures of the people; religion was an integral part of the complex of thoughts and customs. Whereas Christianity is a foreign religion imposed by conversion; it is an immensely powerful religion, claiming universality, and supported by the tremendous sanctities of eternal bliss or eternal torment; and it has been accepted without ever being assimilated. It was an Oriental religion imposed on the West; the excitement and confusions of the convert still persist in western minds. In course of time the new religion, especially in Mediterranean Europe, began to be assimilated to the people; compromises were worked out. The religion was somewhat paganized, the people somewhat Christianized. But then the Protestant Reformation, and the multiplicity of sects that issued from it and the counter-reformation in the old church; these revivified Christianity, and renewed the discordance and tension.

"This tension, of course, is only one determinant among many of the qualities of which I speak, which is ethical and intellectual.

"The intellectual strain may be suggested by the well-known words of one of the fathers of the church, Tertullian, I think: "Credo quia absurdum"—"I believe because it is unbelievable." Or it may be suggested by the spectacle of Newton in his later years, turning his mind from the Mystics and mathematics to works of rather chimerical theology. Or by the heart-searchings of Victorian times, when science and religion were supposed to be antagonists. This strain is considerably relaxed at present, by concessions on both sides; but chiefly because the old Hebraic and what may be called mythological elements of Christianity have been more or less discarded.

"But the ethical strain persists. We obey in fact, consciously or not, two opposed systems of morality. They cannot be reconciled, yet we cling to both of them, and serve two masters. (We have in fact two moralities, which cannot be reconciled, yet most of us cling to both of them.) We believe in the Christian virtues, universal love, self-abnegation, humility, non-resistance; but we believe also, as individuals and as nations, in the pagan virtues of our ancestors: justice with its corollary vengeance, pride and personal honor, will to power, patriotic readiness to meet force with force. Our conduct almost always compromises between these contradictory moralities. And the great movements of Christianity—the Crusades, for instance, or the great colonizations, or the French and Russian revolutions—are inspired and confused by both of them.

"An unresolved conflict in the mind of an individual not only confuses but also often stimulates drives to action; it becomes a source of power. A person who is not at peace inwardly is the more likely to be active outwardly. And a person who cannot subdue himself will be driven to subdue others. He who cannot, or dares not, understand himself, will often be driven to make discoveries outside himself.

"So, I believe, it has been with the culture of Christianity. Other cultures have been comparatively static, ours is dynamic; and I think the tension that I have indicated has been a chief source of these dynamics.

"Now it is my belief that not only the self-contradictions and self-frustrations of our culture are derived from this tension between Western race and Oriental religion; but also a good part of its greatness, genius, energy, which transcend those of any previous culture.

"Compare, for illustration, Greek architecture with Gothic, or the *Iliad* with the *Divine Comedy*, or Greek tragedy with Elizabethan tragedy; the former are simple, limited, well-integrated and self-consistent; the latter strained, aspiring, intense, confused and manifold. Compare the protagonists of Greek tragedy with Shakespeare's tragic heroes; those are only at war with fate; these—Hamlet, Macbeth, Lear—are at war with themselves also, as the soul of Christianity is, and has always been.

"Being neither historian nor philosopher I cannot pursue these themes further; I only suggest them for consideration."

*   *   *   *

Arriving home from Europe on New Year's Day, each of the Jefferses asked himself, "Why, when it is so beautiful here, did we ever leave it?" and each promised, "We'll never leave again." But that was before Mabel Dodge Luhan, with her Indian husband, Tony Luhan, and her secretary Spud Johnson, arrived in Carmel.

Mabel Luhan is the woman who self-admittedly "called" or "willed" the English writer D. H. Lawrence to Taos, New Mexico. She called him half way around the world for the purpose of immortalizing her desert in prose. For years she had been obsessed with the idea of the artistic perpetuation of the New Mexico country. She was responsible for the folio of photographs by Ansel Adams, printed by the Grabhorn Press; at her invitation the painters Maurice Sterne (her former husband), Georgia O'Keefe, John Martin, and Nicolai Feschin went to New Mexico to paint it. Although Lawrence was not known to her personally, she persuaded him to come to her; he came, but wrote sparingly of the desert and died before he had accomplished Mrs. Luhan's purpose. Indomitable, she then "willed" that Robinson Jeffers should come to New Mexico and take up where Lawrence had left off.

Early in 1930, the year the Jefferses had returned from Europe, the Luhans rented the Beckwith house on the Point near Tor House. Through the Steffenses, they effected an introduction to Jeffers. But it was not an easy task Mrs. Luhan had set for herself —to will Jeffers from Carmel to New Mexico. Her secretary, Spud Johnson, who observed the miracle, outlined it step by step in an article which he wrote for *The Carmelite*.[3]

". . . Others who saw it happening may tell you that the first step was an invitation to visit New Mexico; that the second step was a series of urges and insistences, both of which were met by the blank wall of Jeffers' resolution (made when they returned from their strenuous European venture) not to stir again for years—perhaps never; that the third step was a subtle campaign of Taos publicity plus a still more subtle campaigning of breaking down Jeffers' resistance to 'going out' or 'seeing people' and otherwise undermining the studied pattern of their well-ordered lives; that the fourth step was the suggestion that the two boys go to Taos for a vacation (an invitation which was clinched by the educational and broadening advantages of such an adventure, including, as it did, the opportunity to visit the various Indian pueblos with Tony as a guide); and that the fifth and final step was the master stroke of changing the entire plan at the very last moment, a reversal which stipulated that either the whole family should go—or none of them; and how could fond parents disappoint their children after they had been completely 'sold' on the idea and were looking forward to it expectantly.

[3]May 29, 1930.

"But of course I don't believe it was like that at all. I think that it was a simple case of kidnapping. Mabel and Tony Luhan have kidnapped Carmel's poet laureate. . . ."

Although Una was aware of Mabel's clever maneuvering, she liked her and found her company stimulating and enjoyable. In May, the Jefferses left Carmel to drive to Taos with Tony and Mabel Luhan after an unprecedented social whirl with them in Carmel. Mabel was successful in her strategy to convince Una that she should have more social contacts and more fun out of life. Una's unselfishness had successfully sublimated this natural urge until Mabel fanned it to life. The Jefferses spent the month of June in Taos, and upon their return to Carmel Una wrote to Albert Bender:

". . . We had a marvelously interesting and helpful trip. The change of altitude was good for us and that gorgeous country was quite new to us. Mabel Luhan is the most interesting woman I've met in years and she did everything to make our trip a happy one. Tony took us to many secret places in the mountains that only the Indians know. We saw much of his pueblo—he took us to other pueblos too, to Acoma the most interesting of all—and even got us into a council meeting of the old men of his tribe. I think Robin got much inspiration from it all. The boys rode every day and swam and grew an inch apiece.

"Mary Austin came up from Santa Fe and stayed over night to see Robin. She was most gracious and was eager to have Robin write something of that country.

"Witter Bynner telegraphed from New York to lend us his house if we wished but Mabel kept us until we had to come home to look after our own place. So here we are in the spot we still love best of all. . . ."[4]

In the meantime, Mabel was writing a book about D. H. Lawrence in the form of a letter addressed to Jeffers. The book was entitled *Lorenzo in Taos* and was referred to by Sydney S. Alberts in his bibliography of Jeffers as "somewhat of a literary curiosity." In the book, Mabel made a direct appeal to Jeffers to complete Lawrence's unfinished work. She said,

"Well, Jeffers, that is all I have to tell you about Lawrence in Taos. I called him there, but he did not do what I called him to do. He did another thing. Perhaps you are the one who will, after all, do what I wanted him to do: give a voice to this speechless land. Something in-

[4]July 2, 1930. In collection of Bender's correspondence with U. J.

terfered with Lorenzo's chance to do that. Perhaps it was because there was too much willfulness and passion and egotism surrounding him here. The irony of it is that if there is a greater freedom and purity in my wish now, that the life here may become articulate, and that you will be the channel through which it shall speak, it is Lorenzo who released me from my insistent self-will and brought me to the happy immolation that has in it no false desire. You are a clear channel and I think I am become myself a clear one, now, too."

Between their first visit in 1930, and 1938, the Jefferses made many more trips to Taos, sometimes staying for a month at a time. The twins, Garth and Donnan, enjoyed the life there, the trips into the Indian country with Tony, the horseback riding, and the freedom. Una found Mabel's guests and friends interesting, amusing, and sophisticated. Jeffers and Una had their own little guest house where he could work undisturbed. It was as ideal as Mabel could make it, but, despite her success in willing Jeffers to come to Taos, her ambition that he would make her barren land articulate was not realized. He wrote only one poem about her country, "New Mexican Mountain":

I watch the Indians dancing to help the young corn
        at Taos pueblo. The old men squat in a ring
And make the song, the young women with fat bare arms,
        and a few shame-faced young men, shuffle the dance.

The lean-muscled young men are naked to the narrow loins,
        their breasts and backs daubed with white clay,
Two eagle-feathers plume the black heads. They dance
        with reluctance, they are growing civilized; the
        old men persuade them.

Only the drum is confident, it thinks the world has not
        changed; the beating heart, the simplest of
        rhythms,
It thinks the world has not changed at all; it is only
        a dreamer, a brainless heart, the drum has no eyes.

These tourists have eyes, the hundred watching
        the dance, white Americans, hungrily too,
        with reverence, not laughter;
Pilgrims from civilization, anxiously seeking
        beauty, religion, poetry; pilgrims from
        the vacuum.

People from cities, anxious to be human again.
      Poor show how they suck you empty! The
      Indians are emptied,
And certainly there was never religion enough,
      nor beauty nor poetry here—to fill Americans.

Only the drum is confident, it thinks the world has
      not changed. Apparently only myself and the
      strong
Tribal drum, and the rockhead of Taos mountain, re-
      member that civilization is a transient
      sickness.[5]

I have no record of the Jefferses having gone to Taos in 1931 or 1932, but they did return in 1933, and just before leaving, Jeffers wrote to Albert Bender:

"The gift is timely too, for we are starting for a month in New Mexico about a week from now, and Una and I were feeling a little gloomy about it, neither of us really liking the sun and the desert, though we expect to see some fine things, and the motoring and the horseback riding will delight our sons. Well, the etching quite consoles us for the trip, if we can find such a solitary rock and blasted tree to meditate under. . . ."

After their 1934 visit to Taos, Una wrote Bender on August 2nd:

"We are well settled into our usual routine now and quiet after the excitement of Taos. There were more people there this year, some of them very amusing. Frieda Lawrence is a great rollicking person who keeps things stirred up—she and Mabel!"

Although it was hot driving to and from Taos and all of the Jefferses hated the heat, the visits continued. Una wrote me in July of 1935 from Taos:

"I wish you knew amid what distractions I write . . . every moment here is beautiful with excitement. Mabel is determined for us to stay longer than our month and perhaps we will stay a few days longer. . . ."

Because it was difficult to find the time to write letters while at Taos, Una would often wait until returning to Tor House to write of amusing incidents which had occurred during their vacation. On July 26, 1935, Una wrote me from Carmel:

[5]*Thurso's Landing and Other Poems.*

"When we were in Taos a friend of Mabel Luhan's came one evening who is an astrologist and keeps her posted about her chart year by year with events often foretold in a very remarkable way (as it seems to R. J. and me who do not feel much interested in that kind of thing) —well, this friend laid out R. J.'s and mine. What I wish to say to you is that the planet Neptune was constantly and importantly present in R. J.'s chart and he (the astrologer) pointed out to me a paragraph about Neptune and his influence on people in an old book on Astrology which so fitted in with your thesis of its importance to R. J. that I meant to copy it for you. . . ."

There is no mention of a trip to Taos in Una's letters of 1936. But in 1937 the Jefferses stopped there for two weeks on the way home from Europe before visiting us in Palm Springs. Again in 1938 the Jefferses went to Taos, and Una wrote me from there on July 1st:

"Such a rush here—never a moment from rising to sleeping for letters.—The exciting trial, then Brill as houseguest, the great psychoanalyst and really a thrilling man to listen to although I have often disagreed so violently with Freud.

"Friends coming and going, parties. Swimming in a hot springs eight miles away. Riding horseback every day. Reading long mss of Mabel's. Going into the mts. —I can't tell you all the things.

"Brill is a wonderful talker. He loves to expound. We plied him with questions on normal and abnormal psychology and he illustrated everything with case histories. He is very wise in human relations and tolerant and witty!

"Garth is breaking two colts for Tony. The colt he broke last year is fine.

"We are going to Frieda Lawrence's for lunch tomorrow. Went with Dorothy Brett to film *Victoria the Great*. Surprised she didn't like it. Brett's father Viscount Esther was Master of the Household or something and Brett lived for years in Windsor Castle. Very friendly with the younger royalties and seeing V. R. all the time.

"Robin finished his preface to the single volume *Selected Poems* Random House will bring out in the fall. They like it very much and are very excited about the book anyway.

"Taos is very beautiful this year. Not so hot and many thunderstorms. Thickets of fragrant wild roses everywhere and oh the exquisite wild olive fragrance that pervades this house. We are in Mabel's Big House and she and Tony are in the Tony House. Most of the servants are here and Mabel and Tony come here for meals. I have Mabel's great bed room 35 x 37 feet. She says she likes it better than any room she ever saw—it *is* beautiful and windows in all directions toward desert, mts., and garden.

"Here is a roster of dogs on the place:

1 Irish wolf hound
1 Great Dane
2 Boston bull terriers
1 cocker terrier
1 cocker spaniel
2 old English sheep dogs
1 pointer pup
1 Grand white English Bull dog HAIG
3 mongrels belonging to gardener.

"We shall be here for fortnight more at least.
Devotedly,
Una"

On October 24, 1938, Una wrote me from Carmel:

". . . While we were there Mr. and Mrs. Michael Myerberg, (he Stokowsky's manager) came through on their way to New York. . . .

"Robin is writing again after a considerable hiatus. His *Selected Poems* are supposed to appear Nov. 15. Cerf writes that there has been much interest shown already about them."

In 1935, Mabel Luhan had written an article on Una and Robin which Una did not wish to be published. It is now in the collection at Yale University, still unpublished, though Mabel and Una gave copies of it to friends. Both women were eager to share it. In August 1935, Una wrote me about the article:

"I felt it ought not to be done at this time for several reasons. About a dozen people have read it, —several almost with tears for its beauty— Steffens was one of these—several with *greatest dislike* as not being spiritual enough—I must say that in *many ways* I think it is startlingly photographic. . . . I must confess I would like to hear *your* reaction—I wish I had let you read it while here—and talk of it."

I received the sketch the following week, along with a letter from Una (anticipating my reaction!):

"Some of it is good, some bad. I think most of the facts—not all are fairly accurate. She aims more at *her* impression than real history. About Teddy's beacon light for instance, *she* thinks it is. . . ."

Una knew it wasn't good, but out of loyalty to Mabel couldn't bring herself to admit it. As I remember it, it was a sentimental testament of Kuster's undying devotion to Una and very little about Robin and Una. I simply couldn't share Una's enthusiasm for Mabel or for her writing, seeing her only as an upsetting and destructive influence in their lives.

One time in 1939, when I was up in the attic of Tor House with Una, I saw an empty bird cage hanging over the old Franklin stove. I asked about it and she told me the twins once had love-birds in it. All that was in it that day was a large feather, obviously not the property of a love-bird. She laughed when I pointed this out and said: "Oh, that! That's an eagle feather. One day Tony Luhan brought it in and laid it on Robin's desk with great ceremony, saying, 'From one chief to another chief.' So of course I kept the feather for Robin."

XV

MORE STONES AND MORE POEMS

ALTHOUGH JEFFERS' POETRY had been reviewed generously by contemporary poets, he himself wrote only five reviews of the work of fellow poets. Upon the death of George Sterling in November, 1926, Jeffers composed two poems and two long articles, but these were in large part appraisals of the man or memories of associations. Albert Bender was responsible for persuading Jeffers to express himself on the subject of Sterling. A friend of both men, Bender was eager to immortalize their friendship, which had actually existed for less than two years.

Sterling stayed at Tor House on occasion—for a week in December, 1925. Again in February, 1926, he brought Sinclair Lewis to meet Jeffers and, though Lewis stayed at a hotel, Sterling stayed at Tor House.

In a letter Jeffers wrote to Donald Friede on April 30, 1926, he says, "Sterling was coming for a few days visit last week, and telephoned that he couldn't. His voice had a queer note in it. 'Why, George, are you sick?' —'NO, I'm lit.' True poet and true San Franciscan."

Jimmy Hopper told me that both Jeffers and Sterling loved the fog and hated the sun. Sterling's theory was that Jeffers' mother had suffered a sun-stroke before he was born. This theory was never substantiated by any members of the family.

On Sterling's visits to Tor House, he would often take Jeffers and Una on trips of exploration along the coast to share with them his favorite haunts.

Jeffers wrote Friede on May 9, 1926, "When he [Sterling] arrived he was still a bit weak and distraught from two or three days of merriment and a consequent week in bed, but he soon recovered in this spartan household."

In June, 1926, Sterling again spent a week at Tor House, taking notes for the sketch he wrote about Jeffers and which was published later that year by Boni & Liveright, *Robinson Jeffers, the Man and the Artist.*

Over the Fourth of July, Sterling brought Edgar Lee Masters to Tor House, and they spent three days—his last visit before his death on November 17. Jeffers wrote Albert Bender on November 19, 1926:

"It seems incredible even now that he is gone, the face and voice and personality so vivid in our minds, and to be always, I am sure, so intimately present in our thoughts of this place and of this coast . . . .

"It seems to me that what happened, however much it may have been planned for some indefinite future, was purely accidental to this time, as much as being run over in the street. I mean that I don't think he felt himself on the wane, nor had any unusual reason for unhappiness nor feeling of frustration. . . ."

One might think from this letter to Bender that Jeffers had felt a warm friendship for Sterling, but he only accepted him as he would the scenery. He was strangely incapable of responding to friendship. He felt admiration and even affection for a few persons, but any effort to keep the relationship warm depended entirely on Una or the friend. He was stolidly inarticulate except in his poetry. In a day when people were public-relations conscious, such inhibitions were looked on with suspicion and were certainly of no help in forwarding the sale of his books. They had to stand on their own worth and not the charm of the writer's personality.

Jeffers did, however, write three reviews of books by James Rorty, Mark Van Doren, and Babette Deutsch, between 1927 and 1930. He no doubt hoped to express his appreciation for their early reviews of his *Tamar* and his consequent success. The reviews were written with a calm detachment and show none of the emotion expressed in his poetry.

The review of Rorty's book, *Children of the Sun and Other*

Poems, appeared in the magazine *The Advance*, April 1, 1927, under the title "Poetry and True Poetry." Jeffers writes, "James Rorty has the gathered intensity that makes a poet, and the awareness that makes a poet significant." But he qualifies this by suggesting that Rorty should extend his writing into the field of prose. "He is adequate to his art, the question is whether the art is adequate to him."

Mark Van Doren's *Now the Sky and Other Poems* was reviewed by Jeffers in the *New York Herald Tribune*, December 2, 1928. The article isn't a great credit to either poet, as Jeffers labors for words and comes up rather repetitiously with the adjective "imaginative."

In the March 25, 1931, issue of *The New Freeman*, Jeffers reviews Babette Deutsch's *Epistle to Prometheus*. Again Jeffers labors for words of praise, but he even qualifies these. Of the three reviews, the one of Rorty is the one most nearly approaching enthusiasm.

He also wrote an appraisal of D. H. Lawrence as a foreword to the posthumously published *Fire and Other Poems*. It may have been prompted by Mable Luhan's persuasions, but it is written with assurance and sincerity. It is obvious that he has a higher opinion of Lawrence, the man, than he does of his poetry.

The year 1930 saw the start of two new projects for Jeffers: the planning and building of a dining room for Tor House and the writing of a new narrative poem, *Thurso's Landing*. The new room was to be added north of the kitchen, with a door and large window facing seaward, another door into the courtyard, and a large window at the north end of the room. A stone fireplace was planned for the northeast corner, and the room's dimensions were to be large enough to accomodate a long table, as well as one of Una's melodeons and a Welsh dresser for the earthenware dishes. At the south end of the room would be a corner for her grandmother's spinning wheel.

Mornings Jeffers wrote on *Thurso's Landing* and afternoons he carried and cemented rock upon rock for the new dining room. The following excerpts from letters which Una wrote to Albert Bender between January 1931 and January 1932 describe life at Tor House during this year:

". . . We have been desperately busy. Carpenters have been here to put roof on dining-room and cupboards inside. Robin has worked very hard afternoons to finish the stone work. The great chimney being complicated by a dovecot built into one side! A cabinet maker who designed and built Mr. Mack's house and furnishings has made for us a beautiful old English table and benches. . . .

"Robin writes all morning as usual. He will have two books out this next year—a tiny thin (very de luxe) one by Random House long promised them with Liveright's permission—and a regular sized one by Liveright. We expect Liveright to spend a week-end during the latter part of January. . . . So many amusing people have come and gone. . . ."

". . . Robin sits here by my side busily typing ms. for his spring book which I think will be called *Thurso's Landing*. (Thurso is a name he got up near John O'Groat's Scotland. It's a strong downright name.)

"It's a gray day—(Oh we pray for rain!) gray sea, gray rocks—a gray government cutter along our coast searching for bodies from a boat lost yesterday in a gray sea—black cormorants flying low overhead—a striking scene . . . ."

". . . To people who turn out work at high pressure and one thing after another Robin's type of mind must seem strange—the reluctance to undertake set tasks (unless he sets them himself) but I often fear to push things lest I kill my goose who lays the golden eggs. Magazines and magazines (*Forum, Bookman, Sat. Review of Lit.; Nation*, etc. even the *Cosmopolitan*) write for poems and the *Examiner* editor in S. F. wrote to ask Robin to contribute and 'name his own price' to the new literary page. My thrifty soul is grieved that these must all be refused as I have had to do. . . ."

When work on the dining room was completed, Una had great fun deciding on where to place the small stones, some of which she had brought home from her travels, and others given by friends. Robin and the twins then cemented them to the window-frames, into the fireplace, and in the flagstone entrances, as others had been cemented into various portions of the tower. The paving in front of the courtyard entrance to the dining room was a section of petrified wood from Arizona. With such embellishments the new room might have achieved the appearance of a fruit cake, but it is a warm, pleasant room, and one is not uncomfortable in the company of these fragments of Ossian's grave, and of the Egyptian pyramids.

After dinner every evening, Jeffers read for an hour or more to his sons, as he had done for the past six or seven years. In the past two years he had read them all of W. H. Hudson, ten Waverly novels, ten Thomas Hardy novels, three of Dostoevsky, Lawrence's *Revolt in the Desert*, parts of Doughty's *Arabia Deserta*, Synge's *Aran Islands*, and many other books. He read well, particularly poetry (though his sons do not recall that he read much poetry to them).

Jeffers often read to Una while she did the family mending, and then he laid out his work for the next morning. Una sent me a copy of answers to a questionaire which she had written in 1931, outlining Jeffers' daily schedule. (She did not remember who had requested it.)

"Mornings until 1:00 p.m. at his desk, usually in the long attic room over our living room where I can hear his slow pacing, for he writes and paces by turn. Some very quiet days he works in the turret of the tower and paces in the sunshine on top. Afternoon stone work or planting trees; evenings reading to the children and me . . . .

"At least one complete day in a fortnight spent by us back in the hills and Coast Redwood canyons. Examines stones and geological formations closely, trees and flowers and water courses, animals and their tracks and old human abandoned enterprises—many about here. Usually we walk briskly for two or three miles along the shore just before sunset every day . . . . One invariable habit he has. He never goes to bed without going outdoors about midnight and walking around the place—watching the stars in their courses, marking the rising or setting of the Constellations and feeling the direction of the wind and noticing the tides at ebb or flow. He observes the barometer closely in winter—one hangs by his bed—is exhilarated by storms. He passionately loves rain and wet weather, distrusts a blazing sun, thinks people overestimate the health in sun baths—points to the hardy races in Northern Europe who live in dark countries."

As to the new poem *Thurso's Landing*, Jeffers, in his Foreword to *Selected Poetry*, explained that the story was:

". . . suggested entirely, I think, by the savage beauty of the canyon and sea-cliff that are its scene, and by the long-abandoned limeworks there. I cannot remember planning the story at all. When we first saw this place, in 1914, the heavy steel cable was hanging across the sky of the canyon, still supporting a rusted skip. During the war it was taken down for iron."

And to Sydney S. Alberts, Jeffers wrote further:

"A promontory of the coast thirty miles south of Monterey is called Bixby's Landing. The cable for carrying lime from the kilns far up the gorge, and a heavy iron skip stuck midway, were still hanging between the headland and the hill when we first saw the place in 1914. Revisiting it many years later, we found a pair of duck hawks nesting under the headland cliff. I wrote some verses called Bixby's Landing (printed with Cawdor) about the solitary beauty of the place, and brought home a few fire-bricks from a broken hoisting-engine to use in a fireplace that I was building. When it occurred to me to make a story about the place, the name had to be changed, and I called it Thurso's Landing.

"It seems to me that the theme of the poem is courage, and its different colors or qualities, in Reave Thurso, in Helen, and in Reave's mother. This is not a Greek or Mediterranean theme but distinctly northern; perhaps for that reason the Viking name of the northernmost town in Scotland came to my mind as the family name of these people."

And in a letter to James Rorty which Jeffers wrote in April, 1932, he answers questions about both "Thurso's Landing" and the poem "Margrave" which also appeared in the volume:

". . . mainly only wanting to make a display of human courage, in Thurso to endure pain, in his wife to endure and end it, but most of all in his mother. I thought of his as volitional and rather sterile, Helen's as imaginative, of the old woman's as instinctive.

"The chief interest of the verses called 'Margrave' was, for me, in the attempt to bring far separated things into affinity, the flight of the nebulae and a crime like the Hickman case, etc., to combine narrative and lyrical passages like the dramatic and lyrical in Greek tragedy. I don't think industrial civilization is worth the distortion of human nature and the meanness and the loss of contact with the earth that it entails. I think your Marxist industrialized communism—if it were ever brought into existence would be a farther step in a bad direction. It would entail less meanness but equal distortion and would rot people with more complete security.—Civilization will have to go on building up for centuries yet and its collapse will be gradual and tragic and sordid and I have no remedy to propose except for the individual to keep himself out of it as much as he can conveniently and to exercise his instincts and self-restraint and powers as completely as possible in spite of it."[1]

Thurso's Landing was the eighth major work to come from the pen of Jeffers, and from the point of view of most reviewers, the most important. Jeffers himself thought it was the best thing which he had written. And as a result of the popular interest in this new work, *Time* magazine carried Jeffers' picture on its cover. Of this circumstance, Jeffers waggishly wrote his publishers: ". . . The picture is very good; it wouldn't be all a pleasure to have my mug on the news-stands, but fortunately I don't see them. . . ."

The literary world had come to accept Jeffers' new verse form and to belie Humbert Wolfe's contention that it was "not poetry." As to the uneven length of line, the metrical rhythm that so perfectly suited his strange off-beat narratives, the best analysis has been written by H. Arthur Klein who was a student at Occidental College in 1930 and wrote his thesis on the metrics of Jeffers' poetry. Jeffers wrote Klein after reading it, saying in part:

"People talked about my 'free verse' and I never protested, but now I am quite touched that someone has at last discovered the metrical intention in it . . . . Of course you have noticed that (chiefly in my narrative poems) many lines are of irregular length—'free' no doubt, as are many lines in Elizabethan dramatic verse—but it seems to me that there is a metrical pattern, if only, and most irregular, as a background from which to measure departures from the patterns . . . . It seems to me (as you have remarked) that the counting of the stresses is not enough, without some regard to the quantities of the unstressed syllables, to make well-sounding lines. But there I can't propose any rule; it is more a matter of ear and rhythmic sense. A line made up of syllables like 'many' or 'easy' couldn't balance rhythmically with a line made up of syllables like 'storm-bent' or 'oak trees', though the number of syllables were the same . . . . Several modern poets have caught Coleridge's and Bridges' thought, or found it out for themselves, but it seems to me that there remains an infinite field of rhythm as yet untouched or hardly touched. English is a language of very diverse and tolerably stable qualities, besides being a strongly accented language. Great and new things might be done in it if we had time and ear."

[1]Pencilled draft in Tor House Collection.

Jeffers was frequently requested to give his definition of "poetry," and his notes and letters reveal examples of his thoughtful analysis of his craft.

In 1930 he answered a query from Professor Camille McCole of the University of Notre Dame:

"The word 'poetry' is one of those abstract words covering a complex of things—like the word 'beauty'—so various for different persons that the only definition I could give would be a bad one out of a dictionary. I suppose the point is to distinguish poetry from unpoetic verse and from poetic prose.

"As to the latter, it seems to me that the word 'poetry' as used in English implies some form of verse. Verse without looking in the dictionary, I should say, is a form of speech characterized by rhythmic recurrences; so that there is a noticeable and fairly regular correspondence of some sort between lines or the stanzas.

"I think the difference between poetry and unpoetic verse lies in the appeal of poetry to the aesthetic emotion. So then one might say that poetry is beautiful verse. But the beauties of verse may be so various—from sublimity of subject to mere intensity of expression—personal taste in the end must distinguish—that you'll excuse me for not going further into the subject of aesthetics.

"I think the quality that I most value in poetry is of imaginative power activated by powerful emotion, so that the imagination is not displayed idly for a show but as if of necessity and in earnest, under emotional compulsion."

And, in 1932, he attempted to give his definition of poetry to Graham Bickley, a student at the University of California, Berkeley:

"Verse is speech modulated to produce patterns of rhythmic recurrences of a certain number of feet or accents or syllables to a line or recurrences of rhyme or of all these or perhaps only recurrent parallelisms of that or expressions as in old-testament verse.

"Poetic content (the feeling, thought, and expression of poetry) may be found in prose also and is only distinguished from that of prose by having more of certain qualities and less of certain others. The thought is more primitive and less specialized. Language is more figurative, giving concrete images rather than abstract ideas and cares more for its own music. Poetry appeals rather to the emotions than to the intelligence and especially to the aesthetic emotion. It appeals more eagerly than prose does to the imagination and to the bodily senses. It deals with the more permanent aspects of man and nature. It tends to be farther removed from quotidian life in order to be nearer to natural, unspecialized and passionate life. Poetry is more properly a celebration and prose a statement of things."

While in Ireland, in 1937, Jeffers made notes which he evidently intended as an answer to yet another query on his "theory" of poetry, but he couldn't remember for whom the letter was intended or if it was ever written. The notes, however, are among his personal papers at Tor House:

"I have ideas on the subject of poetry but really no theory. To develop the ideas would require a big book—Milton's specifications for good poetry, 'simple, sensuous, impassioned' are the best statement on the subject so far as they go, with exceptions (Milton's own example is not exactly simple!). And poetic prose can fulfill all these specifications yet not be poetry! Therefore something should be added about metrical or at least rhythmical lines and parses; for poetry is poetic expression in verse and something should be added about beauty and sound, assonance, alliteration, etc., and all that more subtle music that distinguishes poetic verse from verse that is metrical but not poetic.

"There would be other things to explain. Poetry is in fact a complex of many efforts and qualities and can only be described in detail not through any general statement. And it is known and valued by quasi-instinctive recognition, not conscious analysis; though this may be helpful in developing appreciation."

Further amplifying this definition of rhythm in other notes, Jeffers says:

"I want it rhythmic and not rhymed—moulded more closely to the subject than in older English poetry, but as formed as Alcaics if that were possible, too. The event is of course a compromise but I like to avoid arbitrary form and capricious lack or disruption of form.

"My feelings are for the number of beats to the line! There is a quantitative element too in which the unstressed syllables have part; the rhythm from many sources—physics, biology, the beat of blood, the tidal environments of life to which life is formed. Also a desire for singing emphasis that prose does not have."

Two other undated notes found in Jeffers' papers, undoubtedly written earlier than those quoted above, are a short observation entitled "Science in Verse:"

"I do not think I am wrong in using even in verse some of the fruits of contemporary psychoanalytic study. Poetry has been called a flower of all knowledge; this is only an ideal desire, but we have to live by the gospel that 'beauty is the effulgence of truth.'"

and another one entitled "Charm in Verse:"

"The most fortunate of idyll writers and lyrists have hived a curious sweetness in every line, so that if the page is torn through the middle there is wealth remaining. I know too well that my longer poems—at least—lack this interpenetration of separable charm; and their poetic effect can only be an effect of the whole, the total rhythm and ascent, for they are built partly of base materials, and even the spires are not gilded but only high. This is a falling short and may be helped with increase of years; but perhaps as charm comes something of truth or strength may go away; except in that central poem which I hope to begin soon, which will not be Californian, and for which I am still awaiting as patiently as I can some high tide or luck and power."

Even before *Thurso's Landing* had been released to the public, Jeffers was working on his next narrative poem, of which he wrote to his publishers in November, 1932:

". . . The name I have in mind for the longish narrative poem that's being written is 'Give Your Heart to the Hawks,' a quotation from something said by one of the people in the story. The hawks have a sort of symbolic value throughout the poem. This would be the name of the book, too. Let me know if you think it is too long or too ferocious a title, though I don't know what else to suggest. I think this poem will be nearly the same length as *Thurso's Landing*. In poetry and dramatic value, and variety of character, it seems to me rather better than *Thurso*, but it is not finished yet, of course. The scene is contemporary.

"The book as a whole will be rather longer and more various than anything of mine since *Roan Stallion*. Probably a little more than 200 pages of typewriting after all. Contents: 'Give Your Heart to the Hawks;' a few short poems; 'Descent to the Dead;' 'Resurrection;' 'Helen in Exile.' The latter three form a sequence in thought, though not in scene, all being progressively concerned with the death-and-resurrection theme, though the scenes are British, contemporary American, and Greek at the end of the heroic age.

"I will try to complete the long poem by January first, but I can't promise. It may be a month later. At least I can send the first half of it, and the rest of the book-manuscript at that time, if you want. . . ."

Liveright, Jeffers' publishers, were assailed by economic difficulties, and the publication of the book was delayed. When Liveright announced bankruptcy, thirteen publishers invited Jeffers to join their lists. Liveright released the manuscript of *Give Your Heart to the Hawks* to Random House, and it was published in the fall of 1933.

That same year Sydney S. Albert's *Bibliography* of Jeffers made its appearance. It was not only an important contribution to the student of Jeffers, but it contained a wealth of unpublished and uncopyrighted material that was to make it a valuable item for Jeffers collectors.

Jeffers had predicted that *Give Your Heart to the Hawks* would be "more human than usual, without the mysticism of scandal, though I hope rather interesting. The story is the Greek story of Phaedra, transferred to this coast. *Desire Under the Elms* but a variant of it; but in mine the young man is inseducible, as in the Greek."

The critics were surprised and happily relieved to find this new book free of perversion and incest. The good press notices promoted the sales of the book which reached a satisfactory high for both publisher and author. Although the setting was the same as his other contemporary poems, he achieved new and powerful descriptive passages and a compelling plot.

The symbol of the hawk has a special significance to Jeffers, and among his papers were these notes which he planned to use in answer to a question about his use of the symbol:

"As to the hawk-verses: note first—'Except the Penalties.' The penalties did not mean only hanging or imprisonment, but also the inner revulsion, the disgust and emotional discord, —which, however, would spring from training, not nature. For people can be trained to kill as easily as they can be trained not to.

"The average hawk seemed to me (and still seems) a more beautiful and nobler creature than the average man; besides that men swarm by millions and hawks are rare. So, if I had stopped to ask myself 'Is that a true statement?' I should have said 'Yes—Except the Penalties.' There was no misanthropy involved, but only a comparison. And there was no question of inflicting pain—that would put a different face on the matter—but only of sudden death.

"And I think it was a salutary statement, for certainly men over-value themselves and their lives."

In another poem, "Hurt Hawks," which had appeared in the volume *Cawdor*, Jeffers uses hawks as a symbol of strength: ". . . pain is worse to the strong, incapacity worse." Thurso in "Thurso's Landing" (1932) is likened to a hurt hawk, also, as is Lance Frazer in "Give Your Heart to the Hawks."

Jeffers had promised that there would be no mysticism in this new narrative, but it is here — the reliance on dreams, the prophecies, the spirits who remained in their old haunts to torment those still living, and the religious fanatic, this time Lance's old father. There are always old people to symbolize the decaying race; in this story Lance's old mother, swollen and unattractive, is dying from a heart ailment, and the father's mind has failed. The setting of the story was decided by a scene and farmhouse that Jeffers saw one day, and he said that they "seemed to fit the title." It was in "Sycamore Canyon, just south of Big Sur; and between the title and the scene the poem unrolled itself."

Also included in this volume is "At the Fall of an Age," (formerly titled "Helen in Exile"), a fine dramatic poem of the story of Polyxo's vengeance on Helen of Troy. The poems written in the British Isles, and formerly published in a single volume by Random House under the title *Descent to the Dead* are included.

Later, referring to this title, Jeffers said, "I had several reasons for calling it *Descent to the Dead*. First, I was tired, and wanted to indulge myself by playing dead for a few months. Foreign travel is like a pleasant temporary death; it relieves you of responsibilities and familiar scenes and duties. Then, the light and the life in those cloudy islands seem to be keyed so much lower than they are at home; everything appeared dim and soft, mournful and old; and the past, in that year of peace, seemed to a foreigner much more present than the present. So it was easy to imagine myself a dead man in the country of the dead."[2]

Give Your Heart to the Hawks received honorable mention from the Commonwealth Club of California when presenting their annual Literary Awards for 1933.

[2]From a lecture given at the Foster Memorial in Pittsburgh, on February 24, 1941.

XVI

FIFTIETH BIRTHDAY

ALTHOUGH THE POETRY OF JEFFERS had received high praise from the critics, it had been consistently ignored by the judges for the Pulitzer award. In 1923, *The Argonaut* magazine protested this neglect and was later supported by *The Saturday Review of Literature* and *Poetry*. William Rose Benét, a fellow poet, stormed, ". . . I would choose first the most incredible omissions made by the Pulitzer Poetry Committee . . . that so outstanding a poet as Robinson Jeffers, a man beside whom most of the versifiers of his day look like pygmies, should not ere this have been awarded the Pulitzer Prize, except that probably he is so big that the little judges, standing in his ample shadow, can't see him at all. . . ." But the committee discredited itself further by ignoring such authorities in a field where they had exhibited their ignorance.

However, after the 1935 publication of Jeffers' *Solstice and Other Poems*, he received generous recognition from the Book of the Month Club and a prize of $2,500. Four authors, whose works had not been read sufficiently, were selected for the reward, the others being James T. Farrell for *Studs Lonigan*, Katherine Anne Porter for her *Flowering Judas*, and Paul B. Sears for *Deserts on the March*. The judges were Edna St. Vincent Millay, Pearl Buck, Christopher Morley, Heywood Broun, and Joseph Henry Jackson. Jeffers had received the largest number of votes and was the first to be selected for an award.

Solstice and Other Poems was considered Jeffers' "highest point" in poetical achievement up to this time. The volume is made up of the title poem, "Solstice," and, deserting the local scene, the poem, "At the Birth of an Age" (a story derived from the closing chapters of the *Volsung Saga*), and sixteen short poems.

In a letter to Frederic Carpenter, July 14, 1937, Jeffers answers a question regarding "At the Birth of an Age":

"Revenge was then a moral obligation: the point is that Gudrun's pre-Christian morality broke down; she did *not* take revenge, but was lost between the past and the future just as the present world is . . . . but found a vision at the end."

The public did not readily understand the poem, and for the first time since the publication of *The Women at Point Sur*, Jeffers attempted to justify himself to a critic.[1]

He wrote Rudolph Gilbert:

"You do not perfectly comprehend 'At the Birth of An Age' and I think no one else does though the verses are clear enough. All the prevalent religions think of God as blessed or happy, or at least at peace; even the pantheist mystic finds peace in God; therefore this conception of God as in pain is hardly admitted by the reader's mind. For this reason I built it through the wall-painting of Prometheus, the self-hanging Odin in Norse mythology, the personality of Gudrun, and the phantom of Christ to make it poetically credible. It is a conception that runs through my verses from 'Heauton timoroumenos' (self-tormentor) in 'Women at Point Sur' (page 174) down to this latest. If God is all, he must be suffering, since an unreckoned part of the universe is always suffering. But his suffering must be self-inflicted, for he is all; there is no one outside him to inflict it. I suppose the idea carried psychological as well as cosmic or religious implications. Man as well as God must suffer in order to discover; and it is often voluntary, self-inflicted suffering."

And in answer to Carpenter's question as to what he intended by the line "I have swallowed the whole snake and the lynx," Jeffers explained:

"The last act of the poem is highly symbolized, in order to express the dream-like unreality of Gudrun's existence after death, and in order to universalize the meaning.—Symbolic imagery is capable of expressing many things at the same time. —The serpent is repulsive, treach-

[1]*Shine, Perishing Republic,* by Rudolph Gilbert, 1936.

erous, and beautiful. It is also—as phallic in appearance—a well-known symbol of life and renewal. (That was probably the meaning of the brazen serpent that the Israelites worshiped in the wilderness.)—'I am willing to accept existence again even on the same terms of pain and disgust, sorrow and self-hatred, etc., —because I have seen how beautiful the universe is, and that my existence was part of it, —The lynx lying dead of it.'

"... The lynx lying dead with the wolves around it, was at first Gudrun's dim vision or memory of herself lying dead with the warriors around her. Later this symbol too is widened to represent the body in general, and once or twice the sexual aspect of the body, contrasted with the universal vision of the hanged God."

These questions came from well-informed men who had undoubtedly read the page-long introduction to the poem included in the volume. So again, in his volume of *Selected Poetry*, Jeffers attempts another explanation of the poem:

"'At the Birth of an Age' had a more calculated origin. I was considering the main sources of our civilization, and listed them roughly as Hebrew-Christian, Roman, Greek, Teutonic. Then it occurred to me that I had written something about the Hebrew-Christian source in 'Dear Judas', and that 'The Tower Beyond Tragedy' might pass for a recognition of the Greek source. About the Roman source I should probably never write anything, for it is less sympathetic to me. Recognition of the Teutonic source might be an interesting theme for a new poem, I thought . . . . and the *Volsung Saga* might serve for a fable. Only as the poem progressed did the Teutonic element begin to warp and groan under the tension of Christian influence. The symbol of the self-tortured God, that closes the poem, had appeared to me long before in 'Apology for Bad Dreams' and in 'Women at Point Sur'—Heauton-timoroumenos, the self-tormentor—but it stands most clearly in the self-hanged Odin of Norse mythology."

Of the eighteen short poems in the volume, four are sonnets. In the poem "Sign-Post," Jeffers clearly states his credo:

> Civilized, crying how to be human again: this
> will tell you how.
> Turn outward, love things, not men, turn right
> away from humanity,
> Let that doll lie. Consider if you like how the
> lilies grow,

158

Lean on the silent rock until you feel its divinity
Make your veins cold, look at the silent stars,
        let your eyes
Climb the great ladder out of the pit of your-
        self and man.
Things are so beautiful, your love will follow
        your eyes;
Things are the God, you will love God, and not
        in vain,
For what we love, we grow to it, we share its
        nature. At length
You will look back along the stars' rays and
        see that even
The poor doll humanity has a place under heaven.
Its qualities repair their mosaic around you,
        the chips of strength
And sickness; but now you are free, even to
        become human,
But born of the rock and the air, not of a
        woman.

Some of the finest short poems which Jeffers has written are included in this volume. Babette Deutsch, who was, in part, responsible for attracting public interest to Jeffers through her review of *Tamar*, wrote a review of *Solstice* for *The New York Herald Tribune Books* (October 27, 1935). She says: "The poem
which opens Jeffers' latest volume relates his familiar themes,
with no loss of power, and with the additional interest of a greater
technical variety." Of the title poem "Solstice" she feels that "it
does not have the weight of ancient legend behind it, and though
Madrone Boswell, who kills her children rather than surrender
them to their father, reminds one of Medea, the piece wants the
power of the longer poem, nor is the passion it celebrates, except
at the very end, touched with the grandeur that rests upon the old
saga" (which was the source of that opening poem). Deutsch goes
on to say that Jeffers "is in love with the universe, not with man,
certainly not with the mob. Again and again he asserts that to
love things—not man-made toys, but the austere or delicate out-
crop of natural energy—is to love God and to share His nature
. . . ."

January, 1937, was a busy month for Jeffers; he not only received the Book of the Month Club award, but he was elected a member of the National Institute of Arts and Letters. And, on January 10, he celebrated his fiftieth birthday, on which day he laid the first stones for an additional room on Tor House. January had set the pace for a busy year. Occidental College, which had also achieved its fiftieth anniversary, conferred on Jeffers the honorary degree of Doctor of Humane Letters. The event was celebrated with a special exhibition of the poet's work in the college library. The college issued a check list of its collection of Jeffersiana with a foreword by the president of the college, Remsen Bird, and a short comment written for the catalogue by Jeffers. Albert Bender had given the college his private collection of Jeffersiana and a handsome case in which to house the books. Jeffers' birthday was also commemorated by the library of the University of California with an exhibition of his books and other items.

In July, the Jefferses sailed for Ireland, and the poet's arrival was announced by the *Irish Times*. They visited many of the places where they had stayed on their previous visit, touring the British Isles for about three months. Una wrote glowing letters home to her friends. Two of these letters, one written on August 8th from Ballymore and one written on October 21st from Devon, give a delightful account of some of their experiences. Una's enthusiasm was even crowded into the margins of her letters. On her letter from Ballymore she squeezed in: "We are two miles from Dunfanaghy on coast, just as I planned. Northwest of Ireland, see map." "Certainly many disadvantages, dim lights, no running water, etc., and meals at queer hours. Breakfast 9, Dinner 1:30, Meat-tea 6, Supper 10:30 or 11:00 but fine simple food, milk, butter, eggs, poultry, etc., jams homegrown!"

Picture postcards supplemented the letters to show the country where the boys went deer-stalking; romantic castles; round towers; and the Orkneys, with a picture of a prehistoric stone circle which Una claimed "far surpasses Stonehenge in magical incomprehensibility and grandeur of size and setting—the edge of the world it seems."

Una's letter to me from Ballymore reads:

"We are staying for a month at a charming old farm house which I just discovered by chance when I was quite desperate about finding a little house (they were scarce indeed—over a radius of 30 miles I found only two for rent and they wouldn't do, too much work to get them in order for a short stay). This place luck led us to right by the sea in a wonderful little valley all ups and downs and flowers and rich little farms. Tiny—10 acres all cut into ¼ acre fields enclosed with stone-walls! They take just a few people and never advertize—at present staying are an Eng. colonel and wife and 3 children and his sister, a doctor (prof. at Queen's College, Belfast, and his clergyman uncle and aunt and we.) There are 3 children of the house the age of our boys or a little older and 4 cousins all make it very gay for Garth and Donnan. They swim, play tennis, tramp, walk, go see Irish dances etc., and so do we. We all climbed Errigal, highest mt. in Donegal two days ago. The ocean here has a warm current through it and is much warmer than our ocean. This house has been in the family generations and is ups and downs and little stairs and peat fires. (Robin and I are sitting in our room this moment with a nice little peat-fire—so warm and cheerful and nice smelling.)

"Outside tumbling clouds and a wild wind and sunlight on the far hills. Muckish Mt. is within sight and the rain all comes from that direction. We always watch the Mt. for weather signs. We have been to Glenveagh Castle (Mrs. Kingsley Porter's home—she is the widow of Kingsley Porter the best known American archeologist—and Clapp's great friend).

"Our 24th wedding anniversary was spent at Glenveagh Castle. Our boys spent yesterday all day deer-stalking with her chief stalker—they were not shooting just locating deer but they saw and learned a lot about mt. climbing in heather and gorse and avoiding the deep bog holes (to fall in some of them is certain death—you can't get out by yourself). And to wade knee-deep in others—Lucy Porter left for Italy yesterday but gave us letters to all the great houses in this part of Ireland (which I mean to use but haven't had one vacant moment yet). Lots of antiquities about but only *one* round tower in Donegal out at Tory Island—that was a wild rough trip in a small boat much more primitive place than Uran, have been to Gran Is. to Yeats tower, Ballylle Castle and climbed all over and in it, spent a day at ruined Moore Hall and rowed out to little island in lake where G. M.'s ashes rest under a cairn. Pursued and found about 20 round towers most of them unseen before, climbed Ireland's holy Mt. Groagh Patrick, two days before the annual pilgrimage. O but that was a stiff climb makes me breathless to remember. 'May it be a profit to you,' said an old lady on the way. I hope so too. Again we went up and down all the roads of Connemara. And so to Donegal which I do think now after loving all the rest, is the most thrillingly beautiful country in Ireland. Wild, formidable, spectacular (like Horn Head and the Bloody Foreland and Poisoned Glen—all close by here) and sweet and appealing in the little lanes shadowed with hawthorne hedges and wild honeysuckle and trees —high wild fuchsia. Little lakes of exquisite color everywhere and tiny rivers threading through meadow or down rocky mts. ravines. Great fields and slopes *covered* with wild disarray of gigantic stones flung one would say by maniac gods. I don't see why the painters in the world are not just *here* in a crowd.

"We came 3rd class on the *Georgic*—in order to afford to bring our car. We were filled with misgivings but found it *excellent*. Quite good-enough for anybody. Better in many ways than 1st class on the great *Königin Augusta Victoria* when I crossed first in 1912.

"It takes a very special technique to travel in Ireland and be comfortable, especially when making one night stands as we do so often when actively sightseeing. This technique I acquired last time and remember to our advantage now.

". . . We are going this p.m. on a jaunt to Rosapenna and some cairns and incised stones at Mevagh. The boys are taking many pictures but haven't had much chance to check up on results, no proper finishing place here. They have to send away to Dublin for rolls.

"We are going to Dublin after our stay here and are promised an evening with all the Dublin characters—then to Scotland and England. We still expect to stop with you on our way home.

"I have on today a *red* knit dress which I *had* to seek out and buy to wear especially on dark days—caught by the red shirts of the women in dark Connemara and the red two-wheeled carts which cross the bog continually, loaded with peat. This dress was knitted nearby in Carregart and it's a joy to all of us. We have gone to see old Mrs. Dorgan in a far away village near Gortahork, she who wove my peacock blue homespun. I saw the loom and the wool being spun and dyed. They dye it all, vegetable dyes. My lovely dress was colored with potato skins, onions, lichen and field fuschia. . . ."

One of the most charming things about Una was her insatiable curiosity about little things. This instance of her dragging her family for miles to find an old woman who had knitted a dress for her! Her letter from Devon was equally enthusiastic:

"This *is* a find—the most thrilling place in England—in Devon near the Cornish coast—it's an old stone farm house (with some new wings added for space) on a flat rock just a few feet above high tide, high jutting cliffs behind and around it, broken jagged rocks in front, a wild

162

sea foaming over them and dashing spray against the windows—old, worn gray without, inside—warm colors, shining brass, open fires every where and *fine* cooking! O what Devonshire clotted cream and raspberry jam. R.'s and my bedroom just above the sea which roars and boils amongst the rocks—I adore it.

"Garth and Donnan went over to Paris by themselves for four days. Robin and I went to a grand weekend house party given by Lady Kathleen Curzon Herrick and Marchioness of Tweeddale. Then another night to Lord Farringdon's beautiful place . . . . we've had lots of fun. Two weeks in London seeing lots of old friends and meeting new ones and swirling around every where. I think I wrote you we went around the Inner and Outer Hebrides, north, way to the Shetlands and Orkneys then back along the west coast. Motored from Cape Wrath down to Glasgow. Wild and beautiful.

"We sail for USA Oct. 30 from Southampton. We have a week's engagements in N.Y., but hope to get away in two days . . . .

"Mabel is in N.Y. being analyzed by Brill again. So we shall not stop at Taos . . . .

"P.S. We had an interesting time in the Bodleian. No other visitors and the curator very friendly and full of information. I had an interesting time about a Shelley manuscript. In 1922 the year of the Shelley centenary, Sara Bard Field was there at the Bodleian and (she was writing a Shelley article at the time) asked to see a mss. of Shelley's which in some queer way she had heard had been there for some years unopened but to be opened centenary year. The whole Bodleian force turned upside down by this. Most of them denied the existence of it, at last one man knew about it but said it was being privately edited in London, by whom or how he knew not. Elinor Wylie also at another time went and made a great commotion but no results. No information. So I brought up the matter. Magical results. My nice curator rushed away with great velocity and brought a special man to talk to me. This man has the mss. in charge and talked at length about it. It is a set of personal correspondence. He says there are no new disclosures or information in it but it is still not open to the public eye. There is something queer about it all. Anyway it made some interesting conversation!

"A full length portrait of present Pope in the Bodleian. Curator said the Pope was once a Reader there. When he was made Pope, the Readers sent him an illuminated address and he responded with his portrait."

In October, on his return home, Jeffers wrote some of his own observations about the journey to a young boy by the name of

William Berkowitz. As was his custom, Jeffers first wrote out his letters in pencil, later typing them. Only occasionally was the address included, so unfortunately we often cannot identify the person.

". . . we have been travelling in Great Britain and Ireland and we are on our way home to California. Orkney and Shetland, the little islands north of Scotland, interested me as much as anything. In the Orkney Islands we sailed through the Scapa Flow, where the Germans sank their great fleet which they had surrendered to the British at the end of the war. While we were there a German warship was being brought up for scrap iron. In Scotland we saw a man from Iceland, who had sailed there all alone in a little motor-skiff, and was going on to Norway. He was a middle-aged man who decided to see the world a little before he grew too old. They are dark and dangerous seas, and he had no charts at all and no navigating instruments except a compass. He sailed from Iceland the year before and had been beaten back by storms, but this time he got through.

"It is interesting too to see the North Star almost straight overhead. At home in California it is quite low in the sky and as you go north it rises higher. . . ."

In the poem "Now Returned Home," Jeffers looks back over his experiences:

> Now, returned home
> After so many thousands of miles of road
>   and ocean, all the hulls sailed in,
>   the houses visited,
> I remember that slender skiff with dark
>   henna sail
> Bearing off across the stormy sunset to
>   the distant island
> Most clearly; and have rather forgotten
>   the dragging whirlpools of London, the
>   screaming haste of New York.[2]

Jeffers had completed work on a new book for his publishers before he went abroad, and it greeted him when he arrived back in the States. Its title was *Such Counsels You Gave To Me.*

His critics and friends had often urged him to lighten his

[2]*Selected Poetry.*

themes, but searching his conscience, he refused to compromise. Even Una said "better use some other theme."

She explained this in a letter written to me on May 8, 1935:

". . . my feeling being that few people today are well enough read in Greek Tragedy, or in Shelley or in Byron to read of incest without surprise. Or know the life on lonely shut-in farms as for instance Edgar Lee Masters knows it I discovered in later talks with him. . . ."

In the volume *Such Counsels You Gave To Me*, there are two poems in which Jeffers acknowledges his critics and answers them:

SELF-CRITICISM IN FEBRUARY

The bay is not blue but sombre yellow
With wrack from the battered valley, it is
    speckled with violent foam-heads
And tiger-striped with long lovely storm-shadows.
YOU LOVE THIS BETTER THAN THE OTHER MASK; BETTER
    EYES THAN YOURS
WOULD FEEL THE EQUAL BEAUTY IN THE BLUE.
IT IS CERTAIN YOU HAVE LOVED THE BEAUTY OF STORM
    DISPROPORTIONATELY.
But the present time is not pastoral, but founded
On violence: pointed for more massive violence
    perhaps it is not
Perversity but need that perceives the storm-beauty.
WELL, BITE ON THIS: YOUR POEMS ARE TOO FULL OF
    GHOSTS AND DEMONS,
AND PEOPLE LIKE PHANTOMS—HOW OFTEN LIFE'S ARE—
AND PASSION SO STRAINED THAT THE CLAY MOUTHS GO
    PRAYING FOR DESTRUCTION—
Alas, it is not unusual in life;
To every soul at some time. BUT WHY INSIST ON IT?
    AND NOW
FOR THE WORST FAULT: YOU HAVE NEVER MISTAKEN
DEMON NOR PASSION NOR IDEALISM FOR THE REAL GOD.
Then what is most disliked in those verses
Remains most true. UNFORTUNATELY. IF ONLY YOU
    COULD SING
THAT GOD IS LOVE, OR PERHAPS THAT SOCIAL
JUSTICE WILL SOON PREVAIL. I can tell lies in prose.

Then what is the answer?—Not to be deluded by
    dreams.
To know that great civilizations have broken down
    into violence, and their tyrants come,
    many times before.
When open violence appears, to avoid it with honor
    or choose the least ugly faction; these
    evils are essential.
To keep one's own integrity, be merciful and uncor-
    rupted and not wish for evil; and not be duped
By dreams of universal justice or happiness.
    These dreams will not be fulfilled.
To know this, and know that however ugly the
    parts appear the whole remains beautiful.
    A severed hand
Is an ugly thing, and man dissevered from the
    earth and stars and his history . . . for
    contemplation or in fact . . .
Often appears atrociously ugly. Integrity is
    wholeness, the greatest beauty is
Organic wholeness, the wholeness of life and
    things, the divine beauty of the universe.
    Love that, not man
Apart from that, or else you will share man's
    pitiful confusions, or drown in despair
    when his days darken.

Such Counsels You Gave to Me includes twenty-one lyric poems and one short narrative, as well as the long narrative title
poem, all unrhymed with the exception of two sonnets. Some of
the poems are set in the Jeffers country, others are universal. They
deal with the fantastic powers and follies of the nations and their
little Caesars, and face wars and destruction. Jeffers calls to the
people to stop deceiving themselves.

    At fifty years of age, Jeffers had published eight books of long
narrative poems and four books composed of groups of short poems. Of the latter, *Poems*, published by the Book Club of California, and *Descent to the Dead*, published by Random House, had
more literary significance than his first books, *Flagons and Apples* or *Californians*. Since the publication of *Tamar*, Jeffers had

averaged almost a book a year. Besides the major works, five books presenting one poem each had been printed in small issues by private presses: *An Artist, Stars, Apology for Bad Dreams, Beaks of Eagles,* and *Return.* Five books had been written about Jeffers by George Sterling, Louis Adamic, Rudolph Gilbert, Lawrence Clark Powell, and the author of this work, as well as the *Bibliography* by Sydney S. Alberts.

In the man himself there was no change. He was content as long as Una held off the world and left him free of distractions, free to build immortality with stone and poems. In Una's own words:

"... he cannot give time to going over past writing or thinking about it. I know some writers enjoy this—my beloved Yeats and Moore revise and revise but R. J. thinks time all too short for work in progress and whenever for one reason or another I have gotten him to break his rule a little to talk or analyse his activities I have always regretted it—it puts him off so. I have therefore become firmer and firmer with negatives."[3]

Without question Jeffers would not discuss work in progress and seldom, except in answer to criticism or the questions of students, would he discuss his published works. But as for making revisions, anyone familiar with his manuscripts knows that they were like quail-tracks across his pages. In his last poems, which I transcribed from manuscript and edited for publication, there were sometimes as many as three or four versions of the same poem.

As closely as I worked with him, the only time he ever discussed an unpublished poem with me was after Una's death when he asked me to read "The Cretan Woman" (then "Phaedra") to see if I thought it worthy of publication. We discussed it then and again later when Eva Hesse, his German translator, asked him to lengthen it. One time, after going through a large envelope of manuscripts marked "For Consideration?," I attached notes to those I felt were definitely worthy of revision and placed them on his desk. But by then he was too ill and too weary to make the effort, and his only reaction was to thank me for my trouble.

[3]Letter from U. J. to M. B. B., June 18, 1935.

XVII

THE PROPHET SPEAKS

JEFFERS' PUBLISHERS had been urging him to make a selection of his poems for a one-volume collection. The task took most of the year 1937 to accomplish, and the book was published in 1938 under the title, *The Selected Poetry of Robinson Jeffers*. It includes most of his poems from "Tamar" through "Such Counsels You Gave to Me," with the exception of the narratives "The Women at Point Sur," "Cawdor," "Dear Judas," and a few of his shorter poems. He omitted the first because "it is the least understood and least liked, and because it is the longest"; "Dear Judas" was omitted because it also was not liked. The omission of "Cawdor" was "purely arbitrary and accidental." It was a choice between "Cawdor" and "Thurso's Landing," and since there was no ground for choice, he says that he "simply drew lots in my mind." In a long foreword, which has been freely quoted in this biography, Jeffers clearly states his intentions. There are four previously unpublished poems in the volume. Of one of these, "Shiva," written in fourteen rhymed lines, Jeffers discusses its right to be called a sonnet:

"A 'Shakespearean' sonnet has four quatrains and a couplet, and so I suppose 'Shiva' is an irregular (or degenerate) sonnet in form. And it is a sonnet in the unity and shape of its content. It is the latest, I think, of a series of such fourteen-line poems that began in 1918 or earlier—(see 'The Truce and the Peace' in my *Roan Stallion* volume) —and were then quite regular, but have been increasingly careless of metrical and rhyming regularity.

"It seems to me that we have come to distrust regularity. In the poetry of classical times we value it; I don't know why. It appears either dull or meretricious in our own time."[1]

A one-man exhibition is a test of quality and originality for any artist. Here are poems set in scenes of frightening beauty, written in rhythms as varied as the tides, with words pregnant with power, and a knowledge and vision that encompass all of the past and much of the future, cosmic in scope.

Jeffers wrote no new major works in the years 1938 to 1940, but another honorary degree was conferred on him in 1939 by the University of Southern California, the degree of Doctor of Humane Letters. And in 1940 he was made an honorary member of Phi Beta Kappa.

But such honors could not compensate for the depression which he felt because he was not writing. In hopes of his finding the stimulant which he needed, Una persuaded him to accept an invitation from his brother Hamilton to fly them to Death Valley during Easter of 1938. Hamilton was an experienced pilot, but Jeffers had, unaccountably, a strong premonition of death. He said nothing about it to Una nor to Hamilton, but he left a letter on his desk, should he die and not return to Tor House. Upon his safe return he undoubtedly crumpled the letter and threw it in his basket, to be retrieved later by Una. It is interesting to note with what fatalistic immobility he could face the imminence of his own death:

"Dear Una—On account of a dream I had in London—for no one knows what previsions the human mind is capable of—and a 'hunch' I have here, it seems possible that we may crash on the way to Death Valley in spite of Hamilton's flying experience. Therefore this note and the enclosed holograph last will and testament. But a 'hunch' is not an assurance; I wouldn't bet money on a 'hunch' and it would be just cowardly to refuse an air-plane ride for one. I say this to avoid misunderstanding because I have no desire to die before writing another poem or two and I should love to know you and the boys for hundreds of years to come, and the beauty of things.

"Aside from these considerations I have no prejudice against dying at any time—no desire to but also no shrinking from it so you are not to mourn me if it should happen, but remember that I loved you dearly and wanted you and the boys to be happy—not sorrowful. Remember

[1]Letter to R. H. Elias of Philadelphia. From undated draft in Tor House collection.

also that it is vulgar for poor people to spend money on funerals. I wish to be cremated as cheaply, quickly and quietly as possible, no speech nor meeting nor music, no more coffin than may be necessary, no embalming, no flowers. A funeral is only a sanitary measure. Put the ashes a few inches deep in the courtyard near our little daughter's ashes—certainly no gravestone nor tablet.

"As to the proposed 'Selected'—in case what I imagine should happen —'*Collected* Poems' go ahead with them. I trust your judgment more than I do my own. I will try to get the preface done more or less; and to copy legibly the two or three bits of recent verse that might be added. I really think that the poems are valuable and memorable but how should I know? Don't forget the dedication to U. J. I will copy it out legibly.

"Finally my dearest love to you and our boys. More than I have ever been able to express. Robin."

Jeffers returned from the jaunt, very much alive, but Una was aware that he was still suffering with low spirits and planned yet another trip—this time to Taos. But instead of stimulating him, he sank even lower mentally. Jeffers dreaded these visits to Taos, but because both Una and the twins enjoyed them, he hid his own feelings. But now he was suffering the terrifying experience of having his mind go "dry," and he expressed his despair in a note to Una:

"Una, *I can't write.* I feel completely half-witted (not to diagnose the case) and 'writing'—during the past 30 years—has become one of the conditions of life for me.

"You see how morbid!

"I believe I'll have a new birth in course of time—not willing yet to grow old at fifty like Wordsworth, and survive myself—something will happen—and *life through this hell come home to me*—something will change, something will happen.

"It is a little like my extravagances of 1917 to '19, except that I was uncritical then, and able to keep myself fairly quiet by not writing a lot of foolishness. (Now I know too much.) After that we began to make Tor House—*and that was worth while,*—quite aside from the accidental new birth of my own mind.

"Something like that will happen again. You were insensitive in Taos. —You thought too much about yourself,—as I am doing now. Either person of a pair of lovers ought to think of the other—.

"(Do you understand? —Our love is something different from the love of people that live in apartments. You might have thought about our own peace here—.)"

These repeated visits to Taos were difficult for friends of the Jefferses to understand. In her letters, Una says over and over how intensely Jeffers disliked being uprooted. Of course, Garth and Donnan had reached the age when they needed more than Tor House had to offer, and Taos represented fascinating adventures for two young boys. It was ideal for Una too. She was not only temporarily free of household duties but was in the company of stimulating conpanionship which the very essence of her being craved. Her insatiable vanity had appreciation and praise to feed it. It was an atmosphere as sophisticated as Tor House was simple. Trouble was inevitable, and it came from the least expected source. There are many versions of the story, but the one told me by Una was that Jeffers became attracted to one of Mabel's guests. Knowing Una, I am quite sure that she created a scene violent enough for the guests to be aware of her emotions. This was followed by Una's shooting herself. Her story was that she had removed a gun from a shelf in the bathroom to clean it; that someone entered the house, and it startled her and the gun accidentally exploded; and that she had no intention of killing herself. Others who were at Taos at the time claim it was no accident. However, in October, Una wrote me, "My accident in Taos is almost forgotten, but I have a startling scar on my torso!"

In 1939, Jeffers sat for three portraits, none of which were a success. Kate Carew, Gale Guthrie, and Michael Werhoff were the artists. Of the latter, Una wrote:

". . . he wanted to do an oil but R. can't spare time so he did two crayons. In some ways they are excellent—one has a *remarkable* reproduction of R.'s eyes—but on the whole I like the sketches much less than many photographs by Weston! . . . One of them started to be very fine, then the painter put a terrifically *inspired* look into it (à la Stokowsky) that ruins it for us. Maybe R.'s soul is like that but I doubt it! Werhoff is a friend of Auslander and looks enough like him to be an identical twin. . . ."

In the year 1940, Jeffers received an invitation from the Library of Congress in Washington, D. C., to inaugurate a Poetry Series. Any circumstances other than those in which he found himself that December would have prompted him to give an immediate refusal to the invitation. He disliked talking to people, and crowds filled him with distress. However, the fact that the Carmel Sanitary District had taken action to extend its sewer lines with WPA labor to serve the Point called for an expenditure of $118,971 (the property owners to pay $31,000 or about $46 per lot). Although the property owners were vigorously opposing the plan, it looked as if they would be over-ruled by the city fathers. The Jefferses owned thirty-six lots, so it meant that they would be called upon to pay over $1600; and that sum was not easily earned by a poet. So when the invitation came from Washington, Una asked her husband, "What is your decision?" He replied with resignation, "Answer as you think best." Una wired Joseph Auslander, "Yes."

This was the first time that Jeffers had ever accepted an invitation to speak before an audience, and the resultant series were his only public appearances as a lecturer.

Through Auslander and the Clapps, eastern universities were notified of Jeffers' acceptance to open the Poet's Congress in Washington; and knowing that he would have prepared a paper for the occasion, several of the universities and colleges wrote to Jeffers inviting him to speak before them. After much juggling of dates, Una finally accepted invitations from Pittsburgh, Princeton, Harvard, Columbia, Buffalo, Butler of Indiana, Kansas City, and Utah. Jeffers refused to let his thoughts dwell on the ordeal ahead of him and sought consolation in their new English bull puppy, "Winnie" (named after Winston Churchill).

To supplement Jeffers' address, the Library of Congress planned an exhibition of his books, photographs, and manuscripts. Audrey Wurdemann, poet-wife of Joseph Auslander, had written to Una:

"Our primary purpose is to make the man come alive and liberate the poet from literary dust and distortion . . . to establish the fact that Robinson Jeffers is not a glacial epoch, but a glorious human being, as well as a poet."

The focal point of the exhibition was to be *Tamar*, because, as Audrey Wurdemann said, ". . . it seems to us that is where Robin's career really began . . . ."

The inauguration was to take place on February 27, 1941, so on February 16, accompanied by their friend Noel Sullivan, Una and Robin set out in their Ford to cross the continent. The schedule that Una had set up was Pittsburgh on February 24th, Washington on February 27th, Princeton on February 28th, Harvard on March 3rd, Columbia on March 6th, Buffalo on March 11th, Butler on March 17th, University of Kansas City on March 19th, and Utah on March 24th.

Una had a helpful habit of making notes on her journeys. In her notebook we find, dated February 17th, the following observations:

"Snow begins west of Williams. Wonderful cold stimulating air. Lovely bare white-trunked aspens grouped in snow. Painted desert all ashes of roses. Ice, a brook ice-edged between black forest trees. Incredibly green—Nile green. Dignified brick houses, plain, old, colonial."

According to her notes they crossed California, Arizona, New Mexico, Texas, Oklahoma, Arkansas, Tennessee, Kentucky, Indiana, Ohio, West Virginia, Pennsylvania. Then Maryland, District of Columbia, Virginia, New Jersey, New York, Connecticut, and Massachusetts. Coming home Una even kept track of the mileage. Every small detail was important to her, even gas consumption.

Their first engagement was at Pittsburgh, and this was the first time, since his family sold their home there, that Jeffers had returned or seen any of his relatives. As I had visited there in 1938 and met all the family, I made the arrangements for them. Una wrote:

"On the Sunday of our arrival we had lunch with cousin Alice, then we drove about Pittsburgh, Allegheny, etc.; and called on various connections and houses associated with the family. We saw the house and room Robin was born in, and the Craigs (44 Thorn St.) were most cordial at their home, then to Twin Hollows . . . . It seemed such a charming house and full of life and happiness.

". . . A thing that surprised me was the small part the river played in Robin's life there . . . it is just a little way below Twin Hollows and there were lots of river boats there . . . .

"[At] Stephen Foster Memorial Hall, a beautiful little building next to the tower . . . Robin talked to an intensely interested audience in a fine little auditorium ... After this talk I had no worry about Robin for he read easily and audibly. Our stay was very happy there and it was pleasant to know how likeable the family are. And Robin's old college was glad to claim him."[2]

After the speech in Pittsburgh, the Jefferses and Noel Sullivan journeyed to Washington, D.C. where they stayed with Eugene and Agnes Meyer, the two persons who were most responsible for stirring the Library of Congress into instituting the lecture series. Eugene Meyer was owner of the *Washington Post* and former head of the Federal Reserve Bank. From Washington, Una wrote me:

"They made our stay completely delightful. Parties, expeditions (Mt. Vernon, Arlington, etc.). One of their guests Mr. Justice Stone took us all over and explained Supreme Court doings. At one of Meyer's stag dinners Robin met Knudson who was doing some off-the-cuff opinions and estimates. The Library of Congress thing was an immense success. Afterwards the Meyers had a lot of people (Alice Roosevelt amongst them) in for drinks and my friends the Matthiases, Sweeneys, Noel and others who had dashed down from N.Y.C. and went back by 2:00 a.m. train."

The crowd that gathered to hear Jeffers' address filled Coolidge Hall and overflowed into an adjoining room. A member of the press wrote that Jeffers was "charmingly ill at ease and diffident," as he no doubt was. But the audience listened raptly to the motionless figure on the platform as he read in a monotone from his book of verses. The subject of his address was "The Poet in Democracy," and in it he set forth his views on democracy, philosophy, and mysticism, clearing up some of the misunderstandings entertained about his poetry. He also gave some interesting quotations from his poems, showing the influence of the war on his thinking.

Although the address has since been printed in a fine press edition,[3] it is difficult for the student to obtain, and because the address is the most important statement which Jeffers has made about his poetry, we shall quote it in full. There are deviations

[2]Letter from U.J. to M.B.B. April 12, 1941.
[3]*Themes in My Poems* (1956), The Book Club of California.

here, from the printed text, as this was quoted from Jeffers' original paper. Nor does the printed text include the opening statement on democracy.

After a few words to open his address, Jeffers launched into his definition of democracy:

"...Our democracy has provided, and still provides, the greatest freedom for the greatest number of people. That is its special glory. It is a means, to a purpose. Freedom is the purpose. Every decent government on earth aims at justice and public welfare, but ours is also aimed particularly at freedom; and that word, I think, best expresses our national ideal, the basic principle on which this republic was founded.

"I will read part of a poem about the love of freedom: it was written three or four years ago, and is called 'Shine, Republic.'"

> The quality of these trees, green height;
>   of the sky, shining; of water, a clear
>   flow; of the rock, hardness
> And reticence: each is noble in its quality.
>   The love of freedom has been the
>   quality of Western man.
>
> There is a stubborn torch that flames from
>   Marathon to Concord, its dangerous beauty
>   binding three ages
> Into one time; the waves of barbarism and
>   civilization have eclipsed but have never
>   quenched it.
>
> For the Greeks the love of beauty, for Rome of
>   ruling, for the present age the passionate
>   love of discovery;
> But in one noble passion we are one; and Wash-
>   ington, Luther, Tacitus, Aeschylus, one
>   kind of man.
> And you, America, that passion made you.[4]

"The word *democracy* means a system of government, the surest means toward freedom, and it has a secondary meaning in common usage. It means an attitude of mind,—tolerance, disregard of class-distinction, a recognition that each person, in certain rights and values, is equal to any other person. It means: no snobbery. And no flunkyism, no indecent humility.

[4]*Solstice and Other Poems.*

"This is a great ideal for all men and women: I should like to emphasize it especially for the men and women who write poetry, and indeed for all creative writers and artists. These are a queer people and have strange aims, and are often quite unsuccessful in attaining the things that most people want. Therefore they sometimes feel that they are regarded with suspicion, or patronage, or even contempt; and sometimes they resent this attitude, whether real or imaginary, by foolish assumption of superiority and special dedication. I do not believe for a moment that a poet, as such, is any better, or any worse, than a congressman—or a carpenter; and this is the special bit of democracy that I should like to emphasize for all artists.

"As to the particular case of the poet: democracy is congenial to poetry, but freedom is essential to it. Democracies, like Athens; aristocracies and monarchies, like historic England; even enlightened dictatorships, like Greek Sicily and Augustan Rome:—all these have produced great poetry. These are all sorts of government; their common quality is that there was freedom under government: Sparta is the prime example of a totalitarian state, and she produced nothing, nothing but militarism: no art, no poetry, no literature of any kind. Because there was no freedom. The state was all-important; the individual existed only to serve it. So, when they wanted poetry for the young people to sing, they had to employ a foreigner, a man who was not even a Greek, a man from Sardis, named Aleman, to make their choruses for them.

"The Spartans produced a formidable military machine and nothing else; but even at that game they were hardly, if at all, superior to democratic Athens. It was Athens that rolled back the Persian invasions, and one of her two greatest poets fought a Marathon, and fought at sea, on the bay of Solomas. Do you remember the verses inscribed on the tomb of Aeschylus? He is supposed to have written them himself: —'Beneath this stone lies Aeschylus, the Athenian, the son of Euphonion. Of his valor the grove of Marathon can speak, and the long-haired Persian who knows it well.'—That is all; not a word about the tragedies. This man took poetry in his stride, as I think all great poets do. He devoted most of his life to it, but he wanted to be remembered as a citizen of Athens, a citizen-soldier.

"I wish I might stop here, at this high place; but it would be dishonest not to add that the conflict between democratic Athens and totalitarian Sparta, between rule by the many and rule by the few, finally ruined all Greece, as a similar conflict is ruining Europe. There is nothing more destructive than a war of ideologies. Of course that struggle, like this one, was much more than ideological; national ambitions, and

Una and Billie. Carmel, 1915 or 1916

Robin, Una, Billie, at Tor, where Tor House was built,
1918 or early 1919

Robin, Una, the twins and goats at the Point

Robinson Jeffers. Tor House, Carmel, 1928

Tony Luhan, Donnan Jeffers, Robinson Jeffers.
Taos, New Mexico, 1930

Robin laying stones

1939. Hawk Tower, Tor House, Carmel. Robinson Jeffers

Jeffers with his two sons, Donnan and Garth, in 1944

Tor House and the Tower

Robin with his granddaughter Una. Taken by his brother
Hamilton. Given to M.B.B. *by Hamilton, 1953*

commerce, and mutual fear, were basic. All the Greek states were drawn into it and pulled down by it; they lost prosperity, and they lost power, and they lost more than democracy, they lost freedom, —until long afterwards it was temporarily given back by the conquering Roman, a 'gift' as Wordsworth wrote—

> 'A gift of that which is not to be *given*
> By all the blended powers of earth and heaven'.

"I say this as a duty. Europe will be physically and morally exhausted after this second world war; and perhaps it will be our destiny to carry the heritage of European culture, and what we have added to it, across a time of twilight to a new age; as Byzantium carried the culture of Greece and Rome across the dark centuries, from that age to this one. Therefore we must guard what we have, for it is precious; and if we feel ourselves forced to intervene in foreign conflicts, we must consult the interests of our people first; and our generosity second, —we have always been generous; and ideology last. But sentimentality, never. We can still afford the material risks of sentimentality, but not the disillusion that follows it."

Having completed his definition of democracy, Jeffers next outlined his preoccupation with the war:

"So I came to the tragic conflict that obsesses all our minds at present, and I think of Victor Hugo's verses—

> '*Soyez maudits, d'abord d'être ce que*
> *vous êtes,*
> *Et puis soyez maudits d'obséder les*
> *poètes!*'

"The war obsessed my mind several years before it began. This poem called 'Rearmament' was written in 1934.

> These grand and fatal movements towards
>   death: the grandeur of the mass
> Makes pity a fool, the tearing pity
> For the atoms of the mass, the persons, the
>   victims, make it seem monstrous
> To admire the tragic beauty they build.
> It is beautiful as a river flowing or a slowly
>   gathering
> Glacier on a high mountain rock-face,

177

Bound to plow down a forest, or as frost in
    November,
The gold and flaming death-dance for leaves,
Or a girl in the night of her spent maidenhood,
    bleeding and kissing.
I would burn my right hand in a slow fire
To change the future. . . . I should do foolishly.
    The beauty of modern
Man is not in the persons but in the
Disastrous rhythm, the heavy and mobile masses,
    the dance of the
Dream-led masses down the dark mountain.[5]

"Then the European cities began their air-raid precaution drills, and this slight poem—slight certainly for the subject—was written in March 1936. It is called 'Air-Raid Rehearsals.'"

Unhappy time, why have you built up your
    house
So high that it cannot stand? I see that it
    has to fall;
When I look closer I can see nothing clearly,
    my eyes are blinded with rain.

I see far fires and dim degradation
Under the war-planes, and neither Christ nor
    Lenin will save you.
I see the March rain walk on the mountain,
    sombre and lovely on the green mountain.

I wish you could find the secure value,
The all-heal I found when a former time hurt
    me to the heart,
The splendor of inhuman things: you would not
    be looking at each others' throats with
    your knives.

"In December 1936 I lay awake hearing a storm roar on the roof, and thought of the flooded streams and rock-slides in the mountain gorges a few miles away, and then of the tyrannies and decline of Europe, and the war that was coming, and thoughts made this poem."

The world's as the world is; the nations rearm and prepare
    to change; the age of tyrants returns;

[5]*Ibid.*

The greatest civilization that has ever existed builds itself
    higher towers on breaking foundations.
Recurrent episodes; they were determined when the ape's
    children first ran in packs, chipped flint to an edge.
        I lie and hear dark rain beat the roof, and
        the blind wind.
In the morning perhaps I shall find strength again
To value the immense beauty of this time of the world, the
    flowers of decay their pitiful loveliness, the
    fever-dream
Tapestries that back the drama and are called the future.
    This ebb of vitality feels the ignoble and cruel
Incidents, not the vast abstract order.
        I lie and hear dark
rain beat the roof, and the night-blind wind.
In the Ventana country darkness and rain and the roar of waters
    fill the deep mountain-throats.
The creekside shelf of sand where we lay last August under a
    slip of stars,
And firelight played on the leaning gorge-walls, is drowned and
    lost. The deer of the country huddle on a ridge
In a close herd under madrone-trees; they tremble when a
    rockslide goes down, they open great darkness-
Drinking eyes and press closer.
        Cataracts of rock
Rain down the mountain from cliff to cliff and torment the
    stream-bed. The stream deals with them. The laurels
    are wounded,
Redwoods go down with their earth and lie thwart the gorge. I
    hear the torrent boulders battering each other,
I feel the flesh of the mountain move on its bones in the
    wet darkness.
        Is this more beautiful
Than man's disasters? These wounds will heal in their time;
    so will humanity's. This is more beautiful . . . at night. . . .[6]

"In 1937 I wrote 'Hope Is Not for the Wise.' "

Hope is not for the wise, fear is for fools;
Change and the world, we think, are racing to a
    fall,

[6]"Night Without Sleep," from *Such Counsels You Gave to Me.*

Open-eyed and helpless, in every news-cast that
    is the news:
The time's events would seem mere chaos but all
Drift the one deadly direction. But this is only
The August thunder of the age, not the November.
Wise men hope nothing, the wise are naturally lonely
And think November as good as April, the wise remember
That Caesar and even final Augustulus had heirs,
And men lived on; rich unplanned life on earth
After the foreign wars and the civil wars, the border
    wars
And the barbarians: music and religion, honor and mirth
Renewed life's lost enchantments. But if life even
Had perished utterly, Oh perfect loveliness of earth
    and heaven.

"This next poem, called 'Watch the Lights Fade,' was written in 1938, the year of Munich, and has not yet been printed in a book. It came to me while I was walking along our shore in a story twilight, in a mood of pure sadness."

Gray steel, cloud-shadow-stained,
The ocean takes the last lights of evening.
Loud is the voice and the foam lead-color,
And flood-tide devours the sands.

Here stand, like an old stone,
And watch the lights fade and hear the sea's voice.
Hate and despair take Europe and Asia,
And the sea-wind blows cold.
Night comes: night will claim all.
The world is not changed, only more naked:
The strong struggle for power, and the weak
Warm their poor hearts with hate.
Night comes: come into the house,
Try around the dial for a late news-cast.
These others are America's voices: naive and
Powerful, spurious, doom-touched.
How soon? Four years or forty?
Why should an old stone pick at the future?
Stand on your shore, old stone, be still while the
Sea-wind salts your head white.[7]

[7] *Be Angry at the Sun.*

"The war came; here is a poem that tried to meet it with a kind of desperate optimism. It was written in June 1940, and is called 'The Bloody Sire':"

It is not bad. Let them play.
Let the guns bark and the bombing-plane
Speak his prodigious blasphemies.
It is not bad, it is high time,
Stark violence is still the sire of all the
    world's values.

What but the wolf's tooth whittled so fine
The fleet limbs of the antelope?
What but fear winged the birds, and hunger
Jeweled with such eyes the great goshawk's head?
Violence has been the sire of all the world's
    values.

Who would remember Helen's face
Lacking the terrible halo of spears?
Who formed Christ but Herod and Caesar,
The cruel and bloody victories of Caesar?
Violence, the bloody sire of all the world's values.

Never weep, let them play,
Old violence is not too old to beget new values.[8]

"I believe this, deeply and faithfully; but it will be a long time before the new values can be realized.

"To go back to the beginning of the war: perhaps you remember that Hitler made a speech to his people in Danzig, September 1939, which was broadcast to America and elsewhere. The verses I shall read next are a literal transcript of my experiences that day, mixed with foreboding of things to come, and—shall I say—sickly attempt at humor at the end."

September 19, 1939

This morning Hitler spoke in Danzig, we
    heard his voice.
A man of genius: that is, of amazing
Ability, courage, devotion, cored on a sick
    child's soul,
Heard clearly through the dog-wrath, a sick
    child
Wailing in Danzig; invoking destruction and
    wailing at it.

[8]*Ibid.*

181

Here, the day was extremely hot; about noon
A south wind like a blast from hell's mouth
    spilled a slight rain
On the parched land, and at five a light
    earthquake
Danced the house, no harm done. To-night I
    have been amusing myself
Watching the blood-red moon droop slowly
Into black sea through bursts of dry lightning
    and distant thunder.
Well: the day is a poem: but too much
Like one of Jeffers' crusted with blood and
    barbaric omens,
Painful to excess, inhuman as a hawk's cry.

Completing this theme, Jeffers developed the idea of tension and civil war at the heart of our civilization. He then took up the religious theme in his poems:

"Another theme that has much engaged my verses is the expression of a religious feeling, that perhaps must be called pantheism, though I hate to type it with a name. It is the feeling—I will say the certainty—that the universe is one being, a single organism, one great life that includes all life and all things; and is so beautiful that it must be loved and reverenced; and in moments of mystical vision we identify ourselves with it.

"This is, in a way, the exact opposite of Oriental pantheism. The Hindu mystic finds God in his own soul, and all the outer world is illusion. To this other way of feeling, the outer world is real and divine; one's own soul might be called an illusion, it is so slight and so transitory.

"This is the experience that comes to my Orestes, at the end of a long semi-dramatic poem called 'The Tower Beyond Tragedy.' He is trying to tell his sister Electra what great vision and freedom he has found, on the far shore beyond duty-bound matricide and the ancestral madness."

ORESTES   I left the madness of the
        house, to-night in the dark, with you it walks
        yet.
How shall I tell you what I have learned? Your mind is
        like a hawk's or like a lion's, this knowledge
Is out of the order of your mind, a stranger language.
        To wild beasts and the blood of kings
A verse blind in the book.

ELECTRA   At least my eyes can see dawn
        graying: tell and not mock me, our moment
Dies in a moment.
ORESTES   Here is the last labor
To spend on humanity. I saw a vision of us move in the
        dark: all that we did or dreamed of ʹ
Regarded each other, the man pursued the woman, the
        woman clung to the man, warriors and kings
Strained at each other in the darkness, all loved or
        fought
        inward, each one of the lost people
Sought the eyes of another that another should praise
        him;
        sought never his own but another's; the net of
        desire
Had every nerve drawn to the center, so that they
        writhed
        like a full draught of fishes, all matted
In the one mesh; when they look backward they see
        only
        a man standing at the beginning,
Or forward, a man at the end; or if upward, men in the
        shining bitter sky striding and feasting,
Whom you call Gods . . .
It is all turned inward, all your desires incestuous,
        the
        woman the serpent, the man the rose-red cavern,
Both human, worship forever . . .
ELECTRA   You have dreamed wretchedly.
ORESTES   I have
        seen the dreams of the people and not dreamed
        them,
As for me, I have slain my mother.
ELECTRA   No more?
ORESTES   And the gate's
        open,
        the gray boils over the mountain, I have greater
Kindred than dwell under a roof. Didn't I say this
        would
        be dark to you? I have cut the meshes
And fly like a freed falcon. Tonight, lying on the
        hillside,

sick with those visions, I remembered
The knife in the stalk of my humanity; I drew and it
    broke; I entered the life of the brown forest
And the great life of the ancient peaks, the patience
    of
stone, I felt the changes in the veins
In the throat of the mountain, a grain in many
    centuries,
    we have our own time, not yours; and I was
    the stream
Draining the mountain wood; and I the stag drinking;
    and I was the stars,
Boiling with light, wandering alone, each one the
    lord of
    his own summit; and I was the darkness
Outside the stars, I included them, they were a
    part of
    me. I was mankind also, a moving lichen
On the cheek of the round stone . . . they have not
    made words for it, to go behind things,
    beyond hours and ages,
And be all things in all time, in their returns and
    passages, in the motionless and timeless center,
In the white of the fire . . . how can I express the
    excellence
    I have found, that has no color but clearness;
No honey but ecstasy; nothing wrought nor remembered;
    no undertone nor silver second murmur
That rings in love's voice, I and my loved are one;
    no
    desire but fulfilled; no passion but peace,
The pure flame and the white, fierier than any passion;
    no time but spheral eternity: Electra,
Was that your name before this life dawned—

"These verses express a mystical experience; they also express a protest against human narcissism. Narcissus, you know, fell in love with
himself. If a person spends all his emotion on his own body and states
of mind, he is mentally diseased, and the disease is called narcissism. It
seems to me, analogously, that the whole human race spends too much
emotion on itself. The happiest and freest man is the scientist investi-
gating nature, or the artist admiring it; the person who is interested in

things that are not human. Or if he is interested in human beings, let him regard them objectively, as a very small part of the great music. Certainly humanity has claims, on all of us; we can best fulfill them by keeping our emotional sanity; and this by seeing beyond and around the human race.

"This is far from humanism; but it is, in fact, the Christian attitude: —to love God with all one's heart and soul, and one's neighbor as one's self: as much as that, but as *little* as that.

"I spoke a moment ago of the beauty of the universe, that calls forth our love and reverence. Beauty, like color, is subjective. It is not in the object but in the mind that regards it. Nevertheless, I believe it corresponds to a reality, a real excellence and nobility in the world; but as the color red corresponds to a reality: certain wave-lengths of light, a certain rhythm of vibrations. It was Plato who defined beauty as the effulgence—the shining forth of truth.

"Here are some verses I made on this subject twenty-three years ago, and have never published them in a book because they did not well express my mind—but perhaps they will serve."

THE EXCESSES OF GOD

Is it not by his high superfluousness we know
Our God? For to equal a need
Is natural, animal, mineral: but to fling
Rainbows over the rain,
And beauty above the moon, and secret rainbows
On the domes of deep sea-shells,
And make the necessary embrace of breeding
Beautiful also as fire,
Not even the weeds to multiply without blossom
Nor the birds without music:
There is the great humanness at the heart of things,
The extravagant kindness, the fountain
Humanity can understand, and would flow likewise
If power and desire were perch-mates.

Having already discussed at some length in a preceding chapter Jeffers' use of the theme of the self-torturing God, we will omit this section of the lecture, and proceed to his discussion of the scenic background for his poems.

". . . it is a relief to turn to the simplest and commonest theme of my verse; and that is just the landscape of the Monterey Coast range. I should say that this rocky coast is not only the scene of my narrative verse, but also the chief actor in it. These mountains rise sheer from the ocean; they are cut by deep gorges and are heavy with brush and forest. Remember this is Central, not Southern, California. There are no orange-groves here, and no oil-wells, and many deer; hawk and vulture, eagle and heron, fly here, as well as the sea-birds and shore-birds; and there are clouds and sea-fog in summer, and fine storms in winter.

"This coast is described throughout my narrative poems, but I will read a brief piece that notices one special part of it, a mile or two along the coast-road. These eleven lines are called 'The Place for No Story' because the coast here, its pure and simple grandeur, seemed to me too beautiful to be the scene of any narrative poem of mine.—And I have kept the promise I made to it."

> The coast hills at Sovranes Creek:
> No trees, but dark scant pasture drawn thin
> Over rock shaped like flame;
> The old ocean at the land's foot, the vast
> Gray extension beyond the long white violence;
> A herd of cows and the bull
> Far distant, hardly apparent up the dark slope;
> And the gray air haunted with hawks:
> This place is the noblest thing I have ever seen.
> No imaginable
> Human presence here could do anything
> But dilute the lonely self-watchful passion.[9]

"One of these lines took note of 'the gray air haunted with hawks,' and as I looked over my things in preparation for this reading, it occurred to me that those birds of prey fly so often through my verses that hawk and falcon might be called a characteristic theme in them. This is partly because there are so many in our mountains, and so many kinds,—marshawk and redtail, Cooper's hawk and sparrowhawk and duckhawk—that is the American peregrine falcon—but I won't continue the list. And partly, because I nursed a broken-winged hawk once; and its savage individualism caught my fancy producing these two pieces of verse that together were called 'Hurt Hawks.'"

Here Jeffers quoted the poem and brought his address to a close with a little poem called "Rock and Hawk." The opening of the reading, as we have quoted it, started out with a definition of democracy. At the college addresses, he substituted an explanation of his theme in contemplation of death, quoting from "Thurso's

[9]*Thurso's Landing and Other Poems.*

Landing" and the two short poems, "The Bed by the Window" and "Antrim."

In this address, Jeffers answers the questions put to him most frequently: what are his religious beliefs; what are his political views; why does he dwell on the decline of the age? What influence did his physical environs have on his poetry?

After the address in Washington, they were scheduled for Princeton, but a terrible snow storm prevented them from keeping the engagement. There were ten inches of snow in Philadelphia and a temperature of five degrees. Pittsburgh had paid Jeffers $100 for his address, and the Library of Congress paid him $500. Princeton was to have paid him only $50 which would hardly have paid for the trip from Washington.

The Harvard address was under the auspices of the Morris Gray Poetry Fund and was given at Warren House. The Jefferses stayed with their friend Mrs. Kingsley Porter (Lucy), at Elmswood, arriving there in time for a tea on March 2nd, staying over the next day to attend a dinner given in their honor by Mrs. Porter at Cambridge. Una wrote me: "Harvard was grand! So enthusiastic and welcoming." They paid Jeffers $125.

The address at Columbia was given in the McMillan Academic Theatre. Jeffers was introduced by the poet Leonora Speyer and was paid $200. While in New York, the Jefferses were entertained by their friends the Clapps, the Matthiases, and Esther Busby. They made a trip up-state to visit Edna St. Vincent Millay and her husband, Eugen Boissevain.

Speeches at the University of Buffalo, Butler University, Kansas City, and the University of Utah followed. In all, Jeffers was paid $1250, and, according to Una's accounting, the trip cost them $630. Jeffers had also made recordings of his readings at Harvard and at the University of the City of New York.

The lecture was published under the title *Themes in my Poems* in 1956 by The Book Club of California, printed by Mallette Dean in a limited edition of 350 copies.

We must close this chapter on an ironic note. When the Jefferses returned to Carmel, they learned that the Sanitation Board had been defeated in its efforts to improve the Point by extending the sewer! So the Jefferses' money didn't go down the drain after all.

XVIII

"FAILURE CANNOT CAST DOWN NOR SUCCESS MAKE PROUD"[1]

JEFFERS WOULD HAVE CONSIDERED the year 1941 overcrowded with trivia even if it had contained nothing more than the unprecedented lecture tour. But it also was to see the publication of his new book of poems *Be Angry at the Sun*, the marriage of his son Donnan, and the revival of his dramatic poem "Tower Beyond Tragedy."

Although the Mortar Board Dramatic Group of the University of California had produced "Tower" in 1932 under the direction of Edwin Duerr, it had yet to come alive with professional actors. The 1941 production of "Tower" was undoubtedly a direct result of the intense interest of Dr. Ben Lehman and Judith Anderson in Jeffers' poetry. However, nothing might have come of this interest if it hadn't been that a young man by the name of Charles O'Neal was having a difficult time attracting interest in his summer theater experiment at Del Monte and felt if he could persuade Judith Anderson to star in a production of *Family Portrait* she would draw the people to the theatre. However, Miss Anderson was difficult to persuade, as she was enjoying a rest between motion pictures at her home in Santa Monica. One of the members of the stock company, Henry Brandon, reminded O'Neal that in 1937 Miss Anderson had unsuccessfully tried to persuade the Theater Guild to present Robinson Jeffers' "Tower Beyond

---

[1]From the poem "Rock and Hawk."

Tragedy," casting her in the role of Clytemnestra. He suggested that O'Neal might tempt Miss Anderson to Del Monte if he would agree to produce the "Tower" as well as *Family Portrait*. The ruse was successful, and Miss Anderson accepted the invitation.

Jeffers had not written the drama with the stage in mind, so he permitted John Gassner to adapt it for the local production. When it had been presented by Duerr at the Greek Theatre in Berkeley, he had used a masked chorus to present the narrative; Gassner used a narrator, also changing the structure of the poem slightly to achieve a better dramatic effect, as the third act was anti-climactic. The play went into rehearsal in June and opened on July 4 at the open-air Forest Theater. Four performances were given, the Jefferses attending three of them.

According to Miss Anderson, the two weeks of rehearsals were fraught with crises, including a switch in directors. She felt insufficiently rehearsed for so important a role. After the performance she was in tears, feeling that she had been a complete failure. Her mother, who seldom favored her with compliments, took her in her arms and said, "Well, Miss Anderson, you have arrived!"

Judith Anderson as Clytemnestra, in a blood-red robe, highlighted by a full moon, accompanied by the music of the sea and the wind in the pines, created a never-to-be-forgotten mood. Her intelligent understanding of the emotional role, coupled with her brilliance as a great dramatic actress, made her interpretation memorable. However, she realized that the limitations of summer stock had not done the play justice, and she was more convinced than ever that it was material for Broadway. So she again set about trying to persuade New York producers to present it.

In the meantime *Be Angry at the Sun* made its appearance. It had been four years since the publication of Jeffers' last major work, *Such Counsels You Gave to Me*. The critic, John Holmes, commented that "history has caught up at last with Robinson Jeffers." From the context of these poems it is evident that Jeffers had been deeply concerned with the abominations of the contemporary scene.

The volume consists of one narrative poem "Mara," which is considerably shorter than his previous narrative poems, one dramatic poem "The Bowl of Blood," and twenty-five short lyrics. In the preface, Jeffers explains his theme:

". . . I wish also to lament the obsession with contemporary history that pins many of these pieces to the calendar, like butterflies to cardboard. Poetry is not private monologue, but I think it is not public speech either; and in general it is the worse for being timely. That is why, for the next-to-latest-written poem of this book, I sought out a drunken fisherman, who lives solitary in his hut, under a cliff, and has no radio, no newspaper, no intelligent friends, nothing but fish and whiskey; drugged hermit his mind should have been as dateless as the ocean. But he too began to babble about public affairs, and I stopped him off.

"Yet it is right that a man's views be expressed, though the poetry suffer for it. Poetry should represent the whole mind; if part of the mind is occupied unhappily, so much the worse. And no use postponing the poetry to a time when these storms may have passed, for I think we have but seen a beginning of them; the calm to look for is the calm at the whirlwind's heart."

In answer to an inquiry from William Turner Levy, about the narrative poem "Mara," Jeffers explained:

"Feeling of right and wrong no doubt comes chiefly from education and social pressure. Or is it to some extent intuitive, and directed by social pressure? I don't know the answer. It is generally supported by religion, and is weakened when it loses that old alliance."

This was the third narrative in which Jeffers had used the husband's brother as the wife's lover. In "Thurso's Landing," Mark, Reave Thurso's crippled brother, kills himself for love of Helen, Reave's wife. In "Give Your Heart to the Hawks," Fayne, Lance Fraser's wife, takes Michael, his brother, for her lover; and in this story "Mara," Fawn takes her husband's brother, Allen, as her lover, but without the provocation which Fayne had. Fawn has no excuse except the weak one of propinquity. In one of the shorter poems in the book, "For Una," Jeffers said,

> Tomorrow I will take up that heavy poem again
> About Ferguson, deceived and jealous man
> Who bawled for the truth, the truth, and failed
>   to endure
> Its first least gleam. That poem bores me, and
>   I hope will bore
> Any sweet soul that reads it, being some ways

190

> My very self but mostly my antipodes;
> But having waved the heavy artillery to fire
> I must hammer on to an end. . . .

Jeffers, like Friedenau in "The Bowl of Blood," "feels form and pressure of future events." This dramatic poem is the story of Hitler's fear of failure and his superstitious reliance on prophets. Three maskers carry the burden of the dialogue. The poem has one interesting divergence new to Jeffers: prose is interposed at one point in the poetic dialogue. Jeffers has said that "democracy is prose" and that "freedom is poetry." The subject of the prose lines is democracy.

The book contains other forms new to Jeffers, and all of the poems are pertinent to the war. In the poem, "For Una," Jeffers cried:

> It is not Europe alone that is falling
> Into blood and fire.
> Decline and fall have been dancing in all men's souls
> For a long while.
> Sometime at the last gasp comes peace
> To every soul.
> Never to mine until I find out and speak
> The things that I know.

Jeffers' custom of making reference to characters in other poems is very prevalent in this volume. Tamar appears in the poem "Come, Little Birds;" Charlie, the drunken fisherman of "Give Your Heart to the Hawks" inspires a poem called "Drunken Charlie." He is also referred to in the poem "For Una," as are Michael and Lance Fraser.

The war drained Jeffers emotionally, and he missed his two sons. Garth had joined the Marines and was overseas, and Donnan was living in Ohio. (In 1941 he had married Patricia Grant of Zanesville and had moved there to work in her father's glass factory.) Una was away from Tor House most of the day, devoting her time to Red Cross administrative work. There was little that Jeffers was equipped to do, though he assisted with the coast-patrol work when he was needed. But his spirit groaned for the troubled world.

In 1941, Herbert Carlin wrote Jeffers asking whether his views had changed since writing the poem "The Answer" in 1937. Jeffers replied:[2]

"I'm afraid my views have not changed. Certainly the present war and Roosevelt's rhetorical 'four freedoms' do not make them more hopeful. Hitler and Germany can be smashed of course, after years; but I wonder whether anyone realizes what the state of Europe and the world will be by that time? Even if those 'four freedoms' were to be honestly established at a peace conference, nobody but the U.S. could enforce them; and we shall never be *Roman* nor *German* enough to police the world for a long time. And if we did—could this be called freedom?

"One thing seems even more clear than when I wrote the verse:—that it is up to each person 'to keep his own integrity. . . .' It is going to be a very difficult job."

There was no surcease, however, of literary honors for Jeffers. In November, 1945, an enterprising New York woman, Mrs. Hugh Bullock, in an effort to encourage new talent, set up the Academy of American Poets. She invited twelve outstanding men in the field of letters to be Chancellors. Jeffers' invitation to represent the Pacific Coast was accompanied by an explanatory letter from Fred Clapp: ". . . to *reward* the accomplished and gifted poet with a fellowship stipend of $5,000 in recognition of his contribution to the intellectual and artistic life of this country." But good or bad though their poetry might be, Jeffers had no capacity nor time, for sitting in judgment on the coming young poets of the Pacific Coast and had to decline the honor.

In November he had received a letter from the American Academy of Arts and Letters informing him that he had been duly elected to membership. Membership in this society was limited to fifty living creative artists, including painters, sculptors, musicians, writers and architects.

Such honors were usually acknowledged by Una, with an explanation that, although Jeffers appreciated the honor, he would be unable to take an active part in the society. Then the embossed parchment was placed in a trunk in the attic and forgotten! This wasn't callousness, but a congenital disinterest—public honors and acclaim simply didn't touch Jeffers. He had work to do, and there was no room in his mind or on his head for laurels.

[2]From draft in Tor House Collection.

The Jefferses had always been generous in lending manuscripts for exhibitions. "Solstice" had been exhibited at the Library of Congress; "The Cruel Sea" and "Distant Rainfall" were lent to the Santa Barbara Museum of Art in the summer of 1942. These two poems were also lent to Raymond Larsson for an exhibition of original manuscripts which he assembled for the University of Wisconsin. They were never returned to the Jefferses, and after several months Mr. Larsson informed Una they had been stolen from him. But no offer was made to reimburse the Jefferses for the loss, nor did they receive any official letter of explanation or apology from the University. As a consequence of this experience, the Jefferses were less trusting and generous with future loans.

From 1942 to 1946, the stormy sea was becalmed but brooding. Una was preoccupied with her worries about Garth who was fighting in Germany and with her duties as chairman of the Red Cross. She had little leisure to devote to her friends, which disturbed her. She wrote, ". . . we have taken on a few more duties at Fort Ord and as I regard all that as my contribution to the war effort, it comes first. . . ."[3]

But her loyalties were strong, and when Pheobe and Hans Barkan came down to Carmel from San Francisco or Blanche and Russell Matthias or the Clapps came out from New York, she managed somehow to be with them. Her friendship with Esther Fish and Lee Tevis, both of whom served with her on the Red Cross, was strengthened during these years of close association.

Somehow Una also found time to write letters no matter how busy her life, particularly if in answer to questions about Robin. One, written at this time in answer to a question as to her opinion of his prose, is of particular interest. She says:

". . . I happen to think very highly of it—almost as highly as I do of his poetry. As for his letters I tell you quite frankly some of them are false & insincere. In his desire to be gentle and kind and generous and *responsive* which isn't natural for him I know that he often said things and praised things and was more or less effusive in a very artificial manner. He has outgrown that somewhat but even now I sometimes —in his rare rare letters about poetry—or something he is being pressed about—ask 'do you really think that?' Of course his natural way is not

[3]Letter to M. B. B. December, 1944.

to answer any letter or respond to any gift of book etc. (*almost* any in both cases) & doesn't seem to realize that *hurts* people. He acknowledges the truth of what I've accused him—When he has laid a book or letter away with the *vague* intention of answering he feels perfectly at ease in his conscience. He & I know deep down he'll never get around to it unless I pummel him & I don't often.

"About his own poems he is always given to understatement. I don't know what letters you have—he can write such good ones if it so happens! It will be interesting to see if you can get an honest opinion out of him about the letters if there are any effusive ones. He has an honest indifference about getting things straight about himself. . . ."[4]

Judith Anderson, living in New York, was doggedly clinging to her determination to make some producer aware of Jeffers' talent as a dramatist. But during the war-years the theatre-going public sought merrier entertainment than Greek tragedy, and Miss Anderson had no success in promoting the production of "Tower Beyond Tragedy." At the conclusion of the war, however, the producer Jed Harris agreed that Judith Anderson should do a Greek drama, but his choice was the bloodiest role in history— Medea. They began looking for a translation that could be used in the modern theatre. Dissatisfied with those submitted to her, Miss Anderson urged Harris to allow her to ask Jeffers to do an adaptation of Euripides' tragedy, insisting that if he would he could, and that it would be brilliant. With Harris' consent, she telephoned Jeffers in Carmel, and he agreed to discuss it with Harris. In April, 1945, Una wrote me:

"Jed Harris has bombarded Robin with telegrams, telephones, letters, etc. to do a translation or completely new version of Euripides' *Medea.* Robin consented to try—much to my surprise as he was in the midst of a poem—and besides he has never been able to bend his mind immediately to suggestions for themes. But "Medea" interested him and when he had 27 typed pages done, Harris flew out from N.Y. to see him. Judith Anderson came up from Hollywood. Two days conference . . . . Harris is the most stimulating person—the first person in a very long time who interested Robin or me by his talk (of art!). Robin never likes discussing art of any kind, as you know, particularly anything of his own. But Harris kept us up very late completely absorbed."

[4]Letter to M. B. B., August 22, 1943.

194

Una wrote me again on the subject:

"Robin did the job with great enthusiasm—much to my surprise for he usually finds it impossible to work at anything *suggested* to him. . . . I actually think it is much finer than my pet, Yeats' version of *Oedipus*."

Medea was completed in July, 1945, a piece in simple words and tight construction, well adapted to the demands of the modern theatre.

The plan was to have produced the play on the publication of the book, in 1946; but suddenly Harris decided against production, having run into difficulties with the casting—a bitter disappointment to Miss Anderson.

The play, in book form, received favorable comments. Dr. Hazel Hansen[5] of the Department of Classics at Stanford University wrote to Jeffers:

". . . Medea is a living, breathing person, no longer the strange witch from the fringe of the Greek world. The three students to whom I read the play yesterday evening felt that at once, and that pleases me immensely for the hardest thing in teaching students today is to bridge the span of time and place. The presentation of the gifts to Jason's bride is so vivid and colorful with its glory of gold and the rage of the flame and the horror of death. You have made it thoroughly Greek in its simplicity, its vividness and awful tragedy. Sometimes I think you write better than the Greeks.

"I rather suspected that you would depart from the Euripidean ending. I like yours, although I well remember a performance years ago by Margaret Anglin in the theatre at Berkeley. In the final scene she appeared in a chariot aglow with lights. As she spoke her farewell to Jason, who seemed so small and weak standing there alone in the empty orchestra, the lights gradually grew dim and faded until the chariot seemed to be floating away in the darkness. The audience was spellbound, but of course no such effect was achieved or even intended in ancient days, especially when the play was given in broad daylight. So I like your version with Medea's words of bitter scorn, and Jason crushed and the sense of utter futility. You have breathed a new spirit into a great play and made it more appealing. We classicists will always be deeply indebted to you."

[5]Teacher of Archaeology, Ancient and Modern Greek Languages and Geography. Honorary citizen of Skyros.

Again Miss Anderson went forth in search of a producer for Jeffers' *Medea,* this time approaching Messrs. Whitehead and Rea, and was successful in interesting them in the play.[6] They accepted the fact that there was little hope of their making money on the production, but they decided to settle for the prestige that the collaboration of Miss Anderson and the poet Jeffers would bring to such a production. So the play went into rehearsal in September 1947, with Miss Anderson in the role of Medea, John Gielgud as Jason, and Florence Reed as the nurse.

In the meantime, during the summer of 1947, Michael Myerberg, also an admirer of Jeffers' dramatic talents, had realized his ambition to present the poem "Dear Judas" as a stage piece. Myerberg had successfully presented such singular shows as Thornton Wilder's *The Skin of Our Teeth* and *Lute Song.* He had planned to take "Dear Judas" to Boston for a trial run before its New York presentation, but Catholic churchmen objected so strenuously that Mayor John B. Hynes of Boston and the city censor Walter L. Milliken strongly advised against bringing the play to that city. In a public statement, the mayor said that it would "violate the beliefs of many Bostonians in God and might even create trouble by stirring religious feeling."

Myerberg then arranged with Mrs. Maude Hartwig, producer of the Playhouse in Ogunquit, Maine, to have the trial run there. Francis Sullivan, prominent Portland, Maine, Catholic attempted to prevent its presentation, but Mrs. Hartwig refused to withdraw it, saying that it contained nothing offensive nor salacious and would offend neither Catholics nor any other Christians.

It opened on August 4, to a small and unenthusiastic audience. It was scheduled to open in New York on October 5th, and Myerberg had persuaded Jeffers to write a "presentation" in hopes that this would overcome some of the prejudice due to ignorance of the poem's intent. This was published in the drama section of *The New York Times* on October 6:

"'Dear Judas' was written nineteen years ago, but it is about ten years since Michael Myerberg told me that he was interested in the poem and would like to put it on the stage. This seemed to me a passing

[6]Miss Anderson took Robert Whitehead to Tor House in January, 1947.

fancy, not to be taken seriously, because—although the poem is dramatic and stageable—it was not written for the stage; the thoughts and attitudes it presents are not those that would be expected by any probable audience, and people are bewildered or repelled by what is strange to them. If they come to see a passion play, I thought, they expect either chromo or technicolor sentimentality; but 'Dear Judas' needs some quickness of intelligence to be understood at all. Therefore I dropped the matter from mind; but Mr. Myerberg did not. Several times during the past ten years he has written to me on the subject; and this year he took the thing in hand. So now it will presently be seen whether I underestimated the grasp and adaptability of the minds I had written for. Mr. Myerberg is an artist, a man of imagination and courage, and attracted perhaps by 'the fascination of what's difficult.' He knows the theatre through long experience, but I think he has been amazed as I have been at the absurdities of boycott and prohibition that this play (since I may now call it so) has met with, first in Maine, then in Boston. We hear often enough of books being 'banned in Boston,' not so often of plays; but this is the first time, so far as I know, that the 'banning' has been not on a moral but frankly on a theological basis. It is ridiculous and I suppose illegal, and clearly it sets the clock back (in Boston) to a time before freedom and before the Protestant Reformation. However, the affair is too far out of time and out of this world to have much importance. I don't think that the heresy trials are about to begin, nor the fagots preparing.

"And certainly 'Dear Judas' was not written with this purpose of disturbing any person's religious faith. It was written, like other poems of mine, because the great passions that produced some significant event came visibly into my mind and sought expression. But these were the passions of Jesus, of Mary, of Judas; I was not fool enough to think that I could depict these passions or these persons directly, and succeed where Milton nobly failed; therefore I chose the method of the Japanese Nō plays, which present a haunted place and passion's afterglow, two or three ghosts or echoes of life, re-enacting in a dream their ancient deeds and sorrows. Certainly, if any place is haunted, the garden of Gethsemane should be, more than the Roman forum or the mounds of Troy; the passion suffered there was so much more intensely concentrated, and the event more important—for all future time—'No man shall live,' Jesus says in the play, 'as if I had not lived.'

"To anyone who reads the gospels attentively—as I was required to do under the stern eye of the Presbyterian clergyman, my father—it soon becomes apparent that, though the deeds and sayings are of a beautiful simplicity, the minds of some of the persons are very far from simple.

Peter's mind was simple, no doubt, faithful, impulsive, bewildered, very human. The mind of Jesus is shown to us as if unintentionally, in wonderful glimpses, through the objective narrative. It is deep, powerful and beautiful; and strangely complex, not wholly integrated. He is the Prince of Peace, and yet He came 'not to bring peace but a sword.' He is gentle and loving yet He drives men with whips from the temple, He calls down destruction on Jerusalem, His curse kills an innocent fig-tree.

"This is not the mind of mere incarnation of love, as the sentimentalists represent Him, but of a man of genius, a poet and a leader, a man of such great quality that He has been regarded as God—literally, God—by successive millions of people, for eighteen or nineteen centuries (and some future ones) of the greatest age of human history. That is why there is no attempt in my play to represent this mind directly; but only through its ghost, its haunting echo or after-flame.

"Again, the mind of Judas, as represented in the gospels, is obscure and sick and divided. It may be tragic, or it may be reptilian, according to the motive that drives him; but surely the motive was not mere lust for money. He was a man who had been entrusted with money, and apparently was honest; he had been accepted among Christ's disciples; his despair at the end was so deep that he threw back the silver to those from whom he had received it, and went and hanged himself. One is left free to imagine his mind, provided only that it tallies with his acts; and I have imagined it as skeptical, humanitarian, pessimistic and sick with pity.

"But finally I should like to say that the play is not about Judas. My title is deceptive perhaps. The emphasis should be on the word 'dear' —'dear' Judas—the man was dear to Jesus even while He was being betrayed by him. The play is about this man of transcendent genius who was capable of loving even His enemies, even Judas; and who deliberately sought crucifixion because He understood that only a fierce and dreadful symbol could capture the minds of a fierce people. Only the cross, and death by torture, could 'fill the wolf bowels of Rome'; and conquer the blond savages from the North, who were about to take over Rome's power and primacy."

Myerberg's production of the play achieved some movement by the addition of Bach chorals and interpretive dancing. But these additions were not sufficient to correct the play's unsuitability to the stage; and although Myerberg wrote Jeffers that it had come off "extremely well," it was not popular and, after a two-week's run, closed.

It must have been a great disappointment to Myerberg for he wrote to Jeffers:

". . . Believe me I produced it as well as it is possible for me to produce anything. I am afraid that the lack was with the people—not with us. My only regret is that you did not see the production. We work in a perishable medium and it is all gone now. Perhaps later people will be more ready.

"Believe me, one of the bright spots has been your confidence and faith in me. You have my gratitude. . . ."

Jeffers, understanding his disappointment, wrote with compassion:

"I am deeply sorry not to have seen 'Dear Judas.' We met a number of people who had seen it and one or two who had acted in it, and all accounts agreed that it could not have had a more beautiful nor more imaginative production.

". . . But I wish I had seen you—if only to say that I appreciate all you did for the poem, and that your labor was not wasted, for those who saw your production saw a very beautiful thing, even if many were not able to understand it.

"This note is only an expression of my thanks and admiration. . . ."[7]

[7]Letters in Tor House Collection.

XIX

THE WITCH BEWITCHES

THE CLOSING OF "Dear Judas" the week prior to the opening of "Medea" at the National Theatre was not an auspicious beginning for Robinson Jeffers' introduction to Broadway. The doubters nodded their heads sagely, and the believers were filled with apprehension.

Although Jeffers had no desire nor intention of going to New York for the opening of "Medea" in the end he submitted to the demands of Judith Anderson and the producers. The enthusiasm with which the play had been received in both Princeton and Philadelphia convinced Miss Anderson that it was due for an enthusiastic reception in New York, and she wanted Jeffers there to share the honors. So Una and Robin flew east for the October 20th opening in New York.

Judith Anderson gave the greatest performance of her career and received a storm of applause from a cheering audience. She stood at the front of the stage beckoning to Jeffers in his box to stand, to share in the applause; but Jeffers, completely absorbed in Miss Anderson's success, continued to clap, until Una finally got him to his feet to take one embarrassed bow. She wrote of that exciting experience:

"All day we had been so busy with various people connected with the play that we hadn't had time to be nervous, but, when we drove up to the theatre that night with Whitehead and I saw the crowds and the long queue, I felt trembly.

"Judith Anderson had left word for us to come back to her dressing room. There we found everyone keyed up but very quiet. We were just seated in our box when the curtain rolled back. . . .

"At intermission the audience was standing in the aisles and shouting. Many old friends rushed into our box, and there was no doubt that the play was a success. At the end, after Judith had taken 13 curtain calls, there began to be cries for 'Author, author.' Robin was slow to understand that he must take a bow, he had been too lost in watching the players to remember his connection with it all."

Night after night, the "Medea" played to a full house, continuing month after month, lauded by the theater's most astute critics, publicized in every newspaper and magazine in the country, with a two-page spread in *Life* magazine. As Miss Anderson took the bows, she insisted that all publicity give Jeffers his share of the credit, and it was she who insisted that he receive a generous royalty. She apparently was more excited over Jeffers' success as a playwright than hers as an actress. She clutched tightly the reluctant hand of Jeffers as she soared starward. It was her faith, her perseverance, and her talent which brought to Jeffers a popularity in the theater that it is most improbable he would have had without her—at least during his life time.

Jeffers' success as a dramatist is incongruous considering the fact that, outside of his attendance at the production of "Tower Beyond Tragedy" in the Forest Theatre in Carmel, he had, as a youth in Europe, seen two plays in German (he couldn't remember what they were) and two by Shakespeare. Literally he was unfamiliar with the theater, though it must be remembered that he had read many Greek dramas.

Jeffers said that Judith Anderson, as an actress, was "not modern, not 19th century, not Shakespearean, not medieval, not peasant,—stripped and timeless."[1]

To quote from Brooks Atkinson in *The New York Times*:

"If Medea does not understand every aspect of her whirling character, she would do well to consult Judith Anderson. For Miss Anderson understands the character more thoroughly than Medea, Euripides or the scholars, and it would be useless now for anyone else to attempt the part. Using a new text by Robinson Jeffers, she set a landmark in the theatre, where she gave a burning performance in a savage part. . . ."

[1]From R. J.'s pencilled notes.

The success of the play also promoted the sale of the book to twice the number of any other single book Jeffers had written. Such success failed to alter the life of this incorruptible man, and he and his wife returned to Tor House and their Spartan routine. But their solitude was broken—although few understood his poems, the world pressed against the gates of Tor House, curious to look at the Titan. Here they found a man even more difficult to comprehend than the poems which he wrote, a man preoccupied with his cosmic philosophy, watering his trees, writing his verses, in a setting also strange: a little Surrey stone house and the Hawk Tower, with their background of the "enormous beauty" of the Jeffers country. And his wife Una:—vivid, sparkling, gregarious —still holding in her little hand the tender love of this solitary, granitic man.

And suddenly the Jefferses were no longer alone: their son Garth, recently returned from Germany with his wife Charlotte and their infant daughter Maeve, were living at Tor House, as were Donnan and his second wife, Lee Wagner, whom he had married in March, 1947, after his separation from Patricia. The attic had been divided into two apartments for the twins and their families.

The public was now ready to listen to Jeffers, and *The New York Times*[2] was finally successful in persuading him to give his definition of poetry which he wrote under the title, "Poetry, Gongorism and a Thousand Years." After its appearance in the *Times*, it was printed in a small edition of two hundred copies by the Ward Ritchie Press of California. It is interesting to compare this mature statement with those Jeffers had written before his success and quoted elsewhere in this biography. It is rewarding to find that he had remained faithful to the rules he had laid down thirty years earlier: "Poetry is bound to concern itself chiefly with permanent things and the permanent aspects of life"; to write not only for his contemporaries but also for the audience "two thousand years away."

POETRY, GONGORISM AND A THOUSAND YEARS

It used to be argued, and I think it is still accepted by many people, that poetry is a flower of racial childhood and must wither away as

[2]*The New York Times Magazine*, January 18, 1948.

civilization advances. For civilization is based on reason and restraint, poetry on imagination and passion; poetry (they say) is dreams, and civilization the daylight that disperses them. This would be an interesting theory if it were true, but there is no truth in it. The greatest Greek poetry, after Homer, was written at the clear and rational summit of Greek civilization, by the Athenian tragic poets in the fifth century B.C.; and then, as civilization declined, Greek poetry declined. It had its revivals, in Sicily, in Alexandria, and these coincided with revivals of civilization. Latin poetry also, though less typcal, because the Romans were not originators but cultivators, has a similar history. It flowered at the peak of Roman civilization, in the late republic and early empire, and declined with it.

These are but two examples out of many that could be cited, but they are enough to scuttle the supposed rule. They do not reverse it, for actually there is no rule at all; or at least none is discernible. Poetry is less bound by time and circumstances than any other of the arts; it does not need tangible materials; good poetry comes almost directly from a man's mind and senses and bloodstream, and no one can predict the man. It does not need a school nor an immediate tradition; and it does not need, though Whitman said so, "great audiences too." How much of an audience did Keats have in his lifetime?

The present is a time of high civilization rapidly declining: it is not a propitious period for any of the arts; men's minds are a little discouraged, and are too much occupied with meeting each day's distractions or catastrophe. Yet there is no final reason why great poetry would not be written by someone, even today. Whether its greatness would be recognized is another question, for greatness is strange, unexpected and sometimes repellent, but probably it would, in time.

What seems to me certain is that this hypothetical great poet would break sharply away from the directions that are fashionable in contemporary poetic literature. He would understand that Rimbaud was a young man of startling genius but not to be imitated; and that "The Waste Land," though one of the finest poems of this century and surely the most influential, marks the close of a literary dynasty, not the beginning. He would think of Gerard Hopkins as a talented eccentric, whose verse is so overloaded with self-conscious ornament and improbable emotion that it is hardly readable, except by enthusiasts, and certainly not a model to found one's work on, but a shrill note of warning.

Aside from these instances, and to put the matter more fundamentally, I believe that our man would turn away from the self-consciousness and naive learnedness, the undergraduate irony, unnatural metaphors, hiatuses and labored obscurity that are too prevalent in contemporary verse. His poetry would be natural and direct. He would have something new and important to say, and just for that reason he would wish to say it clearly. He would be seeking to express the spirit of his time (as well as of all times), but it is not necessary, because each epoch is confused, that its poet should share its confusion.

On the contrary, detachment is necessary to understanding. I do not think that Shakespeare mixed Hamlet or Lear into his life, as Byron did Childe Harold; the greater poet saw his creations objectively, all the way through, but also all the way around; and thus our supposed poet, being distinctly separate from his time, would be able to see it and to see around it. And I do not think he would give much attention to its merely superficial aspects, the neon lights and toothpaste advertising of this urban civilization, and the momentary popular imbecilities; these things change out of recognition, but great poetry is pointed at the future. Its author, whether consciously or not, intends to be understood a thousand years from now; therefore he chooses the more permanent aspects of things, and subjects that will remain valid. And therefore he would distrust the fashionable poetic dialect of his time; but the more so if it is studiously quaint and difficult; for if a poem has to be explained and diagramed even for contemporary readers, what will the future make of it?

There was a seventeenth-century Spanish poet named Gongora, a man of remarkable talents, but he invented a strange poetic idiom, a jargon of dislocated constructions and far-fetched metaphors, self-conscious singularity, studious obscurity. It is now only grotesque, but for its moment it was admired in the best circles, and it stimulated many imitators. Then fashion changed, Gongorism was named and ridiculed, and its poet is now remembered because his name was given to one of the diseases of literature.

Euphuism in England had a similar vogue and a similar catastrophe. It seems to me that the more extreme tendencies of modernist verse —and shall I say also of painting and sculpture?—are diseases of like nature, later forms of Gongorism; doctrinaire corruptions of instinct. It is not generally a failure of execution but a collapse of taste—of critical and creative instinct—that brings an art to eclipse. The error in the artist, which perhaps was only momentary and experimental, is echoed with approval by his admirers and a shoal of imitators, and gregariousness and snobbery complete corruption. ("We understand this art, which the ordinary person can only gape at: we are distinguished people.") So the flock gathers sheep.

But poetry has never fallen so deep into this bog as painting and sculpture have, and I believe is now pulling out of it. Poetry must use language, which has a resistant vitality of its own; while sculpture (for instance) may sink to fiddling with bits of wire and tin trinkets.

On the other hand, let it be far from me to propose the average educated man as an arbiter of poetry or any other art. He has his own perversions of taste or complete nullity, duller than Gongorism. Usually he does not care for poetry—and no harm in that—but alas that he has a deep uneasy respect for it; he associates it vaguely with "ideals" and a better world, and may quote Longfellow on solemn occasions. This piety without instinct or judgment is a source of boredom, insincerity and false reputations; it is as bad as the delusions of the little groups; it is worse, because more constant.

I write verses myself, but I have no sympathy with the notion that the world owes a duty to poetry, or any other art. Poetry is not a civilizer, rather the reverse, for great poetry appeals to the most primitive instincts. It is not necessarily a moralizer; it does not necessarily improve one's character; it does not even teach good manners. It is a beautiful work of nature, like an eagle or a high sunrise. You owe it no duty. If you like it, listen to it; if not, let it alone.

Lately I had occasion to read more attentively the *Medea* of Euripides, and considering the reverence that cultivated people feel toward Greek tragedy I was a little shocked by what I read. Tragedy has been regarded, ever since Aristotle, as a moral agent, a purifier of the mind and emotions. But the story of *Medea* is about a criminal adventurer and his gun-moll: it is no more moral than the story of Frankie and Johnny; only more ferocious. And so with the yet higher summits of Greek tragedy, the Agamemnon series and the Oedipus Rex; they all tell primitive horror-stories, and the conventional pious sentiments of the chorus are more than balanced by the bad temper and wickedness, or folly of the principal characters. What makes them noble is the poetry; the poetry, and the beautiful shapes of the plays, and the extreme violence born of extreme passion.

That is to say, three times, the poetry—the poetry of words, the poetry of structure and the poetry of action. These are stories of disaster and death, and it is not in order to purge the mind of passions but because death and disaster are exciting. People love disaster, if it does not touch them too nearly—as we run to see a burning house or a motor crash—and also it gives occasion for passionate speech; it is a vehicle for the poetry.

To return now to the great poet whom we have imagined arising among us at this time. He would certainly avoid the specialists, the Gongorist groups, and he would hardly expect response from the average, the average educated person: then whom should he speak to?

205

For poetry is not a monologue in a vacuum; it is written in solitude, but it needs to have some sort of audience in mind. Well: there has been a great poet in our time—must I say comparatively great?—an Irishman named Yeats, and he met this problem, but his luck solved it for him. The first half of his life belonged mostly to the specialists, the Celtic Twilight people, the Decadents, even the Gongorists; he was the best among them but not a great poet, and he resented it. He had will and ambition, while Dowson and the others dropped by the way-side.

Yeats went home to Ireland and sought in the theatre his liberation from mediocrity; and he might possibly have found it there if he had been as good a playwright as he was a poet. For the theatre—unless it is a very little one—cannot belong wholly to a group; it has to be filled if possible; and it does not inevitably belong to the average. When many people together see and hear the thing—if it is fierce enough, and the actors and author can make it beautiful—it cuts deep. It cuts through many layers. The average person may even forget his education and delight in it, though it is poetry.

But Yeats found in another way his immortality. He was not a first-rate playwright but he had an insuperable will; and when his Ireland changed he was ready. Suddenly in that magic time when a country becomes a nation, it was Ireland's good fortune that there was a great poet in Ireland. Her unique need, and his will, had produced him.

But the great poet whom we have imagined would not expect all that luck. He might not have a fighting will, as Yeats did, to push on with time and abide its turnings; or his time might never come. If he should write a great poetic play he would probably never see it staged; for that is a matter of luck, and against the odds. And it is not likely that his country will ever feel the need of a great national poet, as Ireland did; or as Germany did in her stormy awakening, and produced Goethe. Yet our poet must feel (in his own mind I mean) the stimulation of some worthy audience. He will look, of course, to the future. "What do I care about the present?" Charles Lamb exclaimed. "I write for antiquity!"

But our man will reverse that. It may seem unlikely that he will have readers a thousand years from now, but it is not impossible, if he is really a great poet; and these are the audience whom he will habitually address. If the present time overhears him, and listens too—all the better. But let him not be distracted by the present; his business is with the future. This is not pleasantry; it is practical advice.

For thus his work will be sifted of what is transient and crumbling, the chaff of time and the stuff that require footnotes. Permanent things, or things forever renewed, like the grass and human passions, are the materials for poetry; and whoever speaks across the gap of a thousand years will understand that he has to speak of permanent things, and rather clearly too, or who would hear him?

"But," a young man cries, "what good will it do me to imagine myself remembered after death? If I am to have fame and an audience I want them now while I can feel them." It seems to me that the young man speaks in ignorance. To be peered at and interviewed, to be pursued by idlers and autograph hunters and inquiring admirers, would surely be a sad nuisance. And it is destructive too, if you take it seriously; it wastes your energy into self-consciousness; it destroys spontaneity and soils the springs of the mind. Whereas posthumous reputation could do you no harm at all, and is really the only kind worth considering.

XX

THE HURT HAWK

EARLY IN MAY, 1948, the Jefferses drove Garth and his family to their new home at McKenzie Bridge in Oregon where Garth had taken a job with the United States Forest Service. After spending a few days to help Charlotte get settled in her new home, Robin and Una returned to Tor House. Problems had arisen over the road-tour for "Medea" and it was necessary for Jeffers to appeal to the Dramatists' Guild for arbitration in the matter. Una feared that they might have to postpone their plan to leave for Ireland, but within a few days prior to their date of departure the situation was resolved, and they left Carmel by plane on June 7, arriving in Shannon, Ireland, on June 12. They had left Donnan and Lee to take care of Tor House.

The first month, the Jefferses toured over the countryside, re-visiting many of the ancient round towers. At Drumcliffe, Una was delighted to learn from the sexton that plans were under way to comply with Yeats' wish and move his remains from France, where he had died in 1939, to the cemetery at Drumcliffe. Una's interest in anything pertaining to Yeats was as lively as ever, and she was as pleased as if she had made the arrangements herself.

But their happy days of vacationing came to an abrupt end, when, on July 11, in a small hotel in Kilkenny, Jeffers caught a severe chill. He complained to Una of a pain in his side, and, since it was unusual for him to have even a mild illness, Una was con-cerned enough to doctor him with aspirin and whiskey and a brisk walk. But during the night the discomfort increased to such an extent that he was forced to leave his bed and sit in a chair the rest of the night, groaning with every painful breath. In the morning, Una called the local physician, Dr. Roche, who diagnosed Jeffers' illness as intercostal rheumatism. After two more days and nights of suffering, the doctor persuaded Jeffers to enter St. John's Hospital for x-rays. These indicated pleurisy.

Una spent anxious hours in the hospital room. She tried to distract her husband from his misery by describing to him the loveliness of the Virginia creeper on the wall outside the window, which had turned red from the cold nights, and the beauty of the hills beyond the bend of the river Norde, which were tufted with yellow hay cocks. But it was Jeffers' first experience in a hospital, and he deeply resented this enforced sacrifice of his privacy.

Una lost track of the endless days of rain, with Robin showing no improvement. Finally Dr. Roche called in an eminent Dublin chest specialist, Dr. Pringle, for a consultation. Anxiously Una listened to the diagnosis: Jeffers was suffering from a streptococcus infection in the pleural cavity with encroachment on the heart. The doctor explained that Jeffers' arteries were hardened beyond his age, making the heart condition more serious, and advised Una to move her husband to Elpi's Private Hospital in Dublin.

The distance from Kilkenny to Dublin is 76 miles, and the ambulance trip taxed Jeffers alarmingly. Una found a cheerful room nearby on Northumberland Road. She was frantic at being alone without family or friends and Robin so seriously ill. But a few days after she had arrived in Dublin the Whiteheads came, having heard in London of his illness. She almost wept with relief, as she had just been told the alarming news that new x-rays showed many lesions in the lung covering which called for a complicated treatment, as this infection had to be dealt with separately. But two days later Jeffers' condition showed a marked improvement, and she urged the Whiteheads to return to London.

August 2 was the Jefferses' thirty-fifth wedding anniversary and the third that they had spent in Ireland. The loveliest anniversary gift that Una had ever received was when Dr. Pringle assured her that Robin was out of danger.

August 15 found Jeffers still improving, though slowly. A wild wind howled down the hospital corridors and whistled through the keyholes. The Jefferses thought nostalgically of Tor House—if they could only get home they would not care if they *never* saw Ireland again! Today was the 29th anniversary of their moving into Tor House—the home they loved so warmly. But Dr. Pringle refused to release Jeffers until he was certain that he could make the journey home without dangerous complications.

On August 23, "Medea" was to open at the Edinburgh Music Festival, and the Whiteheads had urged Una to accompany them. Jeffers was so greatly improved that she yielded to their importunities and flew to Edinburgh to meet them.

Watching the "Medea," Una found it difficult to disassociate herself from the New York performance. Eileen Herlie, who played Medea in the Edinburgh production, was too young for the part, and, despite her sincere efforts, she lacked Judith Anderson's poisonous passion. Others in the cast also fell below Una's expectations, and the recorded music was too faint to be effective. She was surprised that the play was well received by both the public and the press. "The production was adequate but quite uninspired," to put it in the words of Percy Peacock.

Una left Edinburgh the next day and flew to London to spend a few quiet days with her good friend Bess O'Sullivan. She suddenly realized how deadly tired she was and what a tax on her own health the anxiety over Robin had been. Here Percy Peacock called on her—it proved to be the last time that they saw each other, for Percy died the following February. Una wrote of their visit:

"At the time he did not seem ill, but though at times he was exactly the same as of yore, there were moments when he seemed a little vague and confused and dull. . . . The last letter I was ever to have from him was a very loving one in late November. An adorable letter, really, recapitulating our long friendship. . . ."[1]

After thirty-seven years, Percy still held a picture of the young Una in his heart. His letter to her said, in part:

". . . if I were alone I would transfer myself to California to be near you for the rest of my life. How little you have changed! The same

[1] Letter from Una to M. B. B. June, 1949.

gaiety, the same vitality, courage, sincerity, real simplicity and the same wonderful charm that is indescribable! You seemed to me so little changed, and it was so easy for me to picture you as you were once physically, although the changes even there seemed to be comparatively small. In fact you were the old, or rather the young, Una. How changeless for us are the few people we really love. . . ."

By the time Una returned to Dublin on August 30, she was rested, and she found Jeffers in a much more optimistic frame of mind. So it was a great shock when, five days later, he was back in bed with unexpected complications. On September 4, during the drainage of the pleural cavity, Jeffers had collapsed. Frantically the doctors worked over him, and it was well over an hour before his breathing was restored to normal and the crisis was past. It was explained that an embolism had occurred, an air bubble in the bloodstream passing to the brain. Jeffers was delirious for two days and constantly prayed: "God help me, God, I beseech you, help me." He did not recognize Una. The doctors and nurses who had grown so fond of her found her suffering and anxiety heart-breaking.

Miraculously Jeffers rallied again, and his condition steadily improved so that by the 17th of September Una was allowed to take him for a drive in the car. She took him to St. Patrick's Cathedral to see the unique marble stairs which she had found so beautiful, and Swift's and Stella's graves and epitaphs, then to her little room where she had been cared for so lovingly by her landlady, Mrs. Hudson. The outing evidently was good for him, and each day his strength improved.

In the meantime "Medea" had opened in Birmingham where it received a great ovation and had an enthusiastic reception from the press. It may have been that Miss Herlie's performance was more convincing than it had been in Edinburgh. In October the play had a thunderous first-night reception in London, with twelve curtain calls. But the critics disagreed with the public. Geoffrey Tarron, in the *Morning Advertiser*, wrote: "Jeffers' simplification has seriously dulled the play's impact . . . ." He also complained that Eileen Herlie's acting had been "handicapped" by Jeffers! Beverly Baxter, in the *Evening Standard*, wrote: ". . . a vulgar and abreviated version of the tragedy . . . ." Cecil Wilson, in the *Daily Mail*, was almost complimentary with his grudging appraisal: ". . . Mr. Jeffers' free verse treatment has moments of poetic force . . ."

The Glasgow Herald had accepted the play as different, but, ". . . This adaptation, free as it is, intensifies the tragedy for a modern audience . . ." In Birmingham, the critics had been sincerely complimentary, agreeing with the enthusiasm of the audience.

On September 20, nearly two months since Jeffers was first stricken that cold night in Kilkenny, he had recovered his strength sufficiently to be allowed to leave for California. Una's worries would have defeated a less valiant woman. Arriving at the airport at 9:30 in the evening, they had to wait until long after midnight in the discomfort of the terminal before the AOA plane finally took off. They had had a nasty time with customs, and Jeffers had been compelled to have a tiring wait in line. By the time they boarded the plane, they were both exhausted, but further trials awaited them. More than a dozen of the fifty seats were unoccupied, but there were no double seats available despite the assurance of the Dublin AOA office that the Jefferses would have reserved space together. The steward was coolly disinterested in Una's problem of a sick husband, and shrugged them indifferently to separate seats. Una wasn't easily brushed aside, and she wrote in her diary:

"I stood in the aisle and assumed the most determined and hateful air and said, 'I will not sit down except with my husband.' The steward looked hateful too, but I wouldn't budge. Finally the hostess asked several people to move to other seats. They wouldn't. Finally one young American woman volunteered to sit with another woman and so we were adjusted. A very boring trip. Got very hot. It was hard to breathe although the cabin was supposed to be pressurized. It was a Constellation plane. The air got so hot and foul I complained to the steward but he said that at that altitude they couldn't change the air. All the men were in shirt-sleeves and took off their ties. I used my ammonia smelling salts and slept very little. Robin was sweating and took off his coat and I feared he'd get chilled. . . . Arrived in NY hours late."

On September 23, they arrived home. Una describes this happy experience in her diary:

". . . Lovely sunshine and California looking beautiful. Tor House awaited us with flag flying from the top of the tower. (Donnan had hoisted it before dawn.) *A great surprise.* A little plot of lawn by the sun dial, and shellpath in the courtyard and big beds of flowers in bloom. How they worked to accomplish this. The house was spick and span. Robin climbed happily into bed, and looked out over our wonderful rocks with great waves foaming over them. Lindsay was already laughing and playing with us . . . the lovely Rose-a-Lindsay. I felt as if a tractor had run over me several times, but I was very happy to get home again in my own dear place."

While Jeffers was lying ill in Ireland, his fourteenth book of poems, *The Double Axe, and Other Poems,* was published. It was Jeffers' first book in seven years and concerns itself with the theme of wars—the unnecessary wars that were contributing to the decline of our civilization. Through the characters of this tale of fury and foulness, Jeffers cries out, "Deliver us from evil."

The long poem, "The Double Axe," is in two parts. The first, "The Love and the Hate," the second, "The Inhumanist." This, with twenty-seven short poems, makes up the volume.

In the twenty-seven short poems written in the years between 1941 and 1947, Jeffers continues his exploration of the imbecility and betrayals of our political leaders. "We have enjoyed fine dreams; we have dreamed of unifying the world; we are unifying it—against us."[2] Of man's perversities he reminds us, "Truly men hate the truth; they'd liefer/Meet a tiger in the road";[3] of the futility of our wars and the burden of our peace.

Because Jeffers sees our intervention in World Wars I and II as ill spent and believes that future historians will justify his opinion, his publishers inserted a "Note" in the volume *The Double Axe,* stating that they "feel compelled to go on record with its disagreement over some of the political views pronounced by the poet in this volume." This statement proved a great embarrassment to the publishers, Random House. It drew a flood of indignant comment from the reviewers of the book, and there were almost as many words devoted to the statement of the publishers as to the book itself. They even went so far as to state their own po-

[2]"So Many Blood Lakes."
[3]"Cassandra."

213

litical opinions before going on with the review of the book. The ugly truth of these poems, in their setting of beautiful words and beautiful scenery, were, surprisingly enough, received most enthusiastically by the majority of the reviewers. The prose preface is as thought-challenging as any of the poems and merits a careful consideration.

The first part of *The Double Axe* was written during the war and finished a year before the war ended, and it bears the scars; but the poem is not primarily concerned with that grim folly. Its burden, as of some previous work of mine, is to present a certain philosophical attitude, which might be called Inhumanism, a shifting of emphasis and significance from man to not-man; the rejection of human solipsism and recognition of the transhuman magnificence. It seems time that our race began to think as an adult does, rather than like an egocentric baby or insane person. This manner of thought and feeling is neither misanthropic nor pessimist, though two or three people have said so and may again. It involves no falsehoods, and is a means of maintaining sanity in slippery times; it has objective truth and human value. It offers a reasonable detachment as rule of conduct, instead of love, hate and envy. It neutralizes fanaticism and wild hopes; but it provides magnificence for the religious instinct, and satisfies our need to admire greatness and rejoice in beauty.

The shorter poems that tail the book are expressions, in their different ways, of the same attitude. A few of them have been printed previously; three in *Poetry* Magazine, one in the *University of Kansas City Review*, two in *The Saturday Review of Literature*; several in some recent anthologies.

As to the Publishers' Note that introduces this volume, let me say that it is here with my cheerful consent, and represents a quite normal difference of opinion. But I believe that history (though not popular history) will eventually take sides with me in these matters. Surely it is clear even now that the whole world would be better off if America had refrained from intervention in the European war of 1914; I think it will become equally clear that our intervention in the Second World War has been—even terribly—worse in effect. And this intervention was not forced but intentional; we were making war, in fact though not in name, long before Pearl Harbor. But it is futile at present to argue these matters. And they are not particularly important, so far as this book is concerned; they are only the background, or moral climate, of its thought and action.

R. J.

This was a serious breakdown of the harmonious entente which had existed between Random House and Jeffers during the lifetime of Saxe Cummins. Since his death, there had been indications that the publishers had become indifferent to the prestige Jeffers had brought to them or were doubtful about his future. There were other publishers who were ready to place Jeffers on their list, and I pleaded with both Una and Jeffers to make the break. They were, however, loyal to Bennett Cerf and Random House. Later developments proved, however, that it was misplaced for, regardless of pleas of professors and students for long-out-of-print books which were necessary for class room work, the publishers did not even bother to answer the inquiries which eventually reached my desk. After Jeffers' death, the committee of friends, which was formed to honor his memory, urged Random House to publish Jeffers in paper backs and to bring the *Selected Poetry* up to date.

During 1948, Jeffers had started work on another play to be called "Mary Stuart," based on Schiller's version. Although the first act was completed, he stopped work on it because, he said, he was unable sincerely to "feel" the story.

Judith Anderson was pushing Jeffers to adapt "Tower Beyond Tragedy" for the stage, as she had not relinquished her intention to play Clytemnestra to a Broadway audience. But Jeffers couldn't be aroused to enthusiasm for the idea.

XXI

DEAREST, GOOD-BYE

DURING THE YEAR 1949, "MEDEA" thundered across the United States and across the Pacific to Honolulu; it was translated into four languages, was performed in Denmark, Italy, France, and Germany and printed in full in the *Theatre Arts Magazine*; Decca Records produced a "Medea" album. Jeffers' foreword to this album is an excellent exposition on Greek drama. It is the story, in his own words, of the part Judith Anderson played in persuading him to write the adaptation:

Greek tragedy, like the English glory of Elizabethan drama, ran its whole course of production in the space of a man's lifetime, seventy years or so from beginning to end, a brief and blazing explosion of energy. It began in a time of exultation, when the great defensive war with Persia was triumphantly concluded, just as Elizabethan drama began when the epic struggle with Spain ended in victory. Both these happy periods closed in times of disorder and foreboding: in the Peloponnesian War, and in the gloom and gathering anger that prefaced the English Civil War. They were voices of triumph. National triumph inaugurated them; national and social disorder ended them. And there are many other resemblances between these two bursts of dramatic and poetic energy, though the English and Athenian flowerings are separated from each other by a complete change of culture and outlook and circumstance. And by more than two thousand years.

When we think of Elizabethan drama we think first of Shakespeare and then of the many others. But Greek tragedy has three heads instead of one: Aeschylus, Sophocles, Euripides; and whatever we English-speakers may think, it is likely that each one of the three stands as high in world-literature, and surely in world-estimation, as Shakespeare does. Euripides was the youngest of this triumverate, and he was never so entirely accepted by his contemporaries as the others were; but in later time his influence was deeper and wider. When an Alexandrian, or a Roman like Seneca, tried to write tragedy it was generally Euripides whom he imitated. But while Euripides lived, there was always a suspicion, which in fact remains to this day, that his work was not quite moral or solid, not quite "classical," compared to the work of the two older men. Aeschylus labored the theme of sublimity; the persons of his plays, and even the language, the great mouth-filling words, are larger than life. The work of Sophocles was valued for its nobility, the dignity of his characters, the noble sweetness of thought and speech. Euripides understood, no doubt, that he could not be more sublime than Aeschylus nor more noble than Sophocles; he must make his advance in other directions. And perhaps the public showed signs of wearying a little of Aeschylean sublimity, though no one ever confessed it. The younger man had to attract and hold an audience; he had to be interesting at least, whether admirable or not. He had to be a modernist in his time; and the conservatives distrusted him. He introduced romantic incident into his plays, even if it damaged their integrity a little, and realism into character. He presented real and understandable human beings, people you could identify with yourself, rather than ideal heroes and demigods. And he introduced pathos, which is somewhat less than a tragic value; he was accused of dressing his actors in rags, in order to make the audience weep for their misfortunes.

There were other counts against Euripides. His great precursors were more than poets and play-wrights; they were also exemplary citizens. Aeschylus had fought at Marathon, that day of glory; Sophocles had taken an admired part in civic affairs, and was appointed a general of the army. But Euripides remained a private man, a disillusioned student and man of letters. The world had changed in his time, the great dream was fading. Recently Athens had been the savior of all Greece; but now Greece had fallen apart, and Athens, though grown much greater, was only an imperialistic power struggling with Sparta for supremacy, busy with confused battles and oppressions. Therefore, as many honest men have done since his time, Euripides chose to stay aloof from public life; and it seems to me that he was right in his time; but his fellow-citizens judged otherwise.

He was also accused of being a woman-hater—apparently because he was interested in women and understood them, whereas Athenian custom kept them shut up, out of sight, and generally out of mind. The elder dramatists presented types of women—the mother, the faithful wife, the devoted sister—but Euripides was hissed off the stage for showing a real woman desperately in love; his first *Phaedra*. He had to rewrite the play, cancelling half its pity and immediacy, before it could be accepted. And the two greatest plays of Euripides are about women: the *Bacchae*, a study of women gone wild with religious enthusiasm; and the incomparable *Medea*, the subject of this discourse.

Medea is the portrait of a proud woman scorned; a loving woman, whose love, rejected and betrayed, turns terribly to hatred; a barbarian woman who triumphs over Greeks in their own country; a woman of such power and guile—which the Greeks admired, remembering Odysseus—that she is able at last to stand alone against her husband and his friends and the whole city of Corinth, and overturn them. The intensity and fury of this passion is as sublime as anything in Aeschylus, but in another direction. It is as if Euripides were saying to his Athenian audience: "You have prejudices. You think yourselves superior because you are masculine, and because you are civilized Hellenes. Yet consider that you might be mistaken. Be careful. Despise no person." This is a modernist sentiment; it is something that Aeschylus would not have said nor thought. It belongs to the widening afternoon of a civilization, not the arrogant morning. But it did not make Euripides popular with his fellow citizens: the play won third prize.

However—even as I write this—I wonder whether it is wholly true. For it is hard to reconstruct the thoughts of former men, and it is easy to impute one's own interpretation into a great poem. Perhaps, to Euripides as to his audience, Medea was mostly an exciting monster, a deadly wild beast tormented by some qualms of maternal instinct; and Jason and his friends were normal unfortunate people whom the monster destroyed. That astonishing chariot drawn by winged dragons, in which Medea soars away at the end of the play (though not in my version) seems to support this view—or was it only a concession to the well-known Greek love of stage-machinery?

This play by Euripides was not the first *Medea*, for a man named Neophron had written a tragedy on the same subject, which is lost to us, only a six-line fragment surviving. But there is no doubt that Euripides used it as a starting-point, just as Shakespeare used for his own purposes the earlier and otherwise forgotten play about Hamlet . . . and I speak of Neophron's *Medea* because it is vaguely comforting to me to know that— if I have ventured to adapt a Greek tragedy to modern uses—Euripides did it first. Since his time, of course, there have been numberless adaptations; and this one of mine will not be the last—but,

218

I thought, as I watched Judith Anderson's great and creative art, surely the luckiest!

It is nearly four years, I believe, since Miss Anderson asked me to make an adaptation of *Medea* for her. Her reason needs some explanation. She had become interested several years before that in a dramatic poem of mine called "The Tower Beyond Tragedy," in which Greek myth is used more or less in the Greek manner, but it is not an adaptation of any play. Miss Anderson considered that this poem needed but a little clipping in order to fit it for the stage, and she wanted the part of Clytemnestra in it; but producers were naturally suspicious of a poem not primarily intended for acting, and written by an author unknown as a dramatist. The play was finally staged in the village of Carmel, California, in our outdoor theater in the midst of a pine-forest. The direction was spotty, rehearsals hurried, and the cast partly amateur, but the play's allotted four nights were locally very successful; it must have been seen by a good part of the population of this region. Miss Anderson's part in it was of course magnificent; and her desire to have it professionally staged remained unabated. Eventually she was told by one of the most well-known New York producers that he was not willing to undertake "The Tower" but, if she could get me to write a "Medea," he would consider it. She accepted the compromise; in the hope, she says, that it might serve as a stepping-stone toward an eventual production of "The Tower;" and I, though I have never before made a poem to order, was glad to attempt this one, only stipulating that I must be allowed large freedom of adaptation, because every Greek tragedy contains passages that would seem very dull, and others that would seem absurd (on account of changes of taste, interest, and convention) to a present-day audience.

The writing progressed rapidly; and I am bound to say that I had not only the benefit of Euripides for guidance, but also of some invaluable suggestions by Miss Anderson and the proposed producer, visiting me here. But the producer's contract, when it was given to me to sign, proved ridiculously unreasonable; and he would not mend it, and I would not accept it. So the matter rested. After a year or so the play was published as a book; two or three more years passed before it found producers and came to the stage.

I did not want to go to New York on the opening night; simply because I do not like to hear my own verses recited; it is a source of self-consciousness, which (for me at least) does not stimulate either happiness or productiveness. When persuasion was renewed and became compulsive, my wife and I flew to New York and were there three days.

As to my dislike of hearing my own verses recited—I need have felt no anxiety. I heard them and—to confess it—enjoyed them, as if I had had nothing to do with them. They belonged now to Judith Anderson and the others, who had renewed and vitalized the words, and made them beautiful in action. Miss Anderson of course especially—for the play is all Medea's—had taken the somewhat static attitudes and gestures which I in the Greek tradition had imagined, and the monotony with which a man says verses to himself when he is making them, and wrought all into fluid fire.

Jeffers, known formerly only to students of poetry, now became a familiar name to play-goers. But with this he was not concerned; Una was seriously ill. In February, she had been taken to the Stanford Hospital in San Francisco for treatment. Jeffers moved to the Hans Barkan home there to be near her. Una wired their friend Noel Sullivan, "I am very ill. Do what you can for Robin." Noel hastened to San Francisco to Una's bedside. She immediately thanked him for sending the priest. (But he had sent no priest.) She said she had felt much better after the priest's visit, that when she had asked the nurse who the priest was, the nurse had said, "But there was no priest." When Robin came she asked him who the priest was, and he said, "No, there was no priest." She searched Noel's face as she asked, "Who was the priest you sent, Noel?" And he gently explained that his first wish, upon receiving her message, was that he might send a priest to give her comfort, and perhaps it was this wish which had visited her.

Not until late in March was Una released from the hospital and allowed to go to Noel Sullivan's home in the Carmel Valley to convalesce under his watchful eye. She wrote from there a brief note:

"Robin and I have been spending a week with Noel. Lovely rest. Fruit trees all ablossom. I am ashamed not to have thanked you for the Christmas gifts but life has been a whirlwind and a hazard. Both boys and wives and babies were with us a fortnight over Christmas and then I am ashamed to say I got a horrible attack of flu January 5th and followed it up with a major operation. We have hitherto been so amazingly well that this kind of health record for the last year is hard for us to own up to. Robin just finally emerging from his long convalescence when I got sick. . . ."[1]

[1]Letter from Una to M.B.B. March 27, 1948.

It should perhaps be mentioned here that in 1941 Una had an operation for cancer of which few of her friends were aware. She couldn't endure admitting to being ill, although she had visited Dr. Kilgore in Monterey every six months for treatments until 1944, when she had been dismissed as cured.

Although Una was now in frail health, she tried valiantly to keep pace with the busy life at Tor House. To lighten her housekeeping duties she was persuaded, in May, to install electricity —all these years the Jefferses had continued to use their primitive lighting, heating, and cooking devices. The local papers carried the big news. Half gone, the twentieth century was finally catching up with the Jefferses. One story which Donnan tells on his father is about the time a battery of photographers arrived to take pictures of Jeffers and Tor House. Jeffers had accomodatingly assisted in unloading the van of photographic equipment, including large electric photoflash lights. When one of the workmen began futilely searching for an electric outlet, Jeffers mildly reminded them that there were none.

Again the question of installing sewer connections at the Point was raised, and, despite the protests of the property owners, work was to go ahead on it. Jeffers was roused to write a letter of protest to the Editor of the Carmel *Pine Cone*:

"I believe that the Carmel Sanitary Board is acting illegally: first, in opening bids when blocked by a majority of protest; second, in presenting a new estimate (fifty percent less) immediately after their first one was rejected.

"However, I am not going to file an injunction. It is possible, that there are one or two streets where a few houses need sewers. These should be attended to. But that does not make it necessary to dig up every road on the Point and install a complete gridiron of sewer-pipe.

"I only hope (if the protest is not sustained) that some cleverer business man than I am will make sure of two items. First, whether this low bid covers all the work; for one of the three bids opened and read was incomplete, but I did not notice which one. Second if the low bid is a complete one, whether the contractor will carry it through; for he will certainly be operating at a loss, if the first estimate meant anything at all.

"As to our own place, it is ridiculous to assess us more than six thousand dollars (according to the new cut-rate estimate) for a facility which we shall never need; while a big new house covering a little lot, which therefore perhaps really needs the service, will pay less than one hundred and fifty dollars—more than forty times less. But we shall not press this absurdity; but consider ourselves fortunate as long as we are not actually compelled to hook up with a system that at present shockingly defiles the rivermouth and may in future pollute the bay...."

But the City Fathers had little respect for the voice of their distinguished citizen and work on the sewer started in September of that year. The Jefferses were assessed $6,128.10, a high price to pay for pioneering the Point and bringing fame to Carmel. Had it not been for the success of *Medea* the Jefferses could easily have been made bankrupt or forced into selling their property and cherished privacy.

In June, Una was very ill again. She wrote: "... Melba, I've had the most terrible months of my life—from the last of June on. Sciatica. The pain is *excrutiating*...." Noel Sullivan believed that she was fully aware that she was dying of cancer but courageously hoped to keep this knowledge from her family and friends. Although she had a will of iron, by December she was so weak that it was impossible for her to prepare Christmas at Tor House for her family. Noel insisted that they spend Christmas with him at his home, Hollow Hills. Una had to be practically carried from the car into the house, but as the evening progressed she appeared to gather strength and entered into the gaiety of the occasion.

Unfortunately, there were months of suffering ahead for Una. She lay in bed looking out at the sea, while her household moved around her. Lee, Donnan's wife, had taken over the problems of running the house. Her gentleness and thoughtfulness were a great comfort to both Una and Jeffers during those difficult months. Her son, little Lindsay, toddled in and out of his grandmother's room and climbed up on her bed to be loved or read to.

But as summer came to an end, and the first fall days brought rain against the sea-window closing out the world, Una closed her eyes, sighed deeply, and died in her husband's arms, blessedly relieved of her pain.

The heart and the spirit of the graying poet were broken, and there was never a moment of the day or night that he didn't miss his beloved Una. He wrote, despairingly:

"I have been more or less stunned since September—very unhappy and useless. . . . I try to remember the thought and feeling that made my verses and are habitual to me, and I think that they have sustained me against despair—or rather *in* despair—and this loss will come into proportion after awhile. We were married for thirty-seven years and loved each other longer than that. She was so full of life, and all her ancestors and family lived beyond eighty—I never dreamed she would die before me. But it is here. . . ."[2]

Ten years previously, during Una's illness at that time, Jeffers had, though he seems to have forgotten, given thought to the possibility of losing her, for he had written:

FOR UNA

I built her a tower when I was young—
Sometime she will die—
I built it with my hands, I hung
Stones in the sky.

Old but still strong, I climb the stone—
Sometime she will die—
Climb the steep rough steps alone,
And weep in the sky.

The shadow of Una's death hung darkly over Tor House. In the incomparably beautiful poem "Hungerfield," which Jeffers wrote a year later in 1951, he cried, "Una has died, and I am left waiting for death, like a leafless tree waiting for the roots to rot and the trunk to fall. . ."

Shortly after Una's death, Jeffers at long last yielded to Judith Anderson's request to adapt his poem "Tower Beyond Tragedy" for the theater. The American National Theatre and Academy planned to use it to open their winter series, with Miss Anderson in the role of Clytemnestra. For nine years she had worked towards this end, and it was a great personal triumph for her. It seemed incredible that she could top her performance as Medea, but some critics acclaimed her Clytemnestra as the greatest role of her career.

Again Jeffers had no intention of going to New York for the

[2]Letter from R. J. to M. B. B. December 30, 1950.

opening of the play on November 26, 1950, but again he was persuaded. He was in New York for five days, and wrote:

". . . Saw the play twice. Judith is, of course, tremendous, and carried the whole thing on her shoulders. The others were fine actors, but some of them were badly miscast, and it seemed to me there were other serious errors. So I am glad that they will not re-open immediately, as was planned, after their month with ANTA . . . . The reviews were various. Brooks Atkinson, in the N.Y. Times, seemed to say that it was the best thing he had ever seen. His opinion is important, but there were many others who thought otherwise, though all of them praised Judith's extraordinary talent. To me the play seemed less impressive than the production in the Carmel Forest Theatre nine years ago. More polished, of course, but slighter and less interesting. However—I know nothing about the theatre. . . ."[3]

In Jeffers' adaptation for the stage, he cut about two hundred and twenty-five lines of the original text. Most of these lines were descriptive passages, some being replaced by stage-business in the actors' scripts. The first eleven lines of introduction were also cut, and replaced by a strong opening speech by Aeschylus:

I am Aeschylus the Athenian, a poet and a warrior.
Under one hand my sword, in the other my book.
I fought at Marathon, where we broke the enormous
     invasion.
We hunted the haughty Persians and long-haired
     Medes into the sea,
And saved our world. In the time of peace I wrote
     plays.
I wrote about Agamemnon the king of men in triumph
     returning from conquered Troy, and how lovingly
     his wife received him.
That is the theme. See: they are making ready for
     the King's homecoming
Those above are the Queen's men, and those below
Are Agamemnon's. Now the great king approaches.
     (*Entrance of Agamemnon and Clytemnestra*)
You'd never have dreamed that the Queen was Helen's
     sister—Troy's burning flower from Sparta, the
     beautiful sea-flower

[3]Letter from R. J. to M. B. B. December 30, 1950.

Cut in clear flame, crowned with the fragrant golden
 mane, she the age-less, the uncontaminable—
This Clytemnestra was her sister; low-statured, fierce-
 lipped, not dark nor blonde, greenish-gray-eyed.
Sinewed with strength, under the purple folds of the
 queen-cloak, but craftier than queenly.
Standing between the gilded wooden porch-pillars,
Awaiting the King.

Electra's last speech of the original poem has been omitted and replaced by the following dialogue which brings the play to a higher dramatic ending:

ELECTRA: Orestes, today should have been our triumph.
 We labor and conquer—and triumph, we crush our
 enemies and triumph. Oh dull and painful gain,
 that a fool plays with fools. Porter.
PORTER: Here, my lady.
ELECTRA: Fetch me a piece of rope, my brother wants
 me to hang up something—a charm to bring peace.
 Ten feet of rope.
PORTER: Yes, my lady.
ELECTRA: As for the city—let my father's dim ghost
 rule it and make its laws. Waggle old beard,
 sit on the high throne and speak judgment—but
 I'll hang higher. Hush, hush, hush.

But despite Judith Anderson's faith in "Tower" as a theater piece, it was not received enthusiastically by the public. The best analysis has been given by Jeffers' German translator, Eva Hesse, in a letter written in 1959:

". . . I am now busy reworking 'The Tower Beyond Tragedy.' It was well reviewed as a playhouse broadcast some eight years ago and again in a new broadcast last year, and it was an outstanding success when read about two years ago on a Hamburg stage; yet when it was acted for the first time in Vienna it drew very lukewarm reviews, and when it was acted in Germany shortly afterwards it was only a middling success. The two principle trouble factors appear to be (a) it was not, like *Medea*, originally conceived as a stage play and must therefore live by its poetic force rather than by its dramatic structure; (b) the slaying of Cassandra after Clytemnestra does not go well on the stage, two corpses are too many out there in the footlights; also the ensuing dialogue between Orest and Electra is a little confused (due to Orest's derangement) and needs paring down to be properly effective on the stage. When one reads the play or listens to it over the radio these points are not readily noticeable, but when one sees it acted out before one's eyes one realizes what is wrong. . . ."[4]

This same year (1951) Jeffers received the Eunice Tietjens Memorial Prize for a group of poems which appeared in *Poetry* Magazine. True to the inscription over his fireplace: "Seek not to bask you by a stranger's hearth, our own blue smoke is warmer than their fire," Jeffers kept to his even rhythm of verse-making and stone-laying. Lee guarded his privacy as faithfully as had Una. On December 18, Lee gave birth to a lovely baby daughter, named Una Sherwood—fair-haired and blue-eyed, with delicate features. Garth and his wife and three children visited Tor House as often as was possible.

Progress was slow on the stone "annex" which Jeffers and Donnan were building for Lee's and Donnan's growing family. Boulders, which had been Jeffers' for the hauling, suddenly became front yard props of the many houses which had sprung up along "Jeffers Point" and far beyond. In an attempt to complete the house, it was decided to make the garage of brick and to spare what few boulders were available for the house itself.

On October 4, 1952, the Julien Philbert translation of Jeffers' *Medea* opened at Le Théâtre Montparnasse-Gaston Baty in Paris, with Marguerite Jamois in the role of Medea. And in December, Jeffers' poem *Hungerfield* was printed in a private edition of 30 copies by the Grabhorn Press of San Francisco.

The poem *Hungerfield* is addressed to Una—a reminiscence of bright moments shared, but a lamentation in gray:

> It is not that I am lonely for you. I am lonely:
> I am mutilated, for you were part of me:
> But men endure that. I am growing old and my love
> is gone:
> No doubt I can live without you, bitterly and well.
> That's not the cry. My torment is memory
> My grief to have seen the banner and beauty of your
> brave life

[4]Letter from Frau Hesse to M. B. B., 1959.

Dragged in the dust down the dim road to death. To
    have seen you defeated,
You who never despaired, passing through weakness
And pain—
        to nothing.

Jeffers then moves into the story of the man Hungerfield, who
lived at Horse Creek, and his fight against Death. But the opening
and closing passages, addressed to Una, are the most tender and
exquisite that Jeffers has ever written:

. . . You are earth and air; you are in the beauty
    of the ocean
And the great streaming triumphs of sundown; you
    are alive and well in the tender young
    grass rejoicing
When soft rain falls all night, and the little
    rosy-fleeced clouds float on the dawn . . . .

In January, 1954, Random House published a volume of Jeffers' poems under the title *Hungerfield and Other Poems*, which
included "The Cretan Woman" and fourteen short poems, seven
of them being those which had won him the Eunice Tietjens
award. This was the first major book of poems since the publication of *The Double Axe* in 1948. It enjoyed no large sales, and yet
it will probably be the most important of Jeffers' books. After the
success of the theatrical presentation of *Medea*, Random House
was encouraged to reprint the book to meet the demand, which
had resulted in the sale of over 8,000 copies. The furor over *The
Double Axe* drew added attention to the work of the poet, and yet
six years later, this great work was almost passed by.

"The Cretan Woman," based on the *Hippolytus* of Euripides, is
a dramatic poem that Jeffers wrote with Agnes Moorehead in
mind. In structure it differs greatly from "The Tower Beyond
Tragedy" or even "Medea" in that the dialogue is broken down
into very few lines which accelerates the pace of the piece. It was
first acted on the Arena Stage in Washington, D.C., in May, 1954,
enjoying a twelve-week run. And on July 8, the Provincetown
Players presented it, and it was so well received that it played until September. Unfortunately neither company was competent
enough to meet the demands of this dramatic play, which calls

for actors widely experienced in interpreting passionate emotions. In the part of Phaedra there are many nuances which call for the skill of a great actress.

In an interview in *The New York Times* (July, 1954), Jeffers explains his conception of the play:

"How I came to write the version of the play is of no importance to anyone; but I am willing to speak on the subject, if you are to listen. It is not my trade to write plays from the Greek, nor any other kinds of plays, but when Judith Anderson asked me to write a 'Medea' for her I assented, of course; and the play had a considerable success—thanks to Miss Anderson—in New York and across the country. Therefore another actress, who was almost as famous, asked me to write for her a version of 'Phaedra', and again I consented, as I always do at a cocktail party.

"It was a cocktail party, not a contract. My wife and I were going to visit Ireland and the Hebrides again, and I never thought of Phaedra until I fell ill—a brand-new experience for me—and was hospitalized in Kilkenny and Dublin. There—it was a pleasant hospital, with Irish nurses—I remembered my promise and began to write my Phaedra— 'The Cretan Woman'—between the smooth sheets of a bed. It was finished during the lazy weeks of convalescence, after we flew home to California.

"I sent a copy of the manuscript to the actress who had asked for it; but she meanwhile had divorced her husband and developed new ambitions. I did not send a copy to Judith Anderson, because she had told me, long before, that she was not interested in Phaedra.

"So I let the manuscript lie in a drawer for six years and then brought it out to add it to a book of my poems that was being published. I did not remember it well and I read it with interest. The thing was better than I remembered, and seemed not to show any scars of the violent pleurisy that helped me write it."

In the Jeffers version, Phaedra has been made the important character. Hippolytus is frankly drawn as a homosexual who scorns Phaedra's advances—and refuses to do homage to the goddess of love, Aphrodite. But Jeffers explains his shift of emphasis in a letter to Gene de Wild of the Pasadena Play House:

"Hippolytus rashly incurred the anger of Aphrodite and was destroyed by her. That is the Greek story, and more interesting I think than to put all the blame on Phaedra. It provides another dimension. As

228

to Artemis, she didn't interest me. She is only a goddess, Aphrodite is a force of nature.

"As to my Hippolytus being homosexual—I thought I got a hint of it from Euripides. Anyway, it came to my mind and seemed appropriate. You don't write with conscious reasons but take what comes to mind.

"As to Hippolytus' horses running away, scared by a sea-beast, in answer to prayer—it seems a little funny, a sort of superfluous miracle. I don't like miracles, they distract attention from the play. And Theseus, with his record of homicide—it is natural for him to kill his son with a sword, not a prayer.

"I quoted the prayer (in reverse sense) in order to say: 'Yes, I know. I am changing the story a little. I think this way is more likely.'"

Friends had been urging Jeffers to edit Una's diaries which she had written on their travels in the British Isles and Ireland. Theodore Lilienthal, one of Jeffers' long-time friends, took over the responsibility of having it published, and selected The Ward Ritchie Press of Los Angeles for the job. Jeffers proceeded with the editing of the diaries which sharpened his sense of loss and provoked too many memories. But finally his task was completed.

Visits to Ireland was published the latter part of 1954, a small book of only fifty-six pages, representing only a fraction of Una Jeffers' diaries. Una's love of Ireland, her appreciative eye for color, her delight in the Irish people, all shine through. There is no literary effort here, but terse as are the entries, there is style. The only pity is that the diaries were not published in full.

In 1955, the "annex" was nearing completion, and the old garage was successfully converted into a new kitchen. Lee Jeffers wrote:

"We had a door jack-hammered through the wall from the dining-room into the garage. The garage was extended into the court yard with a large bay window—Then Donnan built a wonderful fireplace—and with much, much more work the result is a large and really most charming kitchen—the old kitchen has become the most minute Library to bear so grand a title—very cosy and sweet though, and we all love the changes—gives us so much more room. . . ."[5]

[5]Letter from Lee Jeffers to M. B. B. March 3, 1955.

XXII

SUNSET

JEFFERS TOOK ONE LAST TRIP to Ireland, in 1956, accompanied by his son Donnan, Lee, and their two children, Lindsay and Una. But their trip was cut short by the disturbing news that the City of Carmel planned to start condemnation proceedings against Jeffers' property, intending to use it for a city park. Lee Jeffers wrote:

". . . the dismal and heart-breaking reason for our almost immediate return—a Master Plan for Carmel—a map showing Tor House as a Memorial Library and Robin's land as a public park. The matter upset Robin dreadfully. He detested the thought of having the land tied up by zoning laws, etc., for many years with him paying taxes and not being able to sell if the necessity arose. . . . as soon as we returned Robin resubdivided 10 of the lower lots into three large building sites and sold them, feeling if there were a few more houses and owners to contend with, the plan for a park would be less desirable. . . . seeing the trees go down has been the hardest to bear. . . ."[1]

Although no immediate action was taken by the city, Jeffers suffered constant anxiety. As if in league with the city to harrass the aging recluse who had brought fame to Carmel, the post office then took his rural box number away from him and assigned it to someone else down the street. Letters which continued to come addressed to the old number were stamped with a large warning

[1]Letter from Lee Jeffers to M. B. B., December, 1956.

230

that he must advise his correspondents of his new address. Hundreds of students of poetry, professors, and translators throughout the world knew only that his address was "Carmel," California, and so addressed him, causing considerable inconvenience to the local post office.

From 1954 until 1960, the fields lay fallow. Poems were being written, but not enough to complete a new volume. Voluminous notes were written for a long narrative to be called "Christane," but the effort of making it into a poem was beyond Jeffers' strength. From the winter of 1958 through 1961, one illness followed another, and in each instance Jeffers' doctor, Richard Creedan, despaired of his recovery. But Lee and Donnan lovingly nursed him back to life. After each illness, the Titan was a little weaker until he had no strength for visitors and only faint interest in verse-making.

Donnan took over the task of completing the rock work on the "annex," and in 1958 it was finished, and Lee moved her family from Tor House into their new quarters. However, Lindsay, like his grandfather, cherished his privacy, so he moved back to the loft of Tor House.

The cypresses and eucalyptus trees which Jeffers had planted had grown into an almost impenetrable forest, as had the gorse, dwarfing the houses and the tower and all but concealing them. In answer to a letter of inquiry as to why such an exotic species as the eucalyptus thrived so well on this coast while the Monterey cypress was apparently deteriorating, Jeffers answered,

"I can't answer letters, but I am interested in trees. This Point was bare to the sea-wind when we first came here, and eucalyptus could not have grown up without cypress to shelter it.

"Once in northwestern Ireland we were told that the biggest tree in Ireland grew in a Monastery garden nearby. It was huge, and it was a Monterey cypress. —Also the south of England is full of them—mostly clipped into hedges. . . ."[2]

Although these were not productive years for Jeffers, they brought him added honors. In 1955 he received the Borestone Mountain Poetry Award for *Hungerfield* and a prize of $1,250. In June, 1955, Occidental College celebrated the 50th anniver-

2Letter to Ogden Plumb, July, 1958, Tor House Collection.

sary of Jeffers' graduation with a special exhibition of his works and a handsome check-list printed by The Ward Ritchie Press. A tribute program was held at which Lawrence Clark Powell and Joseph Wood Krutch were the speakers. Powell, also a distinguished alumnus of Occidental, was, at the time, librarian of the University of California at Los Angeles, and is author of several books, including the thesis which he had written in 1932 while at the University of Dijon, *Robinson Jeffers, the Man and His Work.* Jeffers' health prevented his attendance at the event, but a recording was made of his voice reading a few of his poems and accepting the honor which his college was bestowing on him.

In 1958, Jeffers received further honors in the form of a $5,000 award from the Academy of American Poets. Again he declined to appear in person to accept this honor. In the spring of 1960, Stanford University library had an important exhibition of Jeffers' works, arranged by Theodore Lilienthal and including many of the rare items in Mr. Lilienthal's private collection.

Nor had the world of the theater forgotten Jeffers. In the summer of 1955, "The Cretan Woman" was produced at Stanford University as part of its summer theater program, with Marian Seldes as Phaedra and Douglas Watson as Hippolytus. That same summer *Medea* was included as one of the three plays to be presented in the Salute to France program. The Librairie Théâtrale published 1,400 copies of Julien Philbert's translation for the occasion.

In October, *Medea* began a sixteen-week tour of Australia, starring Judith Anderson, enjoying an enthusiastic reception. Both the Berle and the Sullivan television shows included scenes from *Medea* on their network programs. Jerry Wald, of Columbia Pictures, secured the motion picture rights for *Roan Stallion* and *Thurso's Landing*, though nothing came of this, and the rights lapsed in 1962.

The small financial remuneration received for these productions was a welcome addition to Jeffers' income derived from the sale of his books of poetry, amounting to about $600 per year. Although the *Selected Poetry* and *Medea* continued to be reprinted by his publishers, other works were not so fortunate, and were unavailable to teachers, students and book shops, their insistent demands failing to move the publishers.

232

In 1956, Merle Armitage and The Ward Ritchie Press published a beautiful edition of *The Loving Shepherdess*, illustrated by Jean Kellogg, a sensitive and capable young artist whose home is in the Big Sur country. The Book Club of California also published that year the book *Themes in my Poems*, the text of the address which Jeffers had given at the Library of Congress in 1941.

Along with such honors came an attack, in 1957, by one of the lesser American poets, Kenneth Rexroth, in the form of an article published in the *Saturday Review of Literature* under the title, "Decline of a Poet." Rexroth referred to the Yvor Winter attempt to undermine Jeffers' standing in the field of letters, claiming:

". . . it was one of the most devastating attacks in modern criticism, and Jeffers' reputation, then at its height, never recovered, but entered into a slow decline. Today young people simply do not read him. . . ."

"Devastating" perhaps to these two men whose own reputations for critical astuteness would hardly be enhanced by this lack of perception. Had Rexroth had the problem of answering the mound of inquiries from students and young poets which plagued Jeffers daily, he would have wondered what young people *didn't* read Jeffers!

When the article was called to Jeffers' attention, he said, "It is not disturbing but merely obvious. It has happened several times before, and they always say the same things." The editor of the *Monterey Peninsula Herald* wrote an editorial in which he said that the Rexroth attack had been "senselessly embittered, unfair, irresponsible and untrue." Lawrence Clark Powell wrote, "Jeffers is like a sequoia with squirrels running up and down the trunk, squeaking and committing nuisances." In a letter to Jeffers, Merle Armitage said, "You must have cut very deep into these pretenders for them to screech with such violence."

One of the most interesting developments of these years was the success of Jeffers' work in Germany and in Czechoslovakia. From the excellent translations of Eva Hesse, the distinguished publisher Ernst Rowohlt presented an edition of Jeffers' three dramas, "Medea," "Tower Beyond Tragedy," and "The Cretan Woman." "Medea" had been produced at the Theatre Festival in Bad Hersfeld, as well as in three other German theaters, and in

233

two Swiss ones, winning one success after another. Radio broadcasts, magazine reprints, and enthusiastic reviews followed each production. After the Bad Hersfeld presentation, Rowohlt wrote to Jeffers, ". . . we all had the impression that with your play you have enriched the German theatre not only with a new work, but a new "Krafstrom" (source of energy) effecting a new, modern approach to the antique myth. It is for us a real joy to have the privilege of working for your dramatic creations. . . ."

The German critics claimed that Jeffers' "Medea" was "greater than Euripides." So well was it received that a *tournée* was planned with the great dramatic German actress Hilde Krahl, who had scored such a great success in the role of Medea. The *tournée* visited all of the major cities of West Germany for two-night stands, and critics claimed that Hilde Krahl reached the highest point in her career.

Eva Hesse rewrote her stage adaptation of "Tower" which was produced at the Regensburg State Theatre in March, 1961. She said of it, "I am most happy that the play should have had the right sort of success at last. It seems that the producer handled things very intelligently. There were three highlights: Cassandra's long prophetic monologue (this is in two parts in the original, but for the acting version I made a few cuts and combined the two parts into one), the murder of Clytemnestra, and the scene at the end between Orest and Electra. Another important element was that the producer understood how to bring the poetry of Mr. Jeffers' long lines over effectively. . . ."

In October, 1961, "The Cretan Woman," directed by Schalla, was staged in Bochum and was a signal success. Carmen Renate Koper, as Phaedra, won the plaudits of the critics and swept the audience off its feet, and Jeffers, as the author, won his share of the laurels.

In 1958, Czechoslovakia was aroused to the importance of Jeffers' poetry through the translation of the poem, *Mara*, by Kamil Bednár, in a charmingly illustrated edition. Czech magazines printed Bednár's translations of Jeffers' shorter poems, and the translator found himself besieged with requests for further works. In 1960, Bednár's translation of a collection of Jeffers' short poems under the Czech title *Jestrabi Krik* was published, and in the same year *Roan Stallion* and *Hungerfield* appeared. In 1962, a

5,000-copy edition of *The Loving Shepherdess* sold out in two days. This was followed by the translation of *Medea,* first produced in the spring of 1962.

In the meantime, Eva Hesse had introduced Jeffers' poetry to Mary de Rachewiltz, daughter of Ezra Pound, and suggested that she translate it into Italian. In February, 1962, her first translations—a series of ten poems—appeared in the Italian literary magazine, *Segnacola.* In 1963, her translation of "Hungerfield" met with instant success and resulted in a commission to translate "The Cretan Woman" for production.

In 1958, the Voice of America program presented Jeffers' "Tower" in Vienna. Jeffers wrote to the producers:

"It is a great honor for a foreigner to have his play produced in Vienna, that famous city with its proud tradition of the theatre. I recognize the honor, and I hope that you will find the play interesting. I wrote it as a poem, having no idea that it could ever be staged.

"Let me speak also of my translator, Frau Eva Hesse of München. She has extraordinary ability in both languages, German and English, and I am glad to entrust the play to her. My own acquaintance with the great languages of Europe has sadly deteriorated. It is nearly sixty years since I went to school in Leipzig and Zurich; and around the Lake of Geneva. Vevey, Lausanne, Geneva, and so forth. In those days I knew German and French as well as I did English. But now I can only thank Eva Hesse for translating the poem, and you for listening to it.

"Mein Deutsch ist aber vielleicht doch ausreichend, um ihnen-von meinem haus am strand des stillen ozeans—meine besten wunsche und warme grusse senden."

In 1960, Jeffers was seventy-three years old, and his beloved Una had been dead for ten years. Only one major work had been published since her death. Without her inspiration and companionship he was rudderless. He sat in his chair by the sea-window and watched the waves burst in a white spray over the rocks below him. The sea-birds spread their wings between him and the setting sun. Each poem which he wrote took its toll and left him weak, and yet he suffered at the thought that he would write no more. It was at this time that he wrote the poem "My Burial Place."

I have told you in another poem, whether you've
    read it or not,
About a beautiful place the hard-wounded
Deer go to die in; their bones lie mixed in
    their little graveyard
Under leaves by a flashing cliff-brook, and if
They have ghosts they like it, the bones and
    mixed antlers are well content.
Now comes for me the time to engage
My burial place: put me in a beautiful place
    far off from men,
No cemetery, no necropolis,
And for God's sake no columbarium, nor yet no
    funeral.
But if the human animal were precious
As the quick deer or that hunter in the night
    the lonely puma
I should be pleased to lie in one grave with 'em.[3]

There were now four children born to Lee and Donnan—Lindsay, Una, Donnan, and, in April, 1960, John Robinson—the first of Jeffers' twelve grandchildren to be named for him. Garth and Charlotte and their children came to visit Tor House on the brief holidays allowed by the Forestry Service. They now had six children—Maeve, Diana, Morna, Robinson, Stuart, and Garth. It was a miracle of engineering on the part of Lee and Charlotte that they were all bedded and fed and bathed (two small baths for fifteen persons). Jeffers was never too ill to find pleasure in the company of his grandchilden.

Jeffers found the gradual loss of his sight frustrating. A cataract had formed on his right eye which had been injured at birth, and he said of it, ". . . it can see gods and spirits in its cloud/And the weird end of the world: the left one's for common daylight. . . ."[4] By 1961, he could no longer decipher his own writing, and referred to himself as "the old half-blinded hawk." Books, letters and manuscripts arrived daily, demanding acknowledgment for which he had neither the strength nor the sight. Old age and pain were humiliating to him, and though often so ill that Dr.

[3]*The Beginning and the End, and Other Poems.*
[4]Unpublished excerpt.

Creedan insisted on hospitalization or home nursing, the moment he was out of danger, Lee and Donnan assumed the nursing to relieve him of the insecurity he felt in strange places and with strange people. Their love and care kept him alive.

In 1961, Jeffers received the Shelley Memorial Award presented by the National Poetry Society. And in September of that year he entered into a contract with Paul Mason and William Mahan to produce "Tamar" and "Medea" for the screen.

In August he had had a brief return to well-being, no doubt engendered by the arrival in Carmel of Judith Anderson who was to present scenes from "The Tower Beyond Tragedy" and "Medea" at the Wharf Theater in Monterey. Her warm affection and encouragement gave Jeffers the courage to attend her opening night—his first public appearance in a decade and proof of his respect and affection for her.

Television station KQED in San Francisco was planning a program of Jeffers' poems to be read by Dame Judith Anderson against the background of Tor House and scenes in the "Jeffers Country." Jeffers had made an unprecedented promise by consenting to "appear" with Anderson, having been assured that he wouldn't have to speak. However, a lack of funds necessitated the postponement of the program which never took place.

We had been urging Jeffers to bring out another book of poems but the effort of revising and typing the manuscripts was beyond his strength. Finally, he agreed to my transcribing them for him in hopes that his failing eyes could cope with the typewritten copies. So Lee gathered all the papers in one large box and sent it off to me. Sorting the completed poems from the notes, we were delighted to find that there were enough to make up a book. These were returned to Jeffers for his inevitable changes, but even this was too much for him.

From September on, Jeffers' health deteriorated rapidly, his heart but a feeble instrument strengthened by medication. On January 20, 1962, ten days after his 75th birthday, Jeffers died quietly in his sleep at Tor House. The setting had been strangely and beautifully designed, as the entire coast and back country were covered with snow—as beautiful as a Jeffers poem. The sea rose to its full height and dashed itself in anguish against the rocks below Tor House. But on Monday, January 22, the day of

Jeffers' cremation, the sea quieted, promising an easy passage when his spirit set out towards the far horizon to join in the glory of the sunset.

Jeffers' love of solitude was, through a strange set of circumstances, preserved even after death. Newsmen, their attention focused on the Big Storm, the Bing Crosby Golf Tournament and the week-end holiday, were unaware, until Monday, that Jeffers had died. Charlotte and Garth and their children had driven through the storm from Susanville, to be with Lee and Donnan. A few of us joined them, including Rollo Peters, Judith Anderson, and Theodore Lilienthal. There was no funeral service, since it was Jeffers' wish. Tor House was quiet except for the sound of children's voices and the mourning of the surf.

PUBLICATIONS & BIBLIOGRAPHY

CHRONOLOGICAL TABLE OF PUBLICATIONS

1903
DECEMBER / "The Measure;"* "Dawn"* / *The Aurora* (Occidental College magazine).

1904
JANUARY / "Man's Pride;"* "Dreamland"* / *The Aurora*.
FEBRUARY / "A Hill-Top View"* / *The Aurora*.
MARCH / "Death and Resurrection;"* "The Wild Hunt"* / *The Aurora*.
APRIL / "Witches"* / *The Aurora*.
JUNE 9 / "The Condor"* (First poem sold by R. J.) / *The Youth's Companion*.
OCTOBER / "Mountain Pines"* / *The Occidental* (formerly *The Aurora*. R. J. editor).

1905
JANUARY / "Faunus"* / *The Occidental*.
FEBRUARY / "The Lake"* / *The Occidental*.
MARCH / "The Fox"* / *The Occidental*.
JUNE / "The Seniors;"* "The Stream"* / Commencement Annual, Occidental College.
OCTOBER / "The Stream" / *Out West*
NOVEMBER / "The Steadfast Sky"* / *The Cardinal* (University of Southern California literary magazine).
DECEMBER 12 / "The Game"* / *The University Courier* (University of Southern California).

1906
JANUARY 2 / "The City"* / *The University Courier*.
FEBRUARY 6 / "Homeward;"* "The Poultry Lover"* / *The University Courier*.
MARCH 13 / "The Forsaken Cabin"* / *The University Courier*.

1907
MARCH 5 / "The North Pole"* / *The Occidental*.
APRIL / "The Moon's Girls;"* "Age"* / *The Occidental*.
MAY / "Death Valley"* / *Out West*.

*First appearance.

239

1912

DECEMBER 4 / *Flagons and Apples* / Grafton Publishing Co.,
Los Angeles.

DECEMBER 8 / Review of *Flagons and Apples* by R. J. / *Los Angeles Times*.

1913

AUGUST / "Mirrors"* (First and only publication of a short story by
R. J.) / *The Smart Set*.

1916

OCTOBER 11 / *Californians* / The Macmillan Company, New York.

DECEMBER 2 / "He Has Fallen in Love with the Mountains" / *The Literary Digest*.

1917

NOVEMBER / "Let Us Go Home to Paradise" / *Golden Songs of the Golden State*. Anthology compiled by Marguerite Ogden Wilkinson.
A. C. McClurg & Co., Chicago.

1918

DECEMBER / "The Cloud"* / *Palms* (poetry magazine), Guadalajara,
Mexico.

1924

APRIL / *Tamar and Other Poems* / Peter G. Boyle, Publisher, New York.

OCTOBER / "Continent's End" / *Sunset Magazine*, San Francisco.

1925

MAY / "Continent's End," "The Cycle," "To the Stone-Cutters," "Wise
Men in Their Bad Hours," "Invocation" from "Tamar," / *Continent's
End*. Anthology edited by J. H. Jackson. The Book Club of California,
San Francisco.

SEPTEMBER 23 / "Birds," "Haunted Country," "Fog," "Boats in a Fog" /
The Nation.

NOVEMBER 10 / *Roan Stallion, Tamar and Other Poems* (Trade
Edition) / Boni & Liveright, New York.

NOVEMBER / Autobiographical Note in Prospectus of *Roan Stallion,
Tamar and Other Poems* / Boni & Liveright, New York.

NOVEMBER / *Roan Stallion, Tamar and Other Poems* (Author's
presentation copy) / Boni & Liveright, New York.

NOVEMBER / "A California Vignette," "Not Our Good Luck," "Salmon
Fishing," "Suicide's Stone" from "Tamar," "To the Stone-Cutters" /
The Poetry Cure. Anthology compiled by Robert H. Schauffler.
Dodd, Mead & Co., New York.

DECEMBER / "Two Garden Marbles: Alcibiades, Alexander,"
"Adjustment," "Clouds at Evening," "Summer Holiday" / *The
Measure* (A Journal of Poetry).

*First appearance.

FEBRUARY / "Age in Prospect"* / *Overland Monthly*.

MARCH / "Star on the Hill-Crest"* / *San Francisco Review*.

MAY / "Apology for Bad Dreams"* / *New Masses*.

JUNE 9 / "Promise of Peace"* / *The New Republic*.

JULY 13 / "Compensation"* / *The Carmel Cymbal*.

JULY 21 / "Noon"* / *The New Republic*.

AUGUST 7 / "Noon" / *The Literary Digest*.

AUGUST / "The Beach"* / *Overland Monthly*.

NOVEMBER 10 / "All the Corn in One Barn"* (Prose) / *Lights and Shadows from the Lantern*. Gelber, Lilienthal, Inc., San Francisco.

NOVEMBER 24 / "A Great Poet on Sterling"* (Prose) / *The Carmel Cymbal*.

NOVEMBER / "Birds," "Haunted Country," "Fog," "Boats in a Fog," "Promise of Peace" / *Anthology of Magazine Verse for 1926*. Edited by W. S. Braithwaite. B. J. Brimmer Company, Boston.

NOVEMBER-DECEMBER / "George Sterling"* / *San Francisco Review*.

DECEMBER / "Preface"* / *The American Mercury*.

DECEMBER / "Post Mortem"* / *Overland Monthly*.

DECEMBER 22 / "Consciousness"* / *The Carmel Cymbal*.

DECEMBER / "Woodrow Wilson" / *A Day in the Hills*. Anthology edited by Henry M. Bland. Privately printed, San Francisco.

JANUARY / Answers to questionnaire, "Are Artists People?" / *New Masses*.

MARCH / "Winter Sundown"* / *Overland Monthly*.

APRIL 1 / "Poetry and True Poetry" (Book review of *Children of the Sun and Other Poems*, by James Rorty) / *The Advance*.

JUNE 30 / *The Women at Point Sur* (Trade Edition) / Boni & Liveright, New York.

AUGUST 9 / *The Women at Point Sur* (Limited, Signed Edition) / Boni & Liveright, New York.

AUGUST / "Joy" / *Great Poems of the English Language*. Anthology edited by Wallace A. Briggs. McBride & Co., New York.

AUGUST / "Joy" / *Great Poems of the English Language* (English Edition). Edited by Wallace A. Briggs. G. G. Harrap & Co., London.

AUGUST / "Apology for Bad Dreams," "Adjustment," "Compensation," "Age in Prospect," "Ante Mortem,"* "The Beach," "Summer Holiday," "Love-Children,"* "Clouds at Evening," "Noon," "Credo,"* "October Evening,"* "Pelicans,"* "Post Mortem," "Promise of Peace"

*First appearance.

/ *A Miscellany of American Poetry: 1927*. Harcourt, Brace & Co., New York.

NOVEMBER / "A Few Memories" (Prose) / *Overland Monthly*.

NOVEMBER / "Fog," "To the Stone-Cutters," "The Cycle" / *The Third Book of Modern Verse*. Edited by Jessie B. Rittenhouse. Houghton Mifflin Co., Boston.

1928

JANUARY / "Three Poems: The Women on Cythaeron, The Trumpet I-IV,* Birthdues"* / *Poetry*.

FEBRUARY 8 / "Hurt Hawks,"* "To a Young Artist"* / *The Nation*.

MARCH / "Stars"* / *The Bookman*.

MARCH / "Contrast"* / *Sabretooth* (Occidental College).

MAY / "Age in Prospect," "Compensation" / *Modern American and British Poetry*. Edited by Louis Untermeyer. Harcourt, Brace & Co., New York.

JULY / "Wonder and Joy" / *The Book of Poetry*. Selected by Edwin Markham. William H. Wise & Co., New York.

OCTOBER / *Poems* / The Book Club of California, San Francisco.

NOVEMBER / *Roan Stallion, Tamar and Other Poems* (English Export Edition) / *Hogarth Living Poets Series*. The Hogarth Press, London.

NOVEMBER / "The Women on Cythaeron," "Hurt Hawks," "To a Young Artist" / *Anthology of Magazine Verse for 1928*. Edited by W. S. Braithwaite. H. Vinal, Ltd., New York.

NOVEMBER / *An Artist* / Privately printed by John S. Mayfield, Austin, Texas.

NOVEMBER 19 / *Cawdor and Other Poems* (Limited, Signed Edition) / Horace Liveright, New York.

NOVEMBER 23 / *Cawdor and Other Poems* (Trade Edition) / Horace Liveright, New York.

DECEMBER 2 / "Is the Sky Broken?" (Book review of *Now the Sky and Other Poems*, by Mark Van Doren) / *New York Herald Tribune: Books*.

DECEMBER 12 / "Evening Ebb,"* "Hands,"* "Hooded Nights."* Also notes on "Tragic Themes," "The Rhythm." Other excerpts and reprints / *The Carmelite: Robinson Jeffers Number*.

DECEMBER / "Night," "Continent's End" / *An Anthology of World Poetry*. Edited by Mark Van Doren. Albert & Charles Boni, New York.

1929

OCTOBER 10 /*Cawdor* (English Export Edition) / The Hogarth Press, London.

*First appearance.

NOVEMBER 16 / *Dear Judas and Other Poems* (Trade Edition) / Horace Liveright, New York.

NOVEMBER 25 / *Dear Judas and Other Poems* (Limited, Signed Edition) / Horace Liveright, New York.

NOVEMBER / "Boats in a Fog," "Pelicans," "Noon," from *Tamar*, "Night" / *Twentieth Century Poetry*. Edited by J. Drinkwater, H. S. Canby, and W. R. Benét. Houghton Mifflin Co., Boston.

1930

FEBRUARY / *Stars* (First edition with errata) / The Flame Press, Pasadena.

MARCH 10 / *Stars* (Second edition) / The Flame Press, Pasadena.

JULY / "Compensation," "Age in Prospect," "Ante Mortem," "Post Mortem," "Noon," "Clouds at Evening," "To the Stone-Cutters," "Gale in April," "Credo," "Promise of Peace," "Apology for Bad Dreams" / *Modern American Poetry*. Edited by Louis Untermeyer. Harcourt, Brace & Co., New York.

NOVEMBER / "Part III" from "Tamar," "Granite and Cypress," "Wise Men in Their Bad Hours," "Tor House," "Shine, Perishing Republic" / *Lyric America, an Anthology of American Poetry (1630-1930)*. Edited by Alfred Kreymborg. Coward-McCann, New York.

NOVEMBER / *Dear Judas and Other Poems* (English Export Edition) / The Hogarth Press, London.

DECEMBER / *Apology for Bad Dreams* / Harry Ward Ritchie, Paris.

1931

MARCH 25 / "The Stubborn Savior" (Book review of *Epistle to Prometheus*, by Babette Deutsch) / *The New Freeman*.

MAY / "A California Vignette," "To the Rock That Will Be a Cornerstone of the House," "Not Our Good Luck" / *Songs and Stories*. Compiled by Edwin Markham. Powell Publishing Co., Los Angeles.

SEPTEMBER 5 / "New Mexican Mountain"* / *The Saturday Review of Literature*.

DECEMBER 10 / *Descent to the Dead* / Random House, Inc., New York.

DECEMBER / "Joy" / *The Golden Book Magazine*, New York.

1932

FEBRUARY 1 / "Night," "Continent's End" / *The World's Best Poems*. Edited by Mark Van Doren and G. M. Lapolla. Albert & Charles Boni, New York.

FEBRUARY / "Hurt Hawks," "Age in Prospect," "Promise of Peace" / *The Book of Living Verse*. Edited by Louis Untermeyer. Harcourt, Brace & Co., New York.

*First appearance.

MARCH 26 / *Thurso's Landing and Other Poems* (Limited, Signed Edition) / Liveright, Inc., Publishers, New York.

MARCH 26 / *Thurso's Landing and Other Poems* (Trade Edition) / Liveright, Inc., Publishers, New York.

MAY 26 / "First Book"* (Prose) / *The Colophon: Part X.*

JUNE / "Compensation," "Age in Prospect," "Ante Mortem," "Post Mortem," "Noon," "Clouds at Evening," "To the Stone-Cutters," "Gale in April," "Credo," "Promise of Peace," "Apology for Bad Dreams" / *Modern American Poetry* (English Edition). Edited by Louis Untermeyer. Jonathan Cape, London.

AUGUST 19 / "A Triad"* / *The Carmel Pine Cone.*

OCTOBER / "Night," "Birds," "Haunted Country," "Continent's End," "Fawn's Foster-Mother," "The Summit Redwood," "Ascent to the Sierras," "Bixby's Landing," "Ocean," "Hurt Hawks," "Apology for Bad Dreams" / *American Poets 1630-1930*. Edited by Mark Van Doren. Little, Brown & Co., Boston.

OCTOBER / "Night," "Hurt Hawks," "Shine, Perishing Republic," "Joy" / *The New Poetry*. Edited by Harriet Monroe and Alice Corbin Henderson. The Macmillan Co., New York.

DECEMBER / "The Cycle," "Vices," "To the House," "Suicide's Stone," "Salmon Fishing" / *California Poets*. Edited by the House of Henry Harrison, Publisher, New York.

Book Review of *Barabbas* / Albert & Charles Boni's Fall Catalogue.

1933

"Bixby's Landing" / *An American Omnibus*, with an introduction by Carl Van Doren. Doubleday, Doran & Co., New York.

MARCH / "Hurt Hawks," "Age in Prospect," "Promise of Peace" / *The Albatross Book of Living Verse*. Edited by Louis Untermeyer. The Albatross, Paris.

APRIL / "Ode on Human Destinies," "Boats in a Fog," "Gale in April," "To the Stone-Cutters" / *Contemporary Trends: Since 1914*. Edited by J. H. Nelson. The Macmillan Co., New York.

JUNE / A prose note, and "To the Stone-Cutters" / *Fifty Poets: An American Auto-Anthology*. Edited by William Rose Benét. Dodd, Mead & Co., New York.

"Suicide's Stone," "Woodrow Wilson" / *The Modern Muse: British and American Poems Today*. Edited by The English Association. Oxford University Press, London.

Give Your Heart to the Hawks and Other Poems (Trade Edition) / Random House, New York.

*First appearance.

244

Give Your Heart to the Hawks and Other Poems (Limited, Signed Edition) / Random House, New York.

"Lines on Point Lobos" (from *Tamar*) / *The Sierra Club Bulletin*, San Francisco.

1934

(NOTE: Anthologies are not included from this year forward)

Return / The Grabhorn Press, San Francisco.

"Foreword"* to Lawrence C. Powell's *Robinson Jeffers, the Man and His Work* / Primavera Press, Los Angeles.

DECEMBER / *Rock and Hawk* / Privately printed by Frederick Prokosch, Yale University.

1935

JANUARY / "Shine, Republic,"* "Rock and Hawk" / *Scribner's Magazine*.

JANUARY / Letter of George Sterling with comment by R. J. (Prose) / The Book Club of California, San Francisco.

APRIL 6 / "Love the Wild Swan"* / *The Saturday Review of Literature*.

MAY 3 / "Shine, Perishing Republic" / *The Carmel Pine Cone*.

MAY / "E. A. Robinson"* (Prose) / *College Verse*. College Poetry Society of America, Grinnell, Iowa.

OCTOBER / "Cloudy Day"* / *Scribner's Magazine*.

Introductory Comment* / Catalogue, Robinson Jeffers Exhibition, Occidental College.

Roan Stallion, Tamar, and Other Poems / Modern Library, New York.

1936

JANUARY 4 / "Air Raid Rehearsals" / *The Saturday Review of Literature*.

The Beaks of Eagles / The Grabhorn Press, San Francisco.

NOVEMBER 9 / "Sinverguenza" / *Pacific Weekly*.

1937

Such Counsels You Gave to Me, and Other Poems (Trade Edition) / Random House, New York.

Such Counsels You Gave to Me, and Other Poems (Limited Edition) / Random House, New York.

Hope Is Not for the Wise (Folio) / Quercus Press, San Mateo.

October Week-End (Folio) Quercus Press, San Mateo.

1938

APRIL / "Writers Take Sides"* (Prose) / *League of American Writers Magazine*, New York.

The Selected Poetry of Robinson Jeffers (Trade Edition) / Random House, New York.

*First appearance.

MAY / "Review"* on the Lawrence Tibbet award / *College Verse.*
College Poetry Society of America, Grinnell, Iowa.

1939
"Foreword"* to *Of Una Jeffers*, by Edith Greenan. Book also
contains reprint of "The Excesses of God" / The Ward Ritchie Press,
Los Angeles.

SUMMER / "Watch the Lights Fade," "To U. J." "The Excesses of
God" / *The University Review* (University of Kansas City).

OCTOBER / "Come Little Birds"* / *Poetry.*
The House-Dog's Grave—Haig's Grave (Limited Edition) /
Quercus Press, San Mateo.

1940
APRIL 19 / "The Coast Road" / *The Carmel Pine Cone.*

SUMMER / "Thoughts Incidental to a Poem"* (Prose) /
The Personalist.

AUGUST 10 / "May-June, 1940"* / *The Saturday Review* of
Literature.

WINTER / "Prescription of Painful Ends"* / *The Virginia Quarterly
Review.*

DECEMBER / "9/19/39,"* "Finland is Down,"* "Great Men,"* "The
Stars Go over the Lonely Ocean,"* "The Bloody Sire"* / *Poetry.*
The Condor (Folio) / Quercus Press, San Mateo.
Two Consolations (Broadside) / Quercus Press, San Mateo.
"Foreword"* to *Fire and Other Poems*, by D. H. Lawrence /
The Grabhorn Press, San Francisco.

1941
Be Angry at the Sun (Trade Edition) / Random House, New York.
Be Angry at the Sun (Limited Edition) / Random House, New
York.

MAY 2 / "Expect Change" / *The Carmel Pine Cone.*

AUGUST 29 / "The Sirens" / *The Carmel Pine Cone.*

WINTER / "My Dear Love" / *The Virginia Quarterly Review.*

1945
NOVEMBER / "Advice to Pilgrims"* / *Pacific Weekly.*

1946
Medea (Trade Edition) / Random House, New York.

1947
JANUARY / "Continent's End" / *Holiday Magazine.*

SPRING / "The Inquisitors"* / *The University Review* (University of
Kansas City).

*First appearance.

JUNE / "Shine, Perishing Republic" / *Occidental College Alumnus Magazine*.

OCTOBER / "The Greater Grandeur,"* "Real and Half Real,"* "Their Beauty Has More Meaning,"* "Orca"* / *Poetry*.

Natural Music (Folio) / The Book Club of California, San Francisco.

"Foreword" to *Fifty Photographs*, by Edward Weston / Duell, Sloane & Pierce, New York.

OCTOBER 6 / "Comments" on *Dear Judas* / *The New York Times Drama Section*.

1948

JANUARY 18 / "Poetry, Gongorism and a Thousand Years"* (Prose) / *The New York Times Book Review*.

The Double Axe and Other Poems / Random House, New York.

MARCH 28 / "What of It?"* "Original Sin"* / *The Saturday Review of Literature*.

AUGUST 28 / "Greater Grandeur"* / *The Saturday Review of Literature*.

AUGUST-SEPTEMBER / "Medea" / *Theatre Arts Magazine*.

1951

SEPTEMBER 5 / "New Mexican Mountain" / *The Saturday Review of Literature*.

OCTOBER / "Statement on Humanism"* (Prose) / *The Humanist*.

1952

MAY / "Hungerfield"* / *Poetry*.

Hungerfield (Limited Edition) / The Grabhorn Press, San Francisco.

"Point Lobos"* (Prose) / *The Glory of Our West*. Photographs and text by representative Western writers. Doubleday & Co., New York.

DECEMBER / "Eagle Valor, Chicken Mind" / *The Dove in Flames* (poetry magazine briefly published in San Francisco).

1953

*De Rerum Virtute** / The Grabhorn Press, San Francisco.

OCTOBER 9 / "In Tribute"* (Prose) / *The Carmel Pine Cone*.

1954

JANUARY-APRIL / "The Deer Lay Down Their Bones" / *Voices*.

JULY / "Comments"* on "The Cretan Woman" / *The New York Times Book Review*.

Hungerfield and Other Poems (Trade Edition) / Random House, New York.

*First appearance.

"Foreword"* to *Visits to Ireland* (Journal of Una Jeffers, edited by R. J.) / The Ward Ritchie Press, Los Angeles.

1955

MAY 3 / "With All Good Wishes" (Prose) / *Focus* (Occidental College).

1956

Themes in My Poems / The Book Club of California, San Francisco.

"Foreword"* to *The Loving Shepherdess* (Limited Edition) / Random House, New York.

"Foreword"* to *Directions in the Sun,* by Eric Barker / Gotham Book Mart, Inc., New York.

1958

OCTOBER 28 / *The Ocean's Tribute* / The Grabhorn Press, San Francisco.

1961

"First Book"* / *My First Publication* / The Book Club of California, San Francisco.

1963

"Birds and Fishes"* / *Poetry in Crystal* / Steuben Glass, New York.

The Beginning and the End (First edition with errata) / Random House, New York.

The Beginning and the End (Second edition with corrections) / Random House, New York.

SEPTEMBER / *Robinson Jeffers, Selected Poems* / Vintage Books (Random House), New York.

BIBLIOGRAPHY

(BOOKS AND ARTICLES ABOUT ROBINSON JEFFERS)
(Translations Not Included)

1924

OCTOBER / Review of *Tamar and Other Poems* by James Rorty / *Sunset Magazine.*

1925

MARCH 1 / "In Major Mold," a review of *Tamar and Other Poems,* by James Rorty / *New York Herald Tribune: Books.*

MAY 27 / "Brains and Lyrics," a review of *Tamar and Other Poems,* by Babette Deutsch / *The New Republic.*

AUGUST 25 / "Roots Under the Rocks," a review of *Tamar and Other Poems,* by James Daly / *Poetry.*

NOVEMBER / "Rhymes and Reactions," a review of *Tamar and Other Poems,* by George Sterling / *Overland Monthly* (San Francisco).

NOVEMBER / "Two Books," a review of *Tamar and Other Poems* and *Continent's End,* by Virginia Moore / *Voices* (New York).

NOVEMBER 25 / "First Glance," a review of *Roan Stallion, Tamar and Other Poems,* by Mark Van Doren / *The Nation.*

*First appearance.

DECEMBER 30 / "From Pieria to Mediocria," a review of *Roan Stallion, Tamar and Other Poems*, by William Rose Benét / *The Outlook* (New York).

1926

FEBRUARY 10 / "Bitterness and Beauty," by Babette Deutsch / *The New Republic*.

MARCH-FEBRUARY [*sic*] / "A Tower by the Sea," by George Sterling / *San Francisco Review*.

MARCH / "Dark Fire, Black Music," by Joseph Auslander / *The Measure* (New York).
Robinson Jeffers: The Man and the Artist, by George Sterling / Boni & Liveright.

1927

FEBRUARY 19 / "Robinson Jeffers: The Man and the Artist," by George Sterling / *The Argonaut* (San Francisco).

MARCH / "An Occidental Poet," by Albert Croissant / *Occidental Alumnus* (Los Angeles).

JULY 27 / Review of *The Women at Point Sur*, by Mark Van Doren / *The Nation*.

AUGUST 17 / "Or What's a Heaven For?" by Babette Deutsch / *The New Republic*.

AUGUST 28 / "The Deliberate Annihilation," by Genevieve Taggard / *New York Herald Tribune: Books*.

SEPTEMBER / "Satirist or Metaphysician," by James Rorty / *The Masses*.

NOVEMBER / "Robinson Jeffers: Tragic Terror," by Benjamin De Casseres / *The Bookman*.

1928

FEBRUARY / "Jeffers Denies Us Twice," by H. L. Davis / *Poetry*.

MAY 16 / "Robinson Jeffers: The Tragedy of a Modern Mystic," by Lawrence S. Morris / *The New Republic*.

AUGUST / "Robinson Jeffers Receives a Convert," by J. S. Mayfield / *Overland Monthly* (San Francisco).

DECEMBER 12 / "Jeffers, the Neighbor," by Lincoln Steffens, "J. Robinson Jeffers, Stone-Mason," by Ella Winter, and other vignettes / *The Carmelite: Robinson Jeffers Supplement*.

1929

JANUARY 9/ "Bits of Earth and Water," by Mark Van Doren / *The Nation*.

JANUARY 16 / "Brooding Eagle," by Babette Deutsch / *The New Republic*.

MARCH / "Robinson and Una Jeffers: A Portrait of a Great American Poet and His Wife," by Louis Adamic / *The San Franciscan*.

APRIL / "Robinson Jeffers," by Eliseo Vivas / *The New Student* (New York).

MAY / "A Poet of Distinction," by Albert Croissant / *Occidental Alumnus* (Los Angeles).

NOVEMBER 6 / "Robinson Jeffers: A Poet Who Studied Medicine," by M. Webster Brown / *Medical Journal and Record* (New York).

DECEMBER / "Robinson Jeffers: A Lone Titan," by W. H. Hale / *The Yale Literary Magazine.*
Robinson Jeffers: a Portrait, by Louis Adamic / *University of Washington Chap Book* (Seattle).
The Superman in America, by Benjamin De Casseres / *University of Washington Chap Book* (Seattle).
Potable Gold, by Babette Deutsch / W. W. Norton & Co.

1930

JANUARY / "Judas, Savior of Jesus," by Mark Van Doren / *The Nation.*

JANUARY 12 / "Sweet Hemlock," by Babette Deutsch / *New York Herald Tribune: Books.*

FEBRUARY / "Dear Judas," by A. Herbert Klein / *Occidental Alumnus* (Los Angeles).

JULY / "Robinson Jeffers," Part I, by Dwight Macdonald / *The Miscellany* (New York).

SEPTEMBER / "Robinson Jeffers," Part II, by Dwight Macdonald / *The Miscellany* (New York).

1931

MARCH / "Robinson Jeffers: Poet," by Ray M. Lawless / *Present-Day American Literature.*

SEPTEMBER 5 / "Robinson Jeffers" (reprint of "The Most Significant Tendency in American Poetry") by Benjamin H. Lehman / *The Saturday Review of Literature.*

OCTOBER 22 / "Leaves of Grass and Granite Boulders," by Lawrence C. Powell / *The Carmelite.*

DECEMBER 31 / "Jeffers Writes His Testament in New Poem," by Horace Gregory / *New York Evening Post.*

1932

JANUARY 24 / "Robinson Jeffers," by Benjamin De Casseres / *The Daily Tar Heel* (Chapel Hill, North Carolina).

JANUARY 31 / "Comfort in Hell," by Babette Deutsch / *New York Herald Tribune: Books.*

MARCH 31 / "Jeffers Again Hurls Indictment at Civilization," by Horace Gregory / *New York Evening Post.*

APRIL 4 / "Harrowed Marrow," a review of *Thurso's Landing and Other Poems* / *Time*. (Picture of R. J. on cover.)

APRIL 25 / "Jeffers' Mother," by A. C. Robinson / *Time*.

MAY 18 / "Symbolic Melodrama," by James Rorty / *The New Republic*.

An Introduction to Robinson Jeffers, by Lawrence C. Powell / Imprimerie Bernigaud & Privat (Dijon, France).

1933

Fifty Poets: An American Auto-Anthology, by William Rose Benét / Dodd, Mead & Co.

JUNE / *A Bibliography of the Works of Robinson Jeffers*, by S. S. Alberts / Random House (Trade Edition).

JUNE / *A Bibliography of the Works of Robinson Jeffers*, by S. S. Alberts / Random House (Limited, Signed Edition).

1934

Robinson Jeffers: The Man and His Work, by Lawrence C. Powell / Primavera Press (Los Angeles).

SEPTEMBER / "Book Stuff," by Mrs. Jack Valley / *Script Magazine* (Los Angeles).

1935

MARCH / "Robinson Jeffers '05," by Lawrence C. Powell / *Occidental Alumnus* (Los Angeles).

MARCH 9 / "Duel on a Headland," by Niven Busch, Jr. / *The Saturday Review of Literature*.

MAY / "Robinson Jeffers and His Garden," by Lawrence C. Powell / *Sunset* (Menlo Park, California).

1936

Robinson Jeffers and the Sea, by Melba Berry Bennett / Grabhorn Press (San Francisco).

FEBRUARY / "Robinson Jeffers: Bard," by Lawrence C. Powell / *Magazine of Sigma Chi* (Evanston, Illinois).

AUGUST / *Shine, Perishing Republic*, by Rudolph Gilbert / Bruce Humphries, Inc. (Boston).

FALL / "Poets, Paintings and Primroses," by Martha Stewart / *Garden Quarterly* (McDonald Publishing Company, San Francisco).

1937

JANUARY 30 / "Letters on the Pacific Rim," by Idwal Jones / *The Saturday Review of Literature* (New York).

1938

Robinson Jeffers, by William Van Wyck / The Ward Ritchie Press (Los Angeles).

MARCH / "Robinson Jeffers, a California Poet," by Harold Davis /
A radio broadcast, reprinted in the *Pomona College Bulletin.*
SUMMER / "Robinson Jeffers Counterpart of Walt Whitman," by Louis
Wann / *The Personalist* (University of Southern California).
SEPTEMBER / "Robinson Jeffers: Poet of Absolute Negation," by
Charles Glicksberg / *Calcutta Review* (Calcutta, India).
NOVEMBER 11 / "Science and the Poetry of Jeffers," by Hyatt A.
Waggoner / *American Literature* (Duke University).

1939
JANUARY 1 / "Toward a Religious Philosophy of the Theatre," by
Benjamin Miller / *The Personalist* (University of Southern
California).
SUMMER / "Tragic Drama: Modern Style," by R. T. Flewelling /
The Personalist (University of Southern California).

1940
Robinson Jeffers: The Man and His Work, by Lawrence C.
Powell / San Pasqual Press (Pasadena).
Spiritual Aspects of New Poetry, by Amos N. Wilder / Harper &
Bros. (New York).
JANUARY / "Values of Robinson Jeffers," by Frederic I. Carpenter /
American Literature, Duke University (Durham, North Carolina).
MAY / "Demands of the Religious Conscience," by Benjamin Miller /
Review of Religion.
WINTER / "Two Years of Poetry," by Morton D. Zabel / *Southwest
Review,* Southern Methodist University Press (Dallas).
NOVEMBER / "Alumnus Powell on Alumnus Jeffers," by Ben J.
Stelter / *Occidental Alumnus* (Los Angeles).
DECEMBER / "Death Comes for Robinson Jeffers," by Frederic I.
Carpenter / *University Review,* University of Kansas City.
DECEMBER / "Robinson Jeffers," by John F. Stanton / *The Coast
Magazine* (San Francisco).
1941-42
"Tragic and Contemporary: The Poetry of Robinson Jeffers," by
William Turner Levy / *Journal of Social Studies* (Philadelphia).

1943
MAY / "The Savior in the Poetry of Robinson Jeffers," by William
Savage Johnston / *American Literature,* Duke University
(Durham, North Carolina).
1944
MARCH / *Robinson Jeffers: the Philosophic Tragedist,* by Rudolph
Gilbert / Unicorn Press (New York).

SPRING / "Robinson Jeffers in Carmel," by Jean Kellogg / *Voices* (New York).
1945
"Robinson Jeffers," by Mercedes de Costa / *Victory*, Victory Press (London).
1946
OCTOBER / "The Rhythm of Robinson Jeffers' Poetry as Revealed by Oral Reading," by Cornelius Cunningham / *Quarterly Journal of Speech* (New York).
1947
APRIL / "The Hawk and the Rock," by T. J. / *What's Doing* (Carmel).
JUNE / "Point Lobos Photos," with quotes from R. J.'s poems, by W. Connell / *'47 Magazine* (New York).
NOVEMBER 2 / "The Poet: Carmel's Legendary Robinson Jeffers," by Carlton McKinney / *San Francisco Chronicle*.

1948
JULY 31 / "Transhuman Magnificence," by Selden Rodman / *The Saturday Review of Literature* (New York).

1949
SEPTEMBER / "Tragedy: Greece to California," by Ralph Flewelling / *The Personalist*, University of Southern California (Los Angeles).

1950
Some Modern American Poets, by James G. Southworth / Basil Blackwell, Pub. (Oxford).
1953
"Secession," by Lawrence Lipton / *Intro*, a Quarterly of Literature and Art (New York).
People, Places and Books, by Gilbert Highet, Oxford University Press (London).
1954
SEPTEMBER 17-24 / "Robinson Jeffers: Portrait of a Poet," by Thorne Hall / *Carmel Spectator*.
1955
MAY 3 / "Jeffers, the Poet," by Patricia Moisling, "Jeffers, the Man," by Tom Ohlson / *Focus*, Occidental College (Los Angeles).
SUMMER / "The Function of Greek Myth in the Poetry of Robinson Jeffers," by Arthur McTaggart / *Phoenix* (Seoul, Korea).

1956
SUMMER / "The Double Marriage of Robinson Jeffers," by Lawrence C. Powell / *Southwest Review*, Southern Methodist University Press (Dallas).
The Loyalties of Robinson Jeffers, by Radcliffe Squires / University of Michigan Press (Ann Arbor).

1958

"A Poet's Land," by Lawrence C. Powell / *Carmel Magazine.*
Robinson Jeffers: A Study in Inhumanism, by Mercedes Monjian /
University of Pittsburgh Press.
AUTUMN / "The Gentleness of Robinson Jeffers," by Fraser Drew /
Western Humanities (Salt Lake City).

1959

MARCH / "Robinson Jeffers," by Rosalind Wall / *Game and Gossip.*
(San Francisco).
APRIL-MAY / "The Loving Shepherdess of Jeffers and Scott," by Fraser
Drew / *Trace,* Villiers Pub. (London).
SEPTEMBER / "Robinson Jeffers: A Defense," by Sidney P. Moss /
The American Book Collector (Chicago).

1960

The Powers of Poetry, by Gilbert Highet / Oxford University Press
(London).

1961

WINTER / "Jeffers Collection," by Tyrus G. Harmsen / *California Book
Club News* (San Francisco).

1962

FEBRUARY / "Robinson Jeffers," by John W. Caughey / *Pacific
Historical Review* (Berkeley).
SPRING / "In Memoriam: Robinson Jeffers," by Theodore M.
Lilienthal / *California Book Club News* (San Francisco).
Robinson Jeffers, by Frederic I. Carpenter / Twayne Publishers,
Inc. (New York).
Ave, Vale, Robinson Jeffers. A compilation of tributes to Robinson
Jeffers / The Grabhorn Press (San Francisco).

1963

"Robinson Jeffers," by Ward Ritchie / *Impromptu,* Faculty-Alumni
Publication of Occidental College (Los Angeles).
"Poet Without Critics: a Note on Robinson Jeffers," by Horace
Gregory / *New World Writing: Seventh Mentor Selection,* New
World Writing (New York).

1965

"Ideas and Symbols in 'Give Your Heart to the Hawks,' " by Tokubiro
Miura / *Studies in English,* Hosei University pamphlet.

1966

"Robinson Jeffers and the Torches of Violence," by Frederic I.
Carpenter / *The Twenties—Poetry and Prose,* Everett Edwards Press.
Spring / "Robinson Jeffers as Didactic Poet," by William Nolte /
The Virginia Quarterly Review.

254

INDEX

256

261

263